The Limits of
RECIDIVISM
MEASURING SUCCESS AFTER PRISON

Committee on Evaluating Success Among People Released from Prison

Richard Rosenfeld and Amanda Grigg, *Editors*

Committee on Law and Justice
Division of Behavioral and Social Sciences and Education

A Consensus Study Report of

The National Academies of
SCIENCES · ENGINEERING · MEDICINE

THE NATIONAL ACADEMIES PRESS
Washington, DC
www.nap.edu

THE NATIONAL ACADEMIES PRESS   500 Fifth Street, NW   Washington, DC 20001

This activity was supported by contracts between the National Academy of Sciences and the Arnold Foundation (19-02953). Any opinions, findings, conclusions, or recommendations expressed in this publication do not necessarily reflect the views of any organization or agency that provided support for the project.

International Standard Book Number-13: 978-0-309-27697-9
International Standard Book Number-10: 0-309-27697-7
Digital Object Identifier: https://doi.org/10.17226/26459
Library of Congress Control Number: 2022942477

Additional copies of this publication are available from the National Academies Press, 500 Fifth Street, NW, Keck 360, Washington, DC 20001; (800) 624-6242 or (202) 334-3313; http://www.nap.edu.

Suggested citation: National Academies of Sciences, Engineering, and Medicine. 2022. *The Limits of Recidivism: Measuring Success After Prison*. Washington, DC: The National Academies Press. https://doi.org/10.17226/26459.

Acronyms

ADI	Area Deprivation Index
BJS	Bureau of Labor Statistics
EMA	Ecological Momentary Assessment
GED	General Educational Development
MOS	Medical Outcomes Study
NCRP	National Corrections Reporting Program
NCSC	National Center for State Courts
NCVS	National Crime Victimization Survey
NIBRS	National Incident-Based Reporting System
NICS	National Instant Criminal Background Check System
NODS	National Open Court Data Standards
NSDUH	National Survey on Drug Use and Health
PHQ-9	Patient Health Survey-9
PTSD	Post-Traumatic Stress Disorder

SAMHSA Substance Abuse and Mental Health Services Administration
SNAP Supplemental Nutrition Assistance Program

TANF Temporary Assistance for Needy Families

UCR Uniform Crime Reporting
USSC United States Sentencing Commission

Preface

The recidivism rate is a statistical institution in the criminal legal system. It is widely used by policymakers, practitioners, and researchers to refer to the crimes, convictions, and reincarceration of people released from prison. It is the default benchmark for determining the effectiveness of policies and programs to prevent post-release criminal behavior. From the beginning, however, the recidivism rate has had its critics, who argue that it is based on defective data and is commonly misinterpreted and misapplied.[1] Arnold Ventures asked the National Academies of Sciences, Engineering, and Medicine to convene an expert committee to conduct a critical analysis of recidivism and, as needed, propose alternative measures of success for the more than 600,000 persons who reenter society each year after leaving prison. This report is the culmination of the committee's deliberations.

The use of the term "success" in the committee's charge is telling. It reverses the focus on failure that defines the recidivism rate. The committee was asked to consider the multiple meanings and measures of success after prison in addition to the cessation of criminal behavior. We took this charge literally and have devoted extensive attention in our report to measures of post-release progress and improvement across multiple life domains, including physical and mental health, employment, housing, family attachment and community involvement. Our research and presentations by subject matter experts—particularly those by persons with lived experience of incarceration and the practitioners who work with them—convinced us that a sense of hope, efficacy, and overall well-being is of fundamental importance for successful reentry after prison. The challenge is to develop and validate measures of

---

[1]See, for example, Michael Maltz's ([1984] 2001) groundbreaking study.

personal well-being that are both reliable and sufficiently flexible to encompass the diverse experiences, backgrounds, and identities of those leaving prison.

Our analysis of recidivism also poses the same kind of challenge. The recidivism critics, we concluded, are essentially correct: We must move beyond the recidivism rate to adequately measure post-release criminal behavior, which will require reversing the polarity of recidivism from failure to success. In this regard, the committee undertook an extensive review of the research literature on desistance from crime. We were struck by the difference between recidivism and desistance. Recidivism is often operationalized as a binary, either-or, measure of post-release outcomes: You were either rearrested, reconvicted, or reincarcerated after leaving prison, or you were not. By contrast, desistance indicates a gradual process that, like recovery from addiction, illness or disease, can involve relapses. From the vantage point of recidivism, committing a new crime is a mark of failure. From a desistance perspective, committing fewer or less serious crimes is a sign of movement toward desistance. Our review led us to conclude that the concept of desistance more accurately depicts the realities of criminal behavior and its cessation and that measures of desistance should augment the recidivism rate. Measures of recidivism, when used, need to be applied with greater precision. Policymakers, practitioners, researchers, and other users should specify whether recidivism reflects rearrest, conviction, or incarceration and clarify the limitations of such measures.

Little in our analysis of the limitations the recidivism rate is new. Part of our task was to review and draw conclusions from the quite extensive literature on recidivism. We were also charged, however, with formulating recommendations based on our conclusions. In this respect, we broke some new ground. We do not propose that our conclusions about measuring recidivism or the correlates of successful reentry be taken as the last word on these demanding topics. On the contrary, we recommend that foundations and federal agencies use them as points of departure for extensive evaluation of the kinds and quality of the data underlying current recidivism measures and the development of uniform standards for measuring desistance from crime and successful reentry in life domains including but not limited to the criminal legal system.

We recognize that this is a tall order and that, even if our recommendations are taken up by private and government stakeholders, it may be years before they issue their own findings and recommendations. Therefore, the question arises: What is to be done in the meantime? We urge that everyone who cares about what happens to the people who pass through the nation's prisons and reads this report ask themselves the same questions we did as we were writing it: Do current measures of recidivism tell us what we need to know about success after prison? How can we do better?

Richard Rosenfeld, *Chair*
Committee on Evaluating Success
Among People Released from Prison

Acknowledgments

This report was made possible by the contributions of many people. First, we thank the study's sponsor Arnold Ventures, for requesting and supporting this endeavor. We particularly thank Jeremy Travis (Executive Vice President of Criminal Justice) and Jocelyn Fontaine (Vice President of Criminal Justice Research).

Special thanks go to the members of the study committee, who dedicated extensive time, thought, energy, and good humor to the project on such a compressed timeline. In addition to its own research and deliberations, the committee received input from several outside sources, whose willingness to share their perspectives and expertise was essential to the committee's work. We thank Susan Burton (A New Way of Life Reentry Center), George Braucht (Brauchtworks), Kenneth Cooper (Game Changers Reentry Program), Jai Diamond (New York Criminal City Justice Agency), Jennifer Doleac (Texas A&M University), Jerry Flores (University of Toronto), Adam Gelb (Council on Criminal Justice), Peggy Giordano (Bowling Green State University), Diana Good Collins (Metropolitan Community College), Nneka Jones Tapia (Chicago Beyond), Lila Kazemian (City University of New York), Pamela Lattimore (RTI International), Andrea Leverentz (University of Massachusetts, Boston), Sam Lewis (Anti-Recidivism Coalition), Charles Loeffler (University of Pennsylvania), Shadd Maruna (Queen's University, Belfast), Reuben Miller (University of Chicago), Merry Morash (Michigan State University), Daniel Nagin (Carnegie Mellon University), Kara Nelson (True North Recovery), Lisa Puglisi (Yale School of Medicine), William Rhodes, Walter Strauss (New York City Housing Court-retired), Dana Rice (University of North Carolina), John Valverde

(Youthbuild USA), Venus Woods (Cook Inlet Tribal Council), Caryn York (Job Opportunities Task Force).

The committee was also able to gather input from correctional officials and service providers for crime victims and survivors. We extend our gratitude to David Edwards (Missouri Department of Corrections, Department of Planning), Michelle Garcia (DC Office of Victims Services and Justice Grants), Travis Gramble (Multnomah County DCJ Gang Unit and African American Program), Sarah Ohlsen (National Center for Victims of Crime), Alejandro Palacio (National Organization for Victim Assistance), Anne Precythe (Missouri Department of Corrections), Erika Preuitt (Multnomah County Department of Community Justice), Katie Roller (Multnomah County DCJ, Women and Family Services Unit), Bryan Smith (Multnomah County DCJ, Alternative Incarceration Program and Short Term Transitional Leave Program), Bridgette Stumpf (National Network for Victim Recovery D.C.), Glenn Tapia (Colorado Probation Agency), Heather Warnken (Center for Criminal Justice Reform), and Heidi Washington (Michigan Department of Corrections).

The committee also gathered information through a commissioned paper. We thank Lila Kazemian (John Jay College of Criminal Justice) for her contributions to this report and for her willingness to work on an abbreviated timeline. Tyler Harvey (Yale University) contributed valuable research support for Chapters 3 and 4. Finally, we thank John Laub (The University of Maryland) for sharing his enthusiasm and expertise with the committee, and for offering commentary on a report draft.

We also extend our gratitude to the staff of the National Academies of Sciences, Engineering, and Medicine. Briana Smith provided key administrative and logistical support to ensure that the committee process ran efficiently, as well as providing essential support in preparing the report for publication. Ellie Grimes made critical substantive contributions to the committee's information gathering and literature review. Emily Backes provided guidance at every stage of the study process, along with contributing to the writing and editing of the report. Throughout the project, Natacha Blain, director of the Committee on Law and Justice, provided oversight. From the Division of Behavioral and Social Sciences and Education, we thank Kirsten Sampson Snyder and Douglas Sprunger, who expertly shepherded the report through the review process and assisted with its communication and dissemination. We thank librarian Anne Marie Houppert in the National Academies Research Center for her crucial assistance with fact-checking. We also thank Marc DeFrancis for his skillful editing.

This Consensus Study Report was reviewed in draft form by individuals chosen for their diverse perspectives and technical expertise. The purpose of this independent review is to provide candid and critical comments that will assist the National Academies of Sciences, Engineering, and Medicine in making each published report as sound as possible and to ensure that it meets the institutional standards for quality, objectivity, evidence, and responsiveness to the study charge. The review comments and draft manuscript remain confidential to protect the integrity of the deliberative process.

We thank the following individuals for their review of this report: Kristofer Bucklen (Planning, Research, and Statistics, Pennsylvania Department of Corrections), Adam Gelb (Office of the President and CEO, Council on Criminal Justice), Beth Huebner (Department of Criminology and Criminal Justice, University of Missouri–St. Louis), Michael Jacobson (Institute for State and Local Governance and Sociology Department, CUNY Graduate Center), Pamela Lattimore (Research Development, Division for Applied Justice Research, RTI International), Magnus Lofstrom (Criminal Justice, Public Policy Institute of California), and Giovanni Mastrobuoni (Public and Labor Economics, Collegio Carlo Alberto).

Although the reviewers listed above provided many constructive comments and suggestions, they were not asked to endorse the conclusions or recommendations of this report nor did they see the final draft before its release. The review of this report was overseen by James Lynch, Department of Criminology and Criminal Justice, University of Maryland and Ellen Wright Clayton, Vanderbilt Law School. They were responsible for making certain that an independent examination of this report was carried out in accordance with the standards of the National Academies and that all review comments were carefully considered. Responsibility for the final content rests entirely with the authoring committee and the National Academies.

Richard Rosenfeld, *Chair*
Amanda Grigg, *Study Director*
Committee on Evaluating Success
Among People Released from Prison

Contents

Boxes, Figures, and Tables

BOXES

FIGURES

TABLES

Summary[1]

The criminal legal system in the United States has vast reach.[2] Over 75 million American adults have an arrest or criminal record of some kind and 4.3 million remain under community supervision. Over 600,000 people were released from state and federal prisons each year between 2000 and 2019 with the hope that they will successfully reintegrate into their communities.[3] Their success or failure is used as an indicator of our criminal legal system's effectiveness. Tracking the success of those released from prison can tell us whether the criminal legal system is fulfilling its mission and whether public investments are being put to effective use. The successful reintegration of those released from prison is also often used as an indicator of public safety. In fact, the National Institute of Corrections describes successful reintegration as a "critical aspect of correctional missions to improve public safety." Nevertheless, while evaluations of success among individuals released from prison affect perceptions of the performance of our institutions and the safety of our communities, our attempts to evaluate success face serious limitations.

---

[1]Citations to support the text and conclusions of this summary are provided in the body of the report.

[2]In the service of accuracy, the committee uses the term "criminal legal system" to describe the various institutions, agencies, and official actors who enact and enforce criminal law in the United States. See Chapter 1 for further discussion of terminology used in this report.

[3]The number of individuals released from prison in the United States dropped to 549,600 in 2020.

In this context, Arnold Ventures asked the Committee on Law and Justice of the National Academies of Sciences, Engineering, and Medicine to form an ad hoc committee to examine:

1. The strengths and limitations of current measures of recidivism, including variation according to different individual needs and characteristics, and identification of key factors and outcomes that are not adequately captured by this measure alone.
2. The correlates of positive outcomes for individuals who do not return to incarceration and corresponding measures of reentry from prison that go beyond the avoidance of negative outcomes, such as crime, and consider broader measures of success (e.g., health, victimization, family attachment, educational attainment, employment, income, and civic engagement).

The committee members applied expertise from a range of disciplines to their charge, including criminology, law, medicine, political science, sociology, economics, and statistics. Committee members also brought expertise in criminal legal policy and reentry programming, and personal experience of incarceration and reentry. To respond to their charge, the committee examined the existing literature and relevant data sources on recidivism, desistance, and broader post-release outcomes. A public session with researchers, practitioners, and experts with previous experience of incarceration was held and a commissioned paper was secured to fill gaps in evidence and information. The committee also met with and drew on the expertise of correctional officials and crime victims and survivors' service providers in the course of its deliberations.

The committee's conclusions fall broadly into two categories. The first and second conclusions speak to the limitations of current measures of recidivism. The final three conclusions reflect the many broader, positive outcomes of success relevant to those returning from incarceration. Drawing on these conclusions, the committee offers four recommendations for the evaluation of success among those released from prison. The committee offers a range of recommendations for changes in practice, policy, and research, including recommendations whose adoption will require significant time, commitment, and financial investment. Some of the committee's recommendations will require collaboration across organizations and sectors that may be challenging to implement; however, the possible existence of barriers to implementation of a recommendation should not determine the value of pursuing it. Where possible, the committee highlights ways to leverage existing research or programs that offer models from which to build.

From its review of the evidence, the committee concluded that efforts to evaluate success should shift away from exclusive reliance on recidivism, an imprecise proxy at best for measuring return to criminal behavior; clarify the limitations of certain measures of recidivism; draw more heavily on desistance as a measure of post-release outcomes in the criminal legal system; and expand the measurement of post-release success to include well-being in a broad range of life domains. The committee arrived at five key conclusions—supported by evidence presented in chapters 2 through 4—that serve as the basis for the recommendations listed below and discussed in more detail in Chapter 5.

Taken together, the committee's recommendations address two goals: (1) to improve measures of post-release outcomes in the domain of the criminal legal system and (2) to improve the evaluation of post-release success by expanding current concepts and measures to encompass positive outcomes in domains outside of the criminal legal system.

Of particular importance, the committee recognizes that individuals with personal experience of incarceration and practitioners who work with formerly incarcerated individuals have unique insights regarding the conceptualization and measurement of post-release success. Formerly incarcerated individuals and reentry practitioners have made essential contributions to each chapter of this report. The committee strongly recommends that their expertise inform the design and implementation of each of this report's recommendations.

EVALUATING POST-RELEASE SUCCESS: CORE CONCEPTS

The reoccurrence of criminal behavior after release from prison is a key piece of evidence used in evaluating post-release success. Much criminal behavior results in harm to individuals, communities, and society-at-large, and as such is of critical interest to policy makers and the public. To date, the bulk of evaluation of the outcomes of criminal legal system involvement, particularly for people released from prison, has typically relied on measures of recidivism, which purport to measure the likelihood that previously incarcerated individuals will commit new crimes and eventually return to prison. However, existing recidivism measures offer a narrow understanding of reentry and can be misleading if researchers and policy makers are not aware of the varying sampling strategies used to assess how the prison experience affects the life outcomes of individuals after release.

For example, pronounced differences exist between the relatively low recidivism rates of individuals released from prison for the first time and the significantly higher rates among those who have been in prison multiple times. In addition, the administrative data used to measure returns to prison typically include arrests as well as technical violations, which may not always reflect the commission of a new crime. Administrative records are also subject to a number of limitations, the most important of which is that they reflect the recorded actions of legal officials. As a result, administrative records do not count criminal behavior that goes undetected by criminal legal system officials and can include wrongful assignment of criminal behavior to innocent parties. In short, recidivism measures are a limited and imprecise proxy for an individual's return to criminal behavior.

While return to crime is a key piece of understanding post-release success, scientific evidence shows that the cessation of criminal activity is complex and best understood as a slow process that may involve setbacks. Recidivism rates are typically binary (yes/no) measures. Even when they are accurate, they reveal only whether or not a new arrest, conviction, or incarceration has occurred, ignoring factors that would provide a more complete picture of movement toward desistance such as the time elapsed between recidivism episodes, the relative severity of the offense compared to past offenses, and the community and societal factors that influence recidivism.

Research has also documented the persistent and varied barriers facing those attempting to reintegrate in domains beyond criminal legal system involvement. Individuals released from prison today face numerous collateral consequences (impediments beyond conviction and incarceration themselves) with respect to employment, education, housing, health, and community and civic life. Many of these collateral consequences amplify precisely the characteristics that are thought to be associated with continued criminal activity, including weakened social bonds, inadequate and unstable employment, and a diminished sense of well-being. As they are currently applied, recidivism measures encourage a sole focus on negative outcomes in the criminal legal domain when evaluating reentry process. This limits the ability to measure, let alone support, post-release success. It also limits society's collective ability to make informed policy and budgetary decisions regarding the criminal legal system.

MEASURING THE CESSATION OF CRIMINAL ACTIVITY

Broadly speaking, recidivism refers to a return to criminal activity. In practice, recidivism measures rely on administrative records of criminal legal system activity, drawing on rearrest, reconviction, or reincarceration data or some combination of the three. These measures thus reflect the interaction between individuals and the criminal legal system. They can be both over-inclusive, by recording mistaken arrests and wrongful convictions, and under-inclusive, by failing to capture undetected criminal activity. While administrative records capture the most serious criminal behavior reasonably well, victimization surveys indicate that a large fraction of criminal behavior goes undetected.[4] Nor do these measures account for the

---

[4]For example, results from the National Crime Victimization Survey indicate that victims or others reported just 40 percent of violent victimizations and 33 percent of property victimizations to the police in 2020 (Morgan and Thompson, 2021).

disparities in likelihood of arrest, conviction, and reincarceration based on an individual's identity or community context.

Current conceptions of recidivism also tend to treat any return to crime as a failure, without distinguishing between failure as an end state or as part of a desistance process. A robust body of scientific evidence on desistance demonstrates that the cessation of criminal activity occurs incrementally and can involve setbacks. For example, an individual on the path toward ceasing criminal activity may commit additional crimes but with declining frequency or seriousness, indicating that they are on the path to desistance. Common measures of recidivism do not capture this movement toward desistance or other signs of progress highlighted by research on desistance, including changes in self-view and feelings of hope.

In sum, recidivism rates based on administrative records are an imprecise and incomplete proxy for measuring a return to criminal activity (Conclusion 1). Measures of desistance from crime offer a more accurate and realistic account of changes in criminal activity after release from prison (Conclusion 2).

RECOMMENDATION 1: To ensure more precise and accurate use of the construct of recidivism, researchers, policy makers, and practitioners should (a) specify the exact actions taken by legal authorities (arrest, revocation, conviction, incarceration) included in their measures, (b) clarify the limitations of the data used to measure these actions, and (c) supplement binary recidivism measures with measures of desistance from crime such as the frequency and seriousness of offense and length of time until a new offense.

MEASURING SUCCESS

One of the most significant limitations of current measures of recidivism is their limited ability to measure the multiple dimensions of post-release success. In concept and practice, the scope of recidivism is restricted to a single realm—the criminal legal system. But individuals released from prison return to lives and communities that are more complex than avoiding criminal legal system intervention. In addition, the criminal legal system's core aims go beyond punishment to include public safety and rehabilitation—neither of which is captured in full by an exclusive focus on recidivism. The Federal Bureau of Prisons lists successful reentry as a core element of its vision, which will be realized when "through the provision of health care, mental, spiritual, educational, vocational, and work programs, inmates are well-prepared for a productive and crime-free return to society."[5]

---

[5]Federal Bureau of Prisons, "About Our Agency," https://www.bop.gov/about/agency/agency_pillars.jsp.

A more meaningful conception of success views post-release outcomes through the lens of overall healthy adult development across multiple life domains in addition to crime control: education, employment, housing, family and social support, mental and physical health, and civic and community engagement.

An individual's success is also determined in part by their own personal sense of well-being. For example, an individual may prioritize success in certain domains and thus have a sense of well-being despite setbacks in other domains. Neither recidivism nor desistance encompasses this broader conception of success, and researchers and practitioners in the criminal legal space lack adequate methods of measuring it, though promising models have been validated in other disciplines (see Chapter 4 for examples). *Meaningful measures of success traverse multiple life domains including a heightened sense of personal well-being, which is best measured through self-report surveys and validated assessment instruments* (Conclusion 3).

> **RECOMMENDATION 2: Researchers should review existing measures and, as needed, develop and validate new measures to evaluate post-release success in multiple domains, including personal well-being, education, employment, housing, family and social supports, health, civic and community engagement, and legal involvement.**

Individuals released from prison face a number of significant barriers to success across life domains, including ongoing penalties for their criminal behavior. They may return to a community without adequate employment opportunities or training programs. They may not have access to necessary substance abuse treatment or mental health counseling. They may encounter local or state policies that exclude them from accessible housing or social safety net programs. Further, systemic disparities exist along lines of race, socioeconomic status, and geography in access to needed services and supports. As such, post-release outcomes are the product of interactions between individual behavior, institutional actions, and systemic inequalities in exposure to barriers and access to resources. The choices an individual makes, both in prison and after release, play a pivotal role in post-release outcomes, as the listening session with previously incarcerated persons made clear. But an individual's range of choices is shaped by the environments into which they are released, and it can be expanded or constrained by the opportunities or barriers to which they are exposed. *The existence of community and policy facilitators of and barriers to success can be documented in studies that link data on post-release success to local socioeconomic conditions, policies that restrict access to employment, housing, and public benefits, and structural inequalities that disproportionately affect historically marginalized populations* (Conclusion 4).

RECOMMENDATION 3: Researchers should review existing measures and, as needed, develop new measures of facilitators of and structural barriers to post-release success in multiple domains, including personal well-being, education, employment, housing, family and social supports, health, civic and community engagement, and legal involvement. These measures should reflect the particular needs and experiences of historically marginalized groups.

A persistent problem facing the evaluation of post-release success is the lack of shared definitions and methodologies. In the case of recidivism, one reentry program's recidivism rate may refer to rearrests and technical violations of the rules of community supervision while another program's rate may measure only reincarceration. One state's recidivism rate may measure criminal activity in the five years following release, and another's may track recidivism over just three years. As a result, it is difficult to reliably compare recidivism rates across programs or across jurisdictions. A lack of uniform best practices and standards greatly complicates efforts to measure success and limits opportunities to experiment, learn from one another, and scale interventions. The wide variety of definitions and methodologies also invites misinterpretation and misuse. These problems could persist even with a move toward a more robust conception of post-release success.

Individual jurisdictions and agencies are free to retain their own standards and measures of post-release success in addition to uniform standards that allow for reliable comparisons across jurisdictions. *Uniform national standards for measuring success among individuals released from prison would augment the comparability of program evaluations and the utility of administrative and other data across multiple policy domains. The development of a website containing core measures and instruments would hasten the eventual development of uniform measurement standards. These efforts can be supported by federal agencies and private foundations committed to improving success for persons released from prison* (Conclusion 5).

RECOMMENDATION 4: The National Institute of Justice, Bureau of Justice Statistics, Bureau of Justice Assistance, National Institutes of Health, and other federal agencies and centers whose missions are central to the success of persons released from prison should (a) convene interdisciplinary research advisory panels to assess data, methods, and recommendations for measuring post-release success; (b) request grant proposals from researchers and practitioners, in collaboration with formerly incarcerated persons, to review existing measures of success and develop and validate new measures as needed; and (c) consider questions relevant to the measurement of post-release success in existing survey protocols such as the American Community Survey and data collection efforts in other domains such as education, labor, and health. Private foundations committed to improving success among persons released from prison should support this evaluation independently or in partnership with federal agencies. Governmental and private support should be directed, at a minimum, to the following issues:

a) The quality of records from legal and other social institutions used to monitor post-release success;
b) The utility and feasibility of linking records across multiple administrative domains;
c) The utility and feasibility of linking existing administrative data with instruments measuring personal well-being;
d) The development of a website containing core measures of success across multiple administrative domains and the role of qualitative as well as quantitative research in the development of these measures; and
e) The eventual development of uniform national standards for measuring post-release success.

CONCLUSION

The widespread use and misuse of current recidivism measures can generate inaccurate conclusions and ineffective policies and programs. Nonetheless, the committee believes there is great promise for improving the measurement of success among individuals released from prison. Executing the committee's recommended improvements will require the investment of researchers, practitioners, administrators, policy makers, and private funders. It will require advances in data collection, new lines of research, sustained collaboration across disciplines and policy domains, and shifts in shared terminology. These efforts are vitally important. Decisions about what and how to measure can have enormous impact on program and policy outcomes. Improving the measurement of success for those released from prison has the potential to produce more effective policy, safer and more stable communities, and better lives for those who reenter them. Who is included in the process of decision-making is as important as the measurement decisions themselves. Formerly incarcerated individuals and reentry practitioners should be directly involved as partners in each stage of the review, development, validation, and implementation of new measures of success among persons released from prison.

1

Introduction

As of 2019, more than 6.4 million people were on probation, in jail or prison, or on parole in the United States (Minton, Beatty, and Zeng, 2021). Over 600,000 individuals were released from state and federal prisons between 2000 and 2019, and one in three U.S. adults—more than 75 million people—have an arrest or criminal record of some kind (Carson, 2021; Manza and Uggen, 2008; Petersilia, 2003; Prescott and Starr, 2020).[1] The annual budgetary cost of incarceration in the United States has been estimated at $80 billion (Lockwood and Lewis, 2019), though some estimates place it as high as $182 billion (Wagner and Rabuy, 2017). In a system that is this costly and that touches this many lives, accurate and effective measurement of success after release from prison is a high-stakes matter. How do we know whether the system is working?

In the United States, the dominant measure of correctional failure or success is *recidivism*. The National Institute of Justice (NIJ), the research arm of the U.S. Department of Justice, defines recidivism as "a person's relapse into criminal behavior, often after the person receives sanctions or undergoes intervention for previous crime" (National Institute of Justice, 2021). NIJ also states that recidivism is measured by acts that result in arrest, conviction, or incarceration during a specified period (typically three years) following an individual's release from prison. Traditionally, recidivism rates have been used as a near-universal measure to evaluate the success of correctional policies, correctional agencies, and reentry

---

[1]The number of individuals released from state and federal prisons fell to 549,000 in 2020. Numbers for 2021 were not available as of report release.

programs. As documented in this report, however, *common recidivism measures convey an incomplete and often inaccurate and misleading understanding of the success of individuals who enter and are subsequently released from prison.*

Among their other purposes, correctional interventions are intended to reduce criminal behavior and increase public safety, achieve justice for crime victims, and rehabilitate individuals who have committed crimes. Recidivism rates are used to measure the success of these interventions. Yet as this report details, recidivism conveys little about the social reintegration or personal well-being of those returning from prison and nothing about victim satisfaction with correctional interventions.

This report advances our understanding of post-release success in two key ways. First, it discusses multiple limitations of recidivism as a measure of correctional success, and it proposes significant changes in the way post-release criminal behavior is measured. Second, it considers measures of success that go beyond recidivism and provide indicators of post-release success in multiple life domains, including health, family, employment, housing, civic engagement, and personal well-being. In developing this broader notion of success, the committee considered how the outcomes for those released from prison are shaped by the social and policy environments to which they return. We recognize that success depends on the *interaction* among the attributes and choices of individuals, the decisions of legal authorities, and access to services and supports that facilitate reentry.

STUDY CHARGE AND SCOPE

Criticisms of the concept and measurement of recidivism are not new. Researchers in criminology, sociology, economics, psychology, public health, medicine, social work, and other fields have enlarged our understanding of what success in reentry looks like and what it requires. Nevertheless, widely promulgated recidivism data and statistics have not changed in response to these insights. It is against this backdrop that Arnold Ventures requested that the Committee on Law and Justice of the National Academies of Sciences, Engineering, and Medicine convene an expert committee to provide guidance on the measurement and evaluation of success among people released from prison. The committee was charged with critically examining: (1) the strengths and weaknesses of current measures of recidivism; and (2) correlates of positive outcomes for individuals released from prison (see the committee's full Statement of Task in Box 1-1). Twelve prominent scholars and practitioners were included on the committee, representing a broad range of expertise including criminology, sociology, health and medicine, law and policy, statistics, corrections, and reentry (see Appendix A for biographical sketches of the committee members).

BOX 1-1
**Evaluating Success Among People Released from Prison:
Statement of Task**

The National Academies, of Sciences, Engineering, and Medicine will appoint an ad hoc multidisciplinary committee to examine the measurement and evaluation of success among people released from prison to undertake a critical analysis of the following:

1. The strengths and limitations of current measures of recidivism, including variation according to different individual needs and characteristics, and identification of key factors and outcomes that are not adequately captured by this measure alone.
2. The correlates of positive outcomes for individuals who do not return to incarceration and corresponding measures of reentry from prison that go beyond the avoidance of negative outcomes, such as crime, and consider broader measures of success (e.g., health, victimization, family attachment, educational attainment, employment, income, and civic engagement).

A final report will draw conclusions and make recommendations as appropriate and will be subject to institutional review standards.

One of the first tasks facing a National Academies committee is to determine the scope of its statement of task. The committee accordingly made judgments about the bounds of its work. The primary focus of this report is on adults released from incarceration in prisons, which is the principal focus of research and source of data on recidivism. The committee recognizes that measures of success for those under community supervision, in the jail population, and in juvenile correctional settings are undeniably important, and encourages relevant stakeholders—including state, local, and federal agencies—to consider the applicability of the findings and recommendations from this report to those settings.

The measurement of success inevitably invokes normative questions of justice, including the reasonable and proper purposes of punishment and our rehabilitative obligations to those reentering society. Such questions are essential and need to be considered carefully by decision makers, communities, and scholars, but they are beyond the scope of this report. This committee's primary task is to review the relevant research literature on the measurement of recidivism and reentry, call attention to areas needing further research, and draw appropriate conclusions. The measurement of success, however, *does* require consideration of systemic inequalities that shape experiences of reentry for historically marginalized populations. Such considerations are within the scope of the committee's charge when applied to the measurement of post-release success. Accordingly, this report considers evidence about the ways inequalities in the distribution of power, access, and opportunities shape reentry outcomes, and it draws conclusions about how this evidence can inform efforts to improve measures of success.

The issues at hand have broad reach. The measurement of success for those returning from prison has implications for the responsibilities of correctional agencies toward the persons under their supervision, the design of effective reentry policy, community-based programs and services across multiple sectors, the well-being of marginalized communities, victim satisfaction with correctional interventions, and crime control policy. Improving metrics of post-release success is a vital first step in making informed policy decisions and ensuring that taxpayer investments are spent wisely. It is also important for ensuring that the criminal legal system is accountable to those it affects directly, to their families and communities, to their victims and survivors, and to the broader public.

The committee recognizes the pressing need for progress in each of these spaces. It also recognizes that progress will require work beyond that undertaken in this report. The committee's charge focuses on the measurement of success for those returning from prison. The charge does not include evaluating reentry programs or making recommendations for improvements to them, though these are both vital next steps in reimagining reentry. The committee encourages those interested in improving reentry to consider this report a necessary but not sufficient step in that direction.

STUDY APPROACH

Throughout its deliberations, the committee considered several questions relevant to its charge. The following are nine major questions that guided the committee's work:

1. How should "success" be defined for persons released from prison?
2. What are feasible standards for post-release success and how are they related to standards of success for the general population?
3. Do current measures of recidivism adequately capture the multiple dimensions of success and the multiple purposes of the criminal legal system, including crime reduction, rehabilitation, and justice for crime victims and survivors?
4. Do current measures of recidivism draw on the best available knowledge about how desistance from criminal behavior occurs?
5. What are the results of current widely cited studies of recidivism, and how have rates of recidivism based on these studies changed over time?
6. What are the chief limitations of current recidivism measures?

7. How do recidivism, desistance, reentry, and success differ by race, gender, and other salient identities?
8. How do or should measures of post-release success differ across these groups?
9. How should the needs of policy makers and service providers for a feasible method of measuring success be balanced with the need for more accurate and nuanced measures of success?

The committee met and deliberated over a ten-month period to address these questions and reach the findings and recommendations presented in this report. To augment its own expertise, the committee held several information-gathering sessions. The first public session included a moderated conversation highlighting the lived experiences of formerly incarcerated individuals, as well as research presentations focused on data and methods for measuring recidivism and qualitative approaches to studying reentry. The second public session included research presentations on theories of identity change and desistance from crime, as well as moderated conversations highlighting practitioner expertise in reentry, health, employment, education, and housing. Additional listening sessions engaged advocates for crime victims and survivors and correctional leaders, with the aim of better understanding their perspectives on the conceptualization and measurement of post-release success. Insights from these sessions are highlighted in text boxes throughout this report.

The committee conducted an extensive critical review of the literature pertaining to the measurement of recidivism and correlates of positive outcomes for those returning from prison. This review began with an English-language search of online databases, including ProQuest and HeinOnline. Committee members and project staff used online searches to identify additional literature and other resources. Attention was given to consensus and position statements issued by relevant experts and professional organizations. Research reports in peer-reviewed journals of the disciplines relevant to this study received priority. This report also builds on recent publications of the National Academies of Sciences, Engineering, and Medicine, including *The Growth of Incarceration in the United States: Exploring Causes and Consequences*; and *Decarcerating Correctional Facilities during COVID-19: Advancing Health, Equity, and Safety* (National Academies of Sciences, Engineering, and Medicine, 2020; National Research Council, 2014).

LANGUAGE

In the service of accuracy, the committee uses the term "criminal legal system" to describe the various institutions, agencies, and official actors who enact and enforce criminal law in the United States. This terminology can be found in scholarly and popular publications across disciplines, including the *American Journal of Public Health*, the *New York University Law Review*, *Drug and Alcohol Dependence*, the American Bar Association's *Dispute Resolution Magazine*, and the *Encyclopedia of Criminology and Criminal Justice* (Mantha et al., 2021; McDonald and Belknap, 2014; Pinard, 2020; Schneider and Alkon, 2020; Sundaresh et al., 2020).

This report also adopts "person-first" language to refer to people who have experienced incarceration. The use of person-first terminology with reference to people caught up in the criminal legal system recognizes their humanity, their inherent dignity as human beings (Cox, 2020). It avoids labels such as "offender," which defines someone wholly in terms of their criminal legal status and implies that law violation constitutes an immutable social status and personal identity (Solomon, 2021; Tran et al., 2018).

The movement for person-first language originated with people with disabilities in the 1980s. It has since been adopted in other areas of health and medicine and is now regularly applied to people with mental health conditions and individuals diagnosed as obese. By 2016, the Justice Department's Office of Justice Programs had formally adopted person-first language to describe formerly incarcerated people in an effort to "reduce not only the physical but also the psychological barriers to reintegration" (Mason, 2016). Recent commentary in *Academic Medicine* (Bedell et al., 2019) and the *American Journal of Epidemiology* (Bedell et al., 2018) has called for medical professionals to make a similar shift, arguing that the language clinicians use to describe patients influences how they treat patients and noting that histories of medical research abuse were tied to stigmatizing views of the incarcerated population. Using person-centered language also aligns with the current practice of the Centers for Disease Control and Prevention (CDC) (Centers for Disease Control and Prevention, 2020). The committee's use of person-first language is not intended to minimize the impact of crime on victims and survivors or on communities. Our aim in using this language is to accurately describe the communities of interest in this study and to recognize the humanity of people who have been incarcerated.

ORGANIZATION OF THE REPORT

This report is organized into five chapters. Following this introduction, Chapter 2 elucidates the concept of recidivism and provides context on its uses, current methods of measurement, and links to criminological theory, including life course, developmental, and macro perspectives. The chapter also considers the limitations of current measures of recidivism, the quality of the administrative data from which recidivism measures are derived, and how the concept and measurement of post-release success in the criminal legal domain can be improved by taking into account changes in the timing and duration of post-release criminal activity.

Chapter 3 reviews existing research on reentry. It focuses on what is known about the characteristics and mechanisms of success, how success differs by race, gender, and other identity categories, and gaps in research on success. It culminates in an account of what we need to know in order to effectively measure success that is not addressed by current measures of recidivism. Chapter 4 builds on the findings from the previous chapters to identify and analyze alternative measures of success. In addition to considering how best to measure desistance from crime, this chapter examines correlates of positive outcomes beyond desistance and considers broader measures of reentry success in health, education, family, employment, and more.

Finally, Chapter 5 discusses future research needs and presents conclusions and the committee's recommendations. Targets for these recommendations include government agencies, federal, state, and local policy makers, community institutions and organizations providing services to individuals who have been incarcerated, and the research community. Taken together, the recommendations are intended to offer more effective and robust ways of thinking about, evaluating, and measuring success among those released from prison.

REFERENCES

Alper, M., Durose, M.R., and Markman, J. (2018). *2018 Update on Prisoner Recidivism: A 9-Year Follow-Up Period (2005–2014)*. Washington, DC: US Department of Justice, Office of Justice Programs, Bureau of Justice Statistics.

Bedell, P.S., So, M., Morse, D.S., Kinner, S.A., Ferguson, W.J., and Spaulding, A.C. (2019). Corrections for academic medicine: The importance of using person-first language for individuals who have experienced incarceration. *Academic Medicine* 94, 2, 172–175.

Bedell, P.S., Spaulding, A.C., So, M., and Sarrett, J.C. (2018). The names have been changed to protect the. . . Humanity: Person-first language in correctional health epidemiology. *American Journal of Epidemiology* 187, 6, 1140–1142.

Centers for Disease Control and Prevention. (2020). *Health Equity Style Guide for the COVID-19 Response: Principles and Preferred Terms for Non-Stigmatizing, Bias-Free Language.* https://ehe.jhu.edu/DEI/Health_Equity_Style_Guide_CDC_Reducing_Stigma.pdf.

Cox, A. (2020). The language of incarceration. *Incarceration*, 1. Available: https://doi.org/10.1177/2632666320940859.

Federal Bureau of Prisons. About our Agency: Pillars. https://www.bop.gov/about/agency/agency_pillars.jsp.

Lockwood, B., and Lewis, N. (2019). *The Hidden Cost of Incarceration*. Marshall Project. Available: https://www.themarshallproject.org/2019/12/17/the-hidden-cost-of-incarceration.

Mantha, S., Nolan, M.L., Harocopos, A., and Paone, D. (2021). Racial disparities in criminal legal system involvement among New York City overdose decedents: Implications for diversion programs. *Drug and Alcohol Dependence* 226, 108867. Available: https://doi.org/10.1016/j.drugalcdep.2021.108867.

Manza, J., and Uggen, C. (2006). *Locked Out: Felon Disenfranchisement and American Democracy*. Oxford University Press.

Mason, K. (2016). Justice Dept. agency to alter its terminology for released convicts, to ease reentry. Guest Post, *The Washington Post*, May 4. Available: https://www.washingtonpost.com/news/true-crime/wp/2016/05/04/guest-post-justice-dept-to-alter-its-terminology-for-released-convicts-to-ease-reentry/.

McDonald, C., and Belknap, J. (2014). Intimate partner violence. *The Encyclopedia of Criminology and Criminal Justice*, 1–7. Available: https://doi.org/10.1002/9781118517383.wbeccj062.

Minton, T.D., Beatty, L.G., and Zeng, Z. (2021). *Correctional Populations in the United States, 2019 – Statistical Tables*. U.S. Department of Justice, Office of Justice Programs, Bureau of Justice Statistics, NCJ 300655. Available: https://bjs.ojp.gov/library/publications/correctional-populations-united-states-2019-statistical-tables.

Morgan, R.E., and Thompson, A. (2021). *Criminal Victimization, 2020*. U.S. Department of Justice, Office of Justice Programs, Bureau of Justice Statistics, NCJ 301775. Available: https://bjs.ojp.gov/library/publications/criminal-victimization-2020.

National Academies of Sciences, Engineering, and Medicine. 2020. *Decarcerating Correctional Facilities during COVID-19: Advancing Health, Equity, and Safety*. Washington, DC: The National Academies Press. https://doi.org/10.17226/25945.

National Institute of Justice. (2021). *Recidivism*. U.S. Department of Justice, Office of Justice Programs, National Institute of Justice. Available: https://nij.ojp.gov/topics/corrections/recidivism.

National Research Council. (2014). *The Growth of Incarceration in the United States: Exploring Causes and Consequences*. Washington, DC: The National Academies Press. https://doi.org/10.17226/18613.

Petersilia, J. (2003). *When Prisoners Come Home: Parole and Prisoner Reentry*. Oxford University Press.

Pinard, M. (2020). Race decriminalization and criminal legal system reform. *New York University Law Review Online* 95, 119. https://heinonline.org/HOL/P?h=hein.journals/nyulro95&i=119.

Prescott, J.J., and Starr, S.B. (2020). Expungement of criminal convictions: An empirical study. *Harvard Law Review* 133, 2460.

Rhodes, W., Gaes, G., Luallen, J., Kling, R., Rich, T., and Shively, M. (2014). Following incarceration, most released offenders never return to prison. *Crime & Delinquency* 62, 8, 1003–1025. Available: https://doi.org/10.1177/0011128714549655.

Rosenfeld, R., Wallman, J., and Fornango, R. (2005). The contribution of ex-prisoners to crime rates. In J. Travis and C. Visher (Eds), *Prisoner Reentry and Crime in America*, 80-104. New York: Cambridge University Press.

Schneider, A.K., and Alkon, C. (2020). Our criminal legal system: Plagued by problems and ripe for reform. American Bar Association, *Dispute Resolution Magazine* 26, 1.

Solomon, A. (2021). What words we use—and avoid—when covering people and incarceration. Web article posted April 12. *The Marshall Project*. Available: https://www.themarshallproject.org/2021/04/12/what-words-we-use-and-avoid-when-covering-people-and-incarceration.

Sundaresh, R., Yi, Y., Roy, B., Riley, C., Wildeman, C., and Wang, E.A. (2020). Exposure to the US criminal legal system and well-being: A 2018 cross-sectional study. *American Journal of Public Health* 110, S1, S116–S122.

Tran, N.T., Baggio, S., Dawson, A., O'Moore, É., Williams, B., Bedell, P., Simon, O., Scholten, W., Getaz, L., and Wolff, H. (2018). Words matter: A call for humanizing and respectful language to describe people who experience incarceration. *BMC International Health and Human Rights* 18, 1, 1–6.

Wagner, P., and Rabuy, B. (2017). Following the money of mass incarceration. *Prison Policy Initiative*. Available: https://www.prisonpolicy.org/reports/money.html.

2

Measuring Recidivism

By the late 1960s, recidivism had become a widely used metric of correctional performance, appearing in authoritative government reports. The 1967 report of the President's Commission on Law Enforcement and Administration of Justice, *The Challenge of Crime in a Free Society*, emphasized recidivism reduction as a proper goal of corrections. The compilation of recidivism data was identified as a necessary mechanism for assessing the effectiveness of criminal legal system interventions, programs, services, and initiatives (President's Commission on Law Enforcement and Administration of Justice, 1967). The desire for greater accountability for public agencies and individuals in the criminal legal system, combined with the emergence of new arrest and court administrative data, facilitated the calculation of recidivism rates for people released from prison.

Measured as a person's further involvement in criminal behavior after having been sanctioned, recidivism has long been used as an indicator of the success of corrections systems (e.g., Hunt and Dumville, 2016; King and Elderbroom, 2014; Pew Center on the States, 2011). However, this is not the only use of recidivism data. For example, recidivism measured as paroled individuals' readmission to prison has long been a component of prison population forecast models (Austin and McVey, 1989). Both uses of recidivism have important purposes, but problems arise when the purposes of measures are not clearly specified or the limitations of the measures used are not fully addressed.

These concerns are not new. More than 35 years ago, Michael Maltz wrote a treatise that furthered interest in the proper calculation of recidivism, which discussed the perils of faulty or inconsistent measurement and interpretations (Maltz, [1984] 2001). One of Maltz's ([1984] 2001) concerns was that recidivism has been defined in ad hoc ways that do not fully consider the underlying meaning of what is being measured. More recent commentary points out how distinctions in definitions affect conclusions about the performance of corrections systems (Weisberg, 2014) suggests the need for uniformity in measurement to allow for comparisons of outcomes across jurisdictions (Chen and Meyer, 2020; Council of State Governments Justice Center, 2014), and at the same time demonstrates the utility of different measures and definitions (Rhodes et al., 2014).

This chapter explores the ways recidivism is calculated and reported, discusses the strengths and weaknesses of different approaches, and points to conclusions that can—and those that cannot—be drawn from reported recidivism estimates. Consistent with the scope of this study, the chapter focuses primarily on recidivism following release from prison, although recidivism following other criminal legal system contacts is mentioned. Recommendations based on the chapter's findings and conclusions are presented in Chapter 5.

Careful review of the strengths and limitations of current measures of recidivism is important, because ignorance about how data are captured can lead to misuses in policy and practice. Different methodologies and sampling techniques, as discussed below, are needed to answer different kinds of questions related to offending behaviors and involvement with the legal system, and reliance on inappropriate samples can lead to erroneous conclusions. For example, recidivism rates that measure *events* (such as counting each case of admission to prison, in a particular window of time for which one individual could account for more than one event) provide different information from rates that measure *populations* (such as tracking post-release behavior of all those incarcerated during a particular window of time). This distinction between populations and events of interest is often lost, not only when reporting recidivism-related statistics but even when generating such statistics. Too often, errors can be made by those interpreting and relying on recidivism data to make policy and programmatic decisions within the criminal legal system.

ANNUAL PRISON RELEASES

We begin by exploring patterns of prison releases in the United States, one population for whom recidivism rates are regularly calculated, and then review Bureau of Justice Statistics (BJS) statistics on recidivism patterns for release cohorts. In the most recent year (2020) for which data were available from the BJS at the time this report was being written, just under 550,000 sentenced individuals were released from state or federal prisons. As seen in Figure 2-1, although this number is down from its 2008 peak of

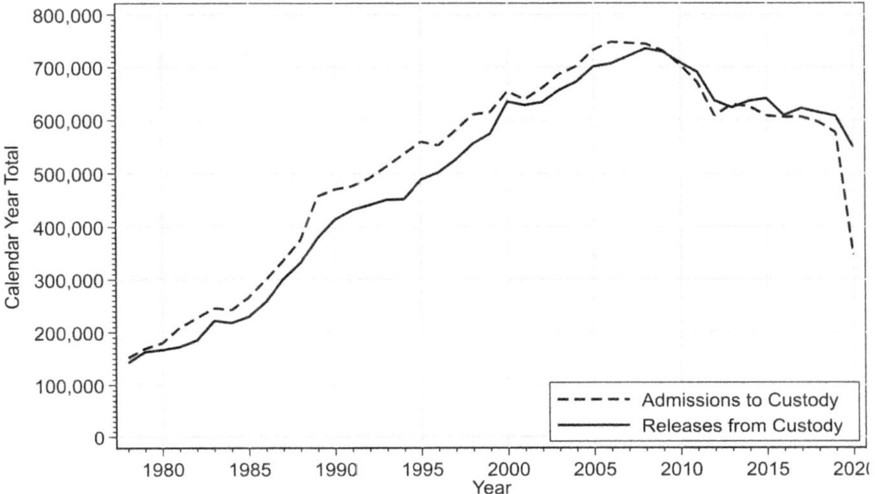

FIGURE 2-1 Annual admissions to and releases from state and federal prisons.
NOTES: Total individuals admitted or released in the calendar year who were sentenced to more than one year under the jurisdiction. Excludes AWOLs, escapes, and transfers.
SOURCE: National Prisoner Statistics (Bureau of Justice Statistics, 2021).

more than 735,000 individuals, it remains four times as high as when the BJS began systematic recordkeeping in 1978, a year when 140,000 individuals returned to the community. The number of people incarcerated in state or federal prison has declined over the last 10 years as annual releases generally exceeded annual admissions. A notable exception to the dominant pattern of alignment between releases and admissions is clearly visible in 2020. In the midst of the COVID-19 pandemic, the volume of releases declined but kept pace with the prior trend, whereas the decline in the volume of admissions was larger than expected by an order of magnitude.

Prison recidivism rates are often measured by the proportion of individuals who left prison in a given year who are later rearrested or reincarcerated (e.g., see "Recidivism in Bureau of Justice Statistics Reports" below). The National Prisoner Statistics data used in Figure 2-1 provide measures of readmission to prison of persons on parole. Such reincarcerations may result from the commission of new crimes or from violation of supervised-release conditions. Among individuals who were under some form of post-custody community supervision (such as parole) and returned to prison custody, the number of those recorded as readmitted for violations of parole conditions has grown steadily over time relative to the number of those

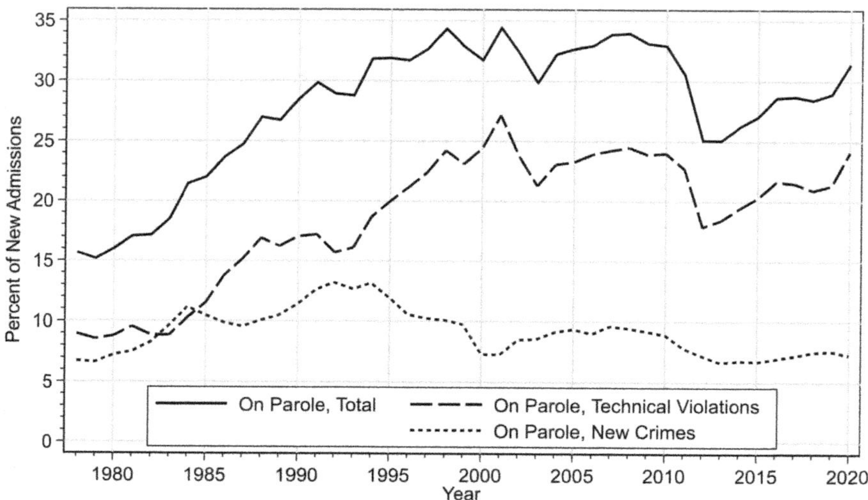

Figure 2-2 Annual percentage of new parole admissions, by type of admission.
NOTES: Only the percentages of new admissions while on parole or other conditional release are shown. The balance of new admissions in this graph comprises new court commitments of individuals who were not on parole.
SOURCE: Original estimates obtained from committee analysis of the National Prisoner Statistics (Bureau of Justice Statistics, 2021).

recorded as readmitted for new crime commission (Figure 2-2). Over the period 1978–2020, growth in the share of prison admissions from parole is accounted for almost entirely by events recorded as parole technical violations rather than new crimes while on parole.

These patterns of readmission illustrate a type of measurement error that arises in using aggregate statistics from administrative data to characterize recidivism. Prison admissions arising from technical violations of conditions of supervision may result from failure to meet conditions imposed on persons supervised in the community following release from prison (such as drug test failures, failure to show up for meetings, or failure to pay fees), or they may arise from new crimes that trigger technical violations. A new crime may trigger a technical violation because conditions of community supervision support an order returning a person to prison if a new crime was committed or a person was arrested, with the execution of the order constituting the technical violation.

The National Prisoner Statistics data are not sufficiently precise to distinguish pure technical violations from violations resulting from new crimes.

Consequently, the extent to which pure technical violations are counted as instances of recidivism or recommission of crime is unknown. Self-report data from the BJS survey of prison inmates offer some insight on this. For example, using data from BJS's survey of individuals incarcerated in state prisons in 2004, Pfaff (2015) showed that 68.3 percent of persons in prison on a technical violation reported that they were later returned to prison on a technical violation following an arrest for a new crime. Pfaff's estimates are for a prisoner stock, which may overstate the number of persons in prison under those conditions relative to the flow from persons admitted for violations. Grattet, Petersilia, and Lin's (2008) analysis of technical violations in California sheds light on the flow issue. Looking at more than 265,000 technical violations occurring in 2003-04, they found that 35 percent consisted of noncriminal or technical violations. The remaining 65 percent consisted of behaviors alleged to have violated the California Penal Code, with more serious violations (e.g., robbery, rape, first-degree burglary) accounting for 10 percent of the code violations. Their work indicates that the behaviors underlying events recorded as technical violations were primarily new offenses and arrests, rather than violations of conditions of supervision (e.g., failure to report, positive drug tests, failure to notify change of address, and so forth).

Violation of the conditions of community supervision, which may include new criminal behavior as well as violations of conditions of supervision, accounted for about a third of prison admissions during the late 1990s through 2011; their share fell in 2011 following the U.S. Supreme Court decision in *Brown v. Plata* that required California to reduce its prison population.

Individuals who violate parole contribute less to the size of the prison population than to the total number of prison admissions.[1] This is because individuals who violate parole serve less time in prison (on average) than persons admitted on a new court commitment. For example, 14 percent of state or federal prison inmates in 2016 reported that they were on parole at the time of the event leading to their current imprisonment (Beatty and Snell, 2021). If pure technical violators serve less time than those admitted on technical violations stemming from new crimes, their contribution to the size of the prison population would be much smaller. Parole supervision issues and their impact on post-release outcomes are discussed in Chapter 3.

---

[1]This text was changed after release of the pre-publication version of the report to correct an error regarding the relative contribution of individuals who violate parole to the total prison population.

COMMONLY USED MEASURES OF RECIDIVISM

In government reports and research papers, the term "recidivism" is used to cover an array of events (e.g., offenses, arrests, convictions, incarceration) and time periods (e.g., within three years of release, within nine years of release). This is not unlike the use of the term "violent offenses" to cover an array of behaviors that range from murder to misdemeanor assault. In both cases, precision is warranted about what is being measured and what portion of the broader concept a measure reflects.

Many current recidivism measures are calculated using administrative data (see below for a discussion of data sources). While older studies of drug courts included self-report offending behavior along with administrative data on rearrest among their recidivism measures (e.g., Harrell, Cavanagh, and Roman, 1998)[2] and surveys of incarcerated people (such as those conducted by Rand and BJS) asked about their prior criminal histories (Peterson, Braiker and Polich, 1980; Beatty and Snell, 2021), recent studies of post-prison release recidivism generally do not rely on self-report behaviors.

In this section, we briefly describe commonly used measures of recidivism in BJS reports, the academic literature, and by state departments of corrections.

Recidivism in Bureau of Justice Statistics Reports

The BJS prisoner recidivism reports are widely cited for providing post-prison recidivism statistics on large samples of persons released from state prisons. Relying on criminal history records from state and federal repositories, BJS has prepared several recidivism measures for five cohorts released from prison in 11 states in 1983 (Beck and Shipley, 1989), 15 states in 1994 (Langan and Levin, 2002), 30 states in 2005 (Alper, Durose, and Markman, 2018; Durose, Snyder, and Cooper, 2015), 24 states in 2008 (Antenangeli and Durose, 2021), and 34 states in 2012 (Durose and Antenangeli, 2021). BJS has devoted a great deal of attention to the standardization of criminal offenses and technical violations from parole across states.

Across its several studies of release-cohort recidivism, BJS has presented several different measures of recidivism, including:

- *Rearrest* for a new crime (as well as rearrest by charge type) both in-state and out-of-state;
- *Volume of arrests* or the total number of arrest offenses among members of a release cohort;

---

[2]Harrell and colleagues generally found that the results from the self-report and administrative data were largely comparable.

- *Readjudication* or an arrest proceeding to sanctioning in a court;
- *Reconviction* or a finding of guilt for a new crime;
- *Reincarceration* or a jail or prison sentence following conviction for a new crime; and
- *Return to prison* or any prison confinement for either a new crime or technical violation (see Durose, Cooper, and Snyder, 2014; Durose and Antenagenli, 2021).

Individuals released from prison after serving a sentence of at least one year are eligible to be included in a BJS release cohort and are identified from reports by state departments of corrections to the National Corrections Reporting Program (NCRP), another BJS product. After drawing a stratified random sample from all eligible individuals, the person-level corrections records are linked using fingerprint-based identification numbers to arrest and prosecution data from state criminal history repositories—"rap sheets" or records of arrest and prosecution—as well as from the Federal Bureau of Investigation (to track out-of-state recidivism). The criminal history data obtained by BJS comprises felonies and misdemeanors and includes information on arrest charges, court dispositions, sentences to incarceration, and custody status. The criminal history data that BJS uses in its studies are the same records that police officers use to determine a suspect's current criminal justice status (e.g., on probation, parole, or bail); that judges use to make pretrial and sentencing decisions; and that corrections officials use to make inmate classification decisions (Durose, Cooper, and Snyder, 2014). Due to state-level differences in tracking modifications to arrest charges or court dispositions, only the originating charges and dispositions are recorded. Information on returns to prison obtained from later rounds of the NCRP is used to supplement incomplete and inconsistent record-keeping in state repositories. With appropriate weighting and survey adjustment, the BJS recidivism program yields generalizable (to the included states) estimates of recidivism using multiple definitions, with corresponding margins of error, for individuals released from state prison and still living within the reference window under study.

In its most recent recidivism study, BJS collected information on a stratified sample of 92,000 people, representing individuals released from prison in 34 states in 2012 who had served a sentence of one year or more (Durose and Antenangeli, 2021). The sample was representative of about 70 percent of individuals released from state prisons in 2012 but is not nationally representative. Some of the findings from this cohort study are summarized in Table 2-1 and described below.

Over one-third of individuals in the 2012 release cohort were arrested for a new crime within one year of their release, three-fifths within three years, and 71 percent within five years (Durose and Antenangeli, 2021).

TABLE 2-1 Recidivism Estimates for 2012 Prison Release Cohort in 34-State Study

	Percent of Sample	Percent Arrested			Percent Convicted			Percent Returned to Prison		
		1 Year	3 Years	5 Years	1 Year	3 Years	5 Years	1 Year	3 Years	5 Years
All Persons	100.0	36.8	61.5	70.8	22.9	45.0	54.4	19.9	38.6	45.8
By sex										
Male	89.0	37.7	62.6	71.7	23.6	46.0	55.4	20.6	39.9	47.2
Female	11.0	29.6	52.9	63.1	16.6	36.7	46.5	13.8	28.2	34.0
By race/ethnicity										
White, Non-Hispanic	43.8	35.1	59.8	69.5	21.7	43.5	53.5	20.1	38.5	45.5
Black, Non-Hispanic	36.2	37.8	64.4	74.0	23.5	47.1	56.7	20.1	40.2	48.0
Hispanic	16.3	38.9	59.4	66.9	24.3	44.0	51.7	19.3	36.3	42.3
American Indian/Alaska Native	1.5	43.3	68.9	78.9	28.0	51.9	63.0	24.6	43.2	51.2
Asian/Native Haw.	0.7	38.0	57.3	64.8	14.8	31.8	39.2	11.4	25.8	28.4
Other	1.5	33.3	59.3	67.8	23.1	47.6	56.7	12.8	31.4	41.0
By age at release										
24 or younger	16.2	46.9	72.3	81.0	29.5	54.8	65.2	25.5	47.8	56.8
25–39	49.9	38.3	64.6	74.4	24.3	48.0	58.2	20.8	41.0	48.8
40–54	28.4	31.6	54.8	63.8	18.9	38.6	46.8	17.2	33.1	38.8
55–64	4.7	22.3	39.0	46.3	12.1	25.1	30.5	11.3	21.1	24.5
65+	0.8	13.8	21.3	25.6	4.8	10.3	13.0	5.1	10.7	14.4
Table number in source document	Table 1	Table 4			Table 7			Table 8		

NOTES: Unweighted $N = 92,100$; weighted $N = 408,300$. *Arrest* refers to either in-state or out-of-state arrest for a new crime. *Conviction* refers to determination of guilt by a court for a new crime; conviction statistics are based on data for 31 of the 34 states in the sample. *Return to prison* refers to any return to prison, including for a technical violation or following conviction for a new crime.
SOURCE: Durose and Antenangeli (2021).

A very large share of these rearrests result in a conviction, as by the fifth year after release, over half of released individuals are convicted of a new crime, typically by plea bargains. Returns to prison are also common, with nearly 46 percent of released individuals sent back to prison for either a technical violation or a new crime within five years. Demographic subgroup estimates indicate that males, members of certain minority groups (Black, American Indian, and Alaska Native), and individuals who are younger at the time of release tend to have a higher likelihood of recidivism, no matter whether the measure reflects interactions with police (rearrest), prosecutors and courts (reconviction), or return to prison.

Among those rearrested within five years of release, the most common offense of rearrest was a public order offense. Over half (54%) of persons released from prison in 2012 were rearrested for a public order offense and 49 percent were rearrested for an "other public order offense" (first column of Table 2-2). The other public order offense category is an undifferentiated category comprising conditional release violations (which include the aforementioned technical violations and arrests for new crimes reported as technical violations) along with lesser felonies and misdemeanors.[3] The next most common arrest offense categories, each characterizing just over 20 percent of released individuals, are assault, larceny or motor vehicle theft, and drug possession.

Table 2-2 shows rearrest offenses by the most serious offense of commitment of those released from prison in 2012. The top row gives the total percent rearrested within each commitment offense category, and the subsequent rows give the percent rearrested by offenses of rearrest. The overall likelihood of rearrest is lowest for individuals who served a prison sentence for violent offenses (65%) and highest for property offenses (78%) (first row in Table 2-2). The single most common group of rearrest offenses is public order offenses, overall and irrespective of the nature of the commitment offense. Arrests for violent offenses accounted for 28.3 percent of all rearrest offenses. Those released from prison with violent offense charges were rearrested for a violent offense at slightly higher rates (32.4%) than those released on property (29.6%) or public order changes (28.1%).

To the extent there is evidence of crime specialization (or rearrest for an offense within the same class as their commitment offense), it is strongest for persons released from prison for property, drug, and public order offenses. This tendency is least pronounced for individuals released after serving a prison sentence for a violent offense, of whom about one-third

---

[3]Durose and Antenangeli (2021, p. 25) define other public order offenses to include probation and parole violations, obstruction of justice, contempt of court, failure to appear, commercialized vice, nonviolent sex offenses, liquor law violations, bribery, invasion of privacy, disorderly conduct, contributing to the delinquency of a minor, and other miscellaneous or unspecified offenses.

TABLE 2-2 Five-Year Rearrest Estimates for 2012 Prison Release Cohort in 34-State Study, by Post-Release Offense Type and Commitment Offense

Post-Release Offense Type	Percent Arrested in 5 Years	Post-release Rearrest Offense by Most Serious Commitment Offense			
		Violent	Property	Drug	Public Order
Any offense	70.8	65.2	78.3	69.8	68.9
Any violent offense	28.3	32.4	29.6	22.6	28.1
Homicide	0.8	1.0	0.7	0.7	0.9
Rape/sexual assault	1.4	1.9	1.2	0.8	1.7
Robbery	4.8	6.2	5.4	3.2	3.7
Assault	21.6	24.6	22.5	17.4	21.5
Other violent	8.8	—	—	—	—
Any property offense	35.7	28.9	51.9	29.7	29.0
Burglary	9.4	6.7	17.1	6.0	6.5
Larceny/motor vehicle theft	21.6	15.8	35.5	16.5	16.3
Fraud/forgery	8.9	6.3	14.3	7.5	6.5
Other property	18.5	—	—	—	—
Any drug offense	32.6	24.1	34.7	43.0	27.7
Possession	21.9	—	—	—	—
Trafficking	11.3	—	—	—	—
Other drug	16.8	—	—	—	—
Any public order offense	54.1	51.1	58.6	51.6	54.9
Weapons	9.4	—	—	—	—
DWI/DUI	8.7	—	—	—	—
Other public order	48.8	—	—	—	—
Number of released prisoners (weighted *N)*	408,300	112,300	115,600	103,900	76,500
Table number in source document	Table 10	Table 11			

NOTES: Arrest refers to either in-state or out-of-state arrest for a new crime. Percentages for any violent, any property, any drug, and any public order offense do not sum to 100 because individuals may be rearrested on more than one occasion, or rearrested and charged for more than one offense type.
SOURCE: Durose and Antenangeli (2021).

are rearrested within five years for a new violent offense, followed by drug commitments, of which 43 percent are rearrested for a new drug offense. The BJS results on specialization are consistent with Pennsylvania data, which show modest degrees of specialization that are highest among property and drug offenses (Bell et al., 2013).

To summarize, while we do not have a national recidivism rate for individuals returning from prison, due to both coverage issues (the limited number of states providing data) and measurement issues (varying definitions, varying measures), the BJS release cohort recidivism program represents the best effort to provide that information. To date, BJS has standardized data collection for 34 states, representing 79 percent of all individuals released from state prisons in the United States (Durose and Antenangeli, 2021). Notably, states differ widely in what constitutes a punishable violation and how (or whether) that information is stored in criminal history repositories in the states that participate in the BJS cohort studies. Close inspection of rearrests indicates that while rearrests for violent crimes exceed the proportion of individuals convicted of violent offenses in the release cohort, many instances of recidivism result from other public order charges that do not necessarily align with measures of serious criminal behavior. These other charges include charges for violations of conditions of supervision, reflecting the operations of the criminal legal system and not necessarily having implications for public safety.

In all of its reports, BJS disaggregates rearrests by type of charge and reports on various characteristics of members of its release cohorts. Drawing on the criminal history records it obtains through the FBI's Interstate Identification Index, BJS also reports on rearrests occurring outside the state in which an individual is released (Durose, Cooper, and Snyder, 2014; Durose, Snyder, and Cooper, 2015). This expands the scope of events covered beyond those included in studies using state-specific criminal history records. When BJS reports on reconviction and reincarceration rates, it generally reports on the cumulate rates of reconviction or imprisonment across the years of its follow-up periods. BJS reconviction statistics are limited to arrests resulting in reconviction.

Recidivism in Academic Literature

Many other studies also rely on official records of arrests, convictions, and imprisonment but vary in the specific measures and periods. Rearrest rates are commonly measured over one or two years and for up to eight years (Bird et al., 2021; Ford and Rector, 2020; Hunt and Dumville, 2016; Seigle et al., 2014). Rather than simply report an overall or summary recidivism number, most of these studies disaggregate rearrests by class or emphasize a particular class of events. For example, in their study of recidivism following the California realignment, Bird and colleagues (2022) focused on felony re-arrests, thereby limiting their recidivism measure to arrests for more serious offenses. Studies conducted by the U.S. Sentencing Commission on persons released from federal prison report rearrest rates for up to eight years and, like BJS, report the annual and cumulative rates, along with median times to first event and recidivism offenses (Hunt and Dumville, 2016; Cotter, 2021). Ford and Rector's study (2020) of the Hawaii Opportunity Probation Evaluation (HOPE) measured rearrests over a one-year period, as did Seigle and colleagues (2014) in their study of recidivism following juvenile placement.

Reconviction measures may appear less frequently in recidivism studies, but generally when they appear, they accompany rearrest measures (e.g., Bird et al., 2022; Durose, Cooper, and Snyder, 2014; Hunt and Dumville, 2016). Recidivism rates that define recidivism as return to prison are commonly used in evaluations of the performance of corrections systems, with a three-year return-to-prison rate appearing commonly (Durose, Cooper, and Snyder, 2014; Gelb, 2018; Hunt and Dumville, 2016; King and Elderbroom, 2014; and Pew Center on the States, 2011, who also report prison return rates by year). A comprehensive recidivism study conducted by the Pew Public Safety Performance group analyzed data for three release cohorts (2005, 2010, and 2012) from 23 states and tracked returns to prison within the state of release for up to five years (Gelb and Velazquez, 2018). The Pew group reported reductions in recidivism rates, as measured by return to prison within three years of release, of nine and 13 percentage points from the 2005 base of 48 percent.

The extent to which studies measuring return-to-prison rates explicitly disaggregate by type of return varies—that is, whether they disaggregate among court commitment, a technical violation, or a new crime covered by a technical violation. State prison population forecaster measures of recidivism typically include readmissions for a parole violation (Harrison, 2021; O'Neil and Koushmaro, 2020; TenNapel et al., 2021) that may include both violations prompted by new crimes as well as technical violations (Hooks, nd). As Gaes and colleagues (2016) point out, distinguishing between a technical violation of a condition of supervision and a technical violation for reasons of a new crime is difficult with the data elements commonly found in corrections administrative databases. They accordingly recommend more extensive data. As noted earlier, evidence suggests that many if not a majority of events recorded as technical violations are actually new crimes or arrests of persons on parole, where the conditions of parole lead to a technical violation for a new crime (Grattet, Petersilia, and Lin, 2008).

The use of different measures of recidivism can cause confusion if one is looking to find out if recidivism rates have increased or decreased. Different studies use different recidivism events, different measures of the severity that constitutes recidivism, and different time periods over which recidivism is measured. They also differ according to whether events occur during periods of correctional supervision or not. These inconsistencies require users of the research literature to take care in interpreting results. Additionally, each of the several measures of recidivism—rearrest, reconviction, or reincarceration for technical violations or new crimes—has limitations. Arrests that do not result in convictions can mean that "the usual suspects" were rounded up but none actually committed a crime. Misclassifying as pure technical violations new crimes that led to a violation can result in underestimates of the severity of behavior.

Although the varieties of definitions of recidivism present challenges for comparing outcomes across places or over time, the use of multiple measures of recidivism has utility. For example, Harding and colleagues (2017) studied the effects of imprisonment on recidivism measured both by reconviction and by reimprisonment. They found no impact of imprisonment on recidivism as measured by reconviction but found an impact on recidivism when measured by reimprisonment. They were able to attribute the difference to technical violations, such as failure to comply with parole restrictions, rather than new criminal behaviors, illustrating a type of analysis that can help illuminate the extent to which recidivism arises from the decisions made by criminal legal system actors versus new offense behaviors.

Comparing outcomes across samples and locations can contribute to an understanding of what may work to help reduce recidivism events. For example, in their review of evidence on the impacts of post-conviction imprisonment on recidivism Loeffler and Nagin (2022) include studies of rearrest and reconviction covering different follow-up periods, including rearrest for periods that include 18 months and 1, 2, 3, 4, 5, and 10 years; reconviction over a 5-year period; and reincarceration within 2 or 3 years. Their review examines differences in recidivism across correctional settings, such as those that give greater emphasis to rehabilitative programming, and they find that the settings that emphasize rehabilitative programming generally lead to less recidivism. While their study does not focus on the "recidivism rate," it takes advantage of the fact that in the studies they reviewed, the authors explicitly defined their recidivism measures. Other cross-jurisdictional comparisons of recidivism have sought to measure the specific deterrent effect of incarceration on future offending (e.g., Nagin, Cullen, and Johnson, 2009; Roodman, 2017; Villettaz et al., 2006). All reached a similar conclusion, that incarceration has at best a null or mildly criminogenic effect on future offending, while Loeffler and Nagin's (2022) review pointed to the importance of rehabilitative programs in achieving recidivism reduction effects. Despite differences in measurement, careful consideration of the definitions and measures used in cross-jurisdiction studies can allow one to draw conclusions about factors that affect recidivism.

Recidivism in Departments of Corrections Reports

Recidivism rates are also often used to gauge the value and effectiveness of criminal legal policies, sometimes alongside other indicators such as "higher rates of employment, supportive family connections, improved health outcomes, and the standing of the formerly incarcerated as citizens in the community" (National Research Council, 2014; see, also, Gelb, 2018; Sabol and Baumann, 2020).

State departments of corrections create and use multiple measures rather than a single, statewide measure of recidivism. An Urban Institute report entitled *Improving Recidivism as a Performance Measure* concludes that a statewide recidivism rate is "too imprecise to draw meaningful conclusions and insufficient for assessing the impact of changes to policy and practice" (King and Elderbroom, 2014). The Pennsylvania Department of Corrections, for example, reports on rearrest and reincarceration rates and breaks these out by many variables such as sentencing offense, geographic location of releases, demographic attributes of released persons, prior criminal history, and type of release. Pennsylvania also studies recidivism-related issues such as crime specialization and recidivism arrests as a fraction of all arrests (Bell et al., 2013). Other state departments of corrections similarly construct multiple measures of recidivism to measure performance. For example, the Minnesota Department of Corrections measures felony reconvictions, reincarcerations, and community supervision recidivism, among other outcomes (Schnell, 2021). The North Carolina Department of Corrections reports on several categories of recidivism admissions, distinguishing between probation and post-release (parole) revocations, and it indicates noncompliance with conditions of supervision including commitment of a new crime as well as technical violations such as positive drug tests, non-reporting, and failing to attend treatment (Hooks, 2021). Similarly, in conversations with representatives of the committee, representatives from the Missouri Department of Corrections noted that they are beginning to capture additional measures such as employment, housing stability, pro-social community activity, and treatment length of stay. In measuring corrections performance, states recognize the value of moving away from binary and unidimensional measurements of recidivism toward more nuanced and detailed indicators (Gelb, 2018).

ELEMENTS OF RECIDIVISM MEASURES

While several events can occur that are defined as recidivism—rearrest, reconviction, reincarceration, technical violation, or graduated sanction—studies vary in the criminal legal system decision point they use to measure recidivism. Each measure has strengths and weaknesses for studying post-release outcomes; here we address some measurement issues that recidivism studies need to consider. Among the most salient limitations of recidivism measures drawn from criminal legal system actions is that the measures reflect the interaction between a person's offending behavior and the system actors' responses to that behavior. We do not attempt to reconcile this discrepancy, but this aspect of measurement error is discussed in detail below.

Purposes and Uses

Central to the measurement of recidivism are the purposes to which measures are put. The purposes and uses determine the samples to be studied, the events to be measured, the durations between them, and the risk environment. Common purposes include program evaluation, program monitoring, performance measurement, forecasting of prison bedspace needs, and research about the correlates of recidivism. Different purposes may impose different requirements on measures and their interpretation. For example, in a drug court setting a treatment provider may want to measure substance use behaviors longitudinally to identify relapse and take appropriate responses. Or an evaluation of the effectiveness of in-prison programs that address criminogenic needs may study persons released from prison in different risk environments (e.g., measured by crime rates or level of police surveillance) to estimate future contacts with criminal legal system agencies. Studies that look at the performance of programs need to be clear about the follow-up periods. For example, if persons are released into parole, should the follow-up period be limited to the period of supervision or extend beyond it? These different periods not only have implications for measured recidivism rates, but they are linked to different research questions about supervision.

Samples and Populations of Interest:
Event-Based and Person-Based Methods

The samples used to study recidivism need to be specified relative to the study purposes and derived from the populations about which inferences are to be made. If a study is interested in focusing on the outcomes of a group of people involved in some treatment program, such as an in-prison substance abuse program, the sample should represent the population of persons involved in that program. If a study seeks to understand the recidivism of persons who entered prison at any point in time, the sample should represent the entering cohort for the period under consideration, even if some members of the entering cohort might still be incarcerated at the end of the study period.

Defining the population, and therefore the sample, to be drawn for a study can present challenges. If measures of corrections system performance are desired, then the population of interest is all persons who were under a system's authority. This population may differ in important ways from the persons released from a system in a given year. A sample of persons released from a system during some period is *event-based* sampling, where the event used to define the sample is release from prison and the population of interest is members of the release cohort. Depending on a number of conditions related to whether a population can be characterized as stationary or as stable, an event-based sample may not represent the system's population (Patterson and Preston, 2008; Rhodes et al., 2014). By comparison, *person-based* samples are drawn from the population of all persons who were in prison during a particular period, regardless of a specific year of release or other event.

The BJS prison recidivism studies of individuals released from prison use event-based samples, and their reports refer to the samples as such by explicitly citing the recidivism rates of persons released from prison during a given year. However, the BJS statistics have also been misused to describe populations other than the ones from which the samples are drawn. In its "Social Determinants of Health" component of Healthy People 2020, the Office of Disease Prevention and Health Promotion uses time-specific prisoner-release recidivism rates to characterize recidivism of persons released from prison or jail.[4] This use represents a misunderstanding of the event-based sample because it generalizes to a population that is not included in the study. More subtly, but still incorrectly, release-cohort event-based sample results have been used to characterize all former prisoners. For example, the *Harvard Political Review* has used the BJS event-based sample to generalize to all former prisoners (Benecchi, 2021) and not just to the persons in the specific release cohort of interest. These distinctions are subtle, but as we show below, the difference in recidivism between an event-based and person-based sample can be large.

The person-based and event-based samples may yield different estimates of recidivism. Rhodes and colleagues (2014) explain that event-based samples of releases from prison (exit-cohort samples) may overrepresent individuals identified as higher risk relative to all persons who entered prison during a period. By comparison, samples of all persons incarcerated during a period contain risk levels in the same proportion as in the

---

[4] See: https://www.healthypeople.gov/2020/topics-objectives/topic/social-determinants-health/interventions-resources/incarceration#:~:text=The%20U.S.%20releases%20over%207, people%20from%20prison%20each%20year.&text=However%2C%20recidivism%20is% 20common.&text=Within%203%20years%20of%20their,than%2050%25%20are%20 incarcerated%20again.

population of all persons incarcerated during the period. Under these conditions, a single exit-cohort-based estimate of recidivism will include a larger proportion of higher-recidivism-risk persons than the population of all persons incarcerated. This contributes to exit-cohort estimates of recidivism that may be higher than those obtained from an entering cohort or from the population of all persons incarcerated during a specific period (Rhodes et al., 2014).

As shown in Table 2-3 below, recidivism rates for event-based release cohorts are higher than those for person-based samples. The event-based releasees have a 21 percent return to prison rate in year 1 with variations across the 17 reporting states. The 2005 cohort has a slightly different reincarceration rate, with 24 states reporting. In both the event-based and person-based samples, *most people released from prison do not return to prison within the observation window*. In the 17-state event-based sample, about half did not return to prison. In the person-based sample, two-thirds did not return.

TABLE 2-3 Illustrating Impact of Type of Sample on Recidivism Rates in 17 States

Years at Risk	Event-Based Release Cohort-Reincarceration (12-year trend for 17 states, percent)	Event-Based Release Cohort by Years at Risk—Reincarceration for 2005 Release (24 states, percent)	Person-Based Sample (percent)	Person-Based Release Cohort by Years at Risk—Reincarceration for 2005 Release (24 states, percent)
Percent Returned to Prison by Follow-up Years				
Average, Year 1	21	22	12	12
25th, 75th Quartile	11–28	n/a	6–16	
Average, Year 3	39	40	23	27
25th, 75th Quartile	29–48	n/a	16–30	
Average, Year 5	46	47	27	29
25th, 75th Quartile	39–54	n/a	22–31	
Percent never returned to prison	51		68	
25th, 75th Quartile	44–53		66–70	
Percent returned to prison 2 times	13		7	
25th, 75th Quartile	16–14		8–7	

SOURCE: Data from Rhodes et al. (2014).

Person-based and event-based samples may have similar recidivism rates when a release cohort represents the population of persons who have been in prison. In demographic parlance, this is when populations can be characterized as stationary. For a prison population to be stationary, the annual number of admissions and admissions by class have to be constant for a long period of time and the number of admissions must equal the number of releases.

Use of exiting event cohorts is most appropriate in answering questions that pertain to a population that experiences an event, such as all persons in a treatment program, or the recidivism rate of a cohort, or whether the recidivism rates of exiting cohorts have changed over time (presuming appropriate adjustments for compositional differences in cohorts). Person-based samples identify an individual as the unit of analysis and follow the history of that person over time. An example is the research on redemption undertaken by Blumstein and colleagues (e.g., Blumstein and Nakamura, 2009; 2010), which follows the criminal careers tradition and identifies "recidivism trajectories" that may eventually lead to desistance. Life-course criminology (Brame, Bushway, and Paternoster, 2003; Laub and Sampson, 2001) is also part of this tradition of following persons over time.

The possible terminological confusion stemming from the use of two types of events (the sampling event and the recidivism event) may be unavoidable, but researchers should be clear so that readers of reports understand the samples used in studies and the populations to which these samples pertain. This understanding can be enhanced by focusing on the purpose of the study, the population about which inferences are to be made, and the sampling procedures. For example, if the purpose is to understand the effects on recidivism of a sentencing regime at a point in time, samples of persons entering prison would be more appropriate than samples of those exiting prison, because the sample of persons exiting prison could contain mixtures of persons sentenced under different regimes. At the same time, entering-cohort samples present the challenge of right-censoring, in that it may take many years for all persons who entered prison at a point in time to exit, which requires appropriate statistical methods to address. Alternatively, a study of an in-prison program on post-prison recidivism would sample from persons released from prison, regardless of the year in which they were sentenced, so long as they participated in the programming.

Recidivism Events

As previously discussed, recidivism measures that are based on contact with criminal legal agencies, such as rearrest measures, consist of some combination of behavior and justice agencies' responses. Although rearrest, reconviction, and reincarceration are commonly used measures of recidivism events, each can be further subdivided by important attributes. For example, rearrest measured by specific charges helps in determining the severity of the arrested behavior. Theoretically, one could expand upon the concept of rearrest to measure the crimes cleared by an arrest or arrests that were not exceptionally cleared by prosecutors. Similarly, reincarceration rates can be refined to distinguish those following from a new sentence from those that did not and, if the data allow, the reasons for technical violations that result in return to prison.

These distinctions among categories of events that measure recidivism indicate that measures of events derived from criminal legal agency records reflect both the actions of criminal legal system officials and the behavior of individuals. Great care is required in making inferences from criminal legal contacts to identify a person's offending behavior. Measuring recidivism in terms of new contacts with criminal legal system agencies is not necessarily equivalent to measuring recidivism as re-offending. Self-report data on offense behaviors may avoid this problem of criminal legal actors' responses, but it can introduce measurement error and bias of its own in estimating the incidence or prevalence of reoffending. Regardless of the source of data, measurement error and potential bias in estimates are major methodological challenges confronting recidivism studies.

Frequency and Duration

Recidivism rates attempt to measure whether a set of individuals has engaged in further criminal behavior over a particular period of time. Reporting on recidivism rates often includes statistics such as time to a first event—the duration of time between release and an individual's first recorded criminal behavior (their first "recidivist event"). Recidivism can also be tracked in terms of patterns or trajectories of recidivist events. Recidivism trajectories that decrease over a duration imply desistance from recidivism.

Connecting the length of a follow-up period to a program or policy purpose may not be simple or obvious. For example, recording recidivism events while a person is under supervision requires a different follow-up period than doing so after they leave supervision. Expecting a program to have long-run effects and therefore measuring recidivism over long periods of time may not reasonable; rather, a shorter follow-up period or sufficiently discrete periods to allow for an understanding of recidivism trends may be more appropriate. In some circles, the three-year follow-up rate has become an implicit standard, reflecting a trade-off between timeliness concerns and allowing a sufficient amount of time to pass for the slope of the rate curve to flatten. For example, the Virginia Department of Corrections routinely reports three-year reincarceration rates (Virginia Department of Corrections Research—Evaluation Unit, 2021).

Ideally, the time frames for follow-up periods should be driven by the theoretical constructs or substantive aims of each recidivism study, but theory may not be sufficiently robust to suggest explicit lengths of follow-up periods; rather, theory may simply indicate that longer or shorter periods are appropriate. A reasonable approach might be for researchers to clearly state their aims, give a rationale for the length of follow-up periods, and maintain information on the timing of events so that the number of events up to different durations can be reported.

DATA SOURCES FOR MEASURING RECIDIVISM

The variations in how recidivism is measured also depend on the sources for the data. The two most common sources are self-report data and official records in administrative data maintained by criminal legal agencies. Table 2-4 summarizes the strengths and limitations of these measures. Private sources, such as consumer reporting agencies, may provide criminal background check information, but we exclude them from this review.[5] The following section reviews the data sources for measuring recidivism and the adequacy of the measures.

Each source is generally associated with specific types of measures. Both classes of data sources have strengths and weaknesses. Self-reports may be a better measure of criminal behavior than administrative data but are costly to obtain and may suffer from recall biases. All classes of administrative data reflect the intersection of individual behaviors and criminal legal responses, and this source of measurement error may not be randomly distributed (see below for a detailed discussion). On the other hand, with administrative data larger samples are available, it is possible to identify trajectories, and the data have utility in demonstrating outcomes such as desistance (Blumstein and Nakamura, 2009) or periods of time when there are no legal system events.

Self-Report Data

Self-report data may provide several measures of recidivism events, primarily through self-reporting on criminal behavior. In addition, self-report data can be used to measure contacts with criminal legal agencies, such as arrests and convictions. Self-report measures of criminal behavior specific to drug use can also be used to evaluate the effectiveness of drug courts

---

[5]For information about Consumer Reporting Agencies, see Lageson, 2020.

TABLE 2-4 Measures Derived from Sources and Strengths and Weaknesses

Measure(s)	Sources	Strengths	Weaknesses/concerns
Crimes committed, contact with justice system agencies, context	Self-report surveys or interviews	Person-based measures that reflect individual behaviors give voice to participants; may allow participants to describe and contextualize the events; can provide very detailed information and uncover rationale for behaviors.	Very costly; mode and setting effects; recruitment and retention issues; nonresponse bias; recall issues; typically small sample sizes.
Rearrest rates	State and local law enforcement agencies; state criminal history repositories	Details about the dates and criminal law charges of arrests, which can be used to assess the severity of the arrest record. State criminal history repositories contain disposition data (nationwide, in about 82% of arrests). Booking (fingerprint) records indicate an official action. Fingerprints allow for linking records within persons over time and place.	Local law enforcement agency data contain little disposition data on the arrest, other than crimes cleared and exceptional clearances; need to go to the state repository to obtain these records. State law is variable on the content of what must be submitted to the repositories (e.g., other than felonies, what misdemeanor, citation, or infraction arrests) and on non-criminal legal uses of criminal history data. State repositories cover within-state criminal history; the FBI's Interstate Identification Index provides for the decentralized interstate exchange of criminal history record information; records are supported by fingerprint submissions (CJIS 2005).
Reconviction rates	County courts; state administrative offices (where available); and state criminal history repositories	Conviction is a well-measured event, even if a conviction is for a lesser charge. Dates of events are measured. Data on each charge are recorded, and the data on multiple charges can be used to assess severity.	Convicted behavior is not always the same as the underlying offense behavior. Not all states have statewide court record systems; access to court records in these states is county-by-county. Often includes the conviction offense only. Does not detail whether offense was plea-bargained. Generally, no universal ID; linkages across places and events need to be done by name and related matches.

continued

TABLE 2-4 Continued

Measure(s)	Sources	Strengths	Weaknesses/concerns
Reincarceration	State departments of corrections (prison records) and local (county) jails	Dates of entry into and exit from custody are well defined; data are on persons with events attached to person records; data on misconduct and treatment are available; prison records indicate release to supervision or not.	Reasons for entry into custody are not always well-defined (e.g., technical violations vs. new crimes); movements may reflect changes in status (e.g., conviction).
Technical violations of conditions of supervision	Probation supervising agencies, which may be federal, state or county; parole supervising agencies (state-level); departments of corrections	Indication of a supervising agency's decisions, which when associated with other agency data provide indications of the probability of revocation conditional upon repeated measured behaviors (e.g., the number of failed drug tests before revocation). Generally include records of the supervision histories and interactions.	Records typically do not detail the nature of the events that led to a technical violation/revocation, or include the dates or severity of the violation behavior. Few systems track the nature of the events. Supervisory agency decisions involve discretion even with the use of risk instruments, which makes it difficult to disentangle the effects of an individual supervisee's behavior from the agency decision making. Variability across systems in data definition and access.
Graduated responses	Supervising agencies	Indications of management strategy to address issues of noncompliance (or incentives for compliance). Typically indicate a date of the event occurring.	Variability in use of graduated responses. Often do not detail the dates when events occurred. Variability in data definitions, lack of complete records of the incremental measures for addressing non-compliance.

and treatment or aftercare programs to alleviate drug use and drug-related problems (Harrell, Cavanagh, and Roman, 1998); and to gauge drug use prior to incarceration in inmate surveys (e.g., Beatty and Snell, 2021).

Self-report data are typically derived from interviews with individuals or the collection of ecological movement assessment data (e.g., from smartphones or emails). Persons are asked whether they engaged in certain offense behaviors. Questions about offense behaviors are typically based on descriptions of the events (e.g., types of crimes such as burglary, larceny, robbery) rather than legal codes.

Self-report data suffer from known problems related to precision and recall. Respondents' reports of offending may be influenced by modes of survey administration, characteristics of the interviewer, anonymity, use of techniques to reduce response bias, and the length of the survey instrument (Gomes et al., 2019). Descriptive terms may have different meanings to different respondents. For example, one person may think of or characterize a burglary as a robbery even though the event was breaking and entering and did not involve use of force to take property. Self-report surveys that allow respondents to self-define criminal events or to affirm behaviors that fall into broad categories introduce measurement error into the classification of events. Alternatively, attribute-based interviewing uses cues to identify events, and the responses to cues result in an event's classification into an offense category. For example, rather than ask a person if they committed a burglary, a respondent may be asked if they "broke into or attempted to break into a home by forcing a door or window, jimmying a lock, cutting a screen, or entering through an open door or window" along with questions about items stolen following entry.

Respondent recall problems have been studied at length, especially in national surveys such as the National Crime Victimization Survey (Bureau of Justice Statistics, 1989; Cantor et al., 2021; Rand and Catalano, 2007) and surveys of incarcerated individuals (Marquis and Ebner, 1981; Peterson et al., 1982). More prominent and rehearsed events are more likely to be recalled than less prominent events. Consequently, more serious offending behaviors are more likely to be recalled than, say, a rash of petty crimes such as shoplifting, larcenies, and simple assaults. If events are to be dated, two forms of telescoping may affect the dating of events. Forward telescoping includes events as having taken place during a specified time frame that was more recent than the event occurred. Backward telescoping includes events reported as occurring at a less recent time than specified.

The reliability of self-report data is improved by bounding interviews (as in the National Crime Victimization Survey) or by calendaring, by time line follow-back and anchoring procedures, and by the inclusion of redundant questions as a way to check the reliability of responses (Peterson et al., 1982). If studies are designed to re-interview persons over time, self-report data are subject to attrition (loss of sample) and panel bias or respondent fatigue, which means that a respondent provides less information as the number of interviews increases.

Self-report surveys also have recruitment and nonresponse challenges. Sampled participants may choose not to participate for many reasons even if an honorarium is offered. Finding sampled participants to conduct an interview is challenging, especially for studies of recidivism, where sampled persons are generally known to be highly mobile. For program evaluations, conducting interviews at a program site, such as a drug court or probation office, may give an appearance of coercion whereby the sampled person thinks that she or he must participate in the survey as part of a program even if participation is voluntary. Despite researchers' pledges of confidentiality to respondents, persons under supervision may be inclined to under-report criminal activity if they believe disclosing these activities could lead to violations. These challenges affect inferences about self-report offense behavior. The inferences can be improved if sources of nonresponse bias are accurately identified and addressed.

Inaccurate reporting of events is another concern with self-report data. Respondents may not report all criminal activity or may report some of it as less serious than it was. Alternatively, they may be predisposed to "boast" about behaviors and describe what they did as more serious than it was in reality. In their analysis of participants in the Cambridge Study in Delinquent Development, Auty, Farrington, and Coid (2015) found that respondents who had several convictions or convictions for more serious offenses were more likely to under-report them, while older persons were less likely to over-report seriousness. Overall, the authors found a high level of concurrent validity between the self-report and official records.

A final concern about inaccurate reporting relates to concerns that respondents may have in talking about ongoing criminal activities. This is especially the case if respondents report activities that could be suspected to be child abuse. Depending upon state law, researchers collecting these data may be mandatory reporters.

Despite the challenges of obtaining reliable self-report data, self-report data are of value, as this type of person-specific data can provide details not otherwise available about post-release behaviors, including the context or risk setting. But most recidivism studies do not use self-report data because of their cost and the need for skilled staff to conduct the interviews.

BOX 2-1
Listening Session:
The Expertise of Individuals with Lived Experience of Incarceration

During a public information-gathering session held by the Committee on Evaluating Success Among People Released from Prison, practitioners and those with lived experience spoke about the importance of including the perspectives of formerly incarcerated individuals in measures of post-release success.

Diane Good-Collins, Director of Metropolitan Community College's 180 Re-entry Asssitance Program: "Qualitative interviews are very important to those that are re-entering. Their input is critical to know whether these programs are doing what they say they are doing. Are they providing the correct services?" (Good-Collins, 2021)

Venus Woods, Director of HIV Prevention and Education with the Alaskan AIDS Assistance Program: "Who should you get the information from? Us! People with lived experience. That's something I've seen that has changed over the years too. When I was first released 10 years ago we weren't talking about our stories out loud. We weren't talking about the criminal legal system the way we are today. We have to be at the table. We aren't just redemption stories, we're leaders who have something to say and something to offer and we will be the ones with the solutions to make that change" (Woods, 2021).

Nneka Jones-Tapia, managing director of Justice Initiatives at Chicago Beyond and former warden of the Cook County jail, discussed the importance of having previously incarcerated people deeply involved in the research process. She emphasized that people with lived experience not only need to be able to participate in research, but should be able to review the research questions being asked before a study begins. Likewise, researchers should make sure that this community is made aware of the study.

SOURCE: See: https://www.nationalacademies.org/event/07-27-2021/evaluating-success-among-people-released-from-prison-meeting-2-public-information-gathering-session-1.

Administrative Data

Most recidivism studies use data from official records of arrests, convictions, and incarceration that are drawn from the operational databases of criminal legal agencies. These are most often referred to as administrative data. See Box 2-2 for a description of administrative data.

Measures using administrative data indicate arrested, charged, and convicted offending behaviors and not necessarily all actual offense behaviors. Charged behaviors reflect the interactions of individuals with the legal system.

BOX 2-2
Administrative Data

Administrative data are the manual or automated records maintained by criminal legal agencies to document the activities of their agents and personnel. The record of events occurring throughout the criminal legal process constitutes criminal history record information (CHRI), also known as a "rap sheet" or record of arrest and prosecution. A criminal history record describes offenses and persons, including fingerprint identification, information about arrests and, depending upon completeness, subsequent dispositions. CHRI is compiled using data provided by local, county, state, and federal law enforcement agencies; local and regional jails; pretrial services agencies; state and federal prosecutors' offices, courts, and prison departments; and state, federal, and local probation and parole agencies. Agencies record events occurring under their jurisdiction or authority. Individual agencies differ in their use of biometric (fingerprint-based) identification numbers, which can facilitate linking records of unique persons across place and time. Law enforcement and corrections agencies generally do better at obtaining fingerprints, while prosecutors' offices and courts tend not to obtain and record biometric data.

Aggregators of criminal history information recorded by the various agencies exist. For example, in some but not all states, an administrative office obtains records from individual courts. Every state has established a criminal history repository that maintains CHRI and identification data; these repositories are generally maintained by state departments of police or public safety. These repositories hold arrest and criminal case-processing information, such as information about arrest dates, statutory offenses and charges, and court dispositions, for the records reported to them. The criminal record is invoked by an arrest record that law enforcement agencies submit to their state repositories.

Arrest records are supplemented by information provided by prosecutors' offices, courts, and correctional agencies, each of which contributes data to complete the CHRI by submitting information about subsequent dispositions of charges. A completed criminal history record contains information about arrest charges, including their dispositions, sentences, and custody dates. The completeness of the CHRI record varies among the states. According to the most recent survey of criminal history repositories, in 2018, 49 states (that responded) reported having final disposition data for 68 percent of all arrests in state databases (Goggins and DeBacco, 2020). Accessing administrative data through a central repository is more efficient than collecting the data from individual agencies in various jurisdictions. Access to and use of CHRI by entities outside the criminal legal system, such as researchers, requires use of strict data security protocols.

For example, if two individuals engage in the same criminal activity but the second lives in an area with a larger police presence, that second individual may be rearrested while the other's crime goes undetected. Differences in the rate at which victims report crimes to the police affect the likelihood of an arrest. An individual may also be wrongfully rearrested or reconvicted of a crime they did not commit and still appear in recidivism rates.

Administrative data may underreport offending and reoffending based on a number of factors, including victims' willingness to report offenses to the police, the rate at which crimes go unsolved, the extent of police presence, and the scope of community supervision. Discretionary policing activities and the intensity of supervision may lead to over-reporting of criminal legal system outcomes relative to underlying offense behavior. Failure to distinguish between a parole revocation that occurs because of a new offense and a technical violation may lead to an overestimate of criminal behavior if violations of supervision such as drug test failures are included as criminal behaviors.

While criminal history records can provide researchers with the most comprehensive and accessible source of data on recidivism as measured by criminal legal agencies, a number of reliability concerns are associated with administrative data. These include clerical issues, such as missing arrest records, purged records, and duplicate records in jurisdictions with centralized booking. Some records may be in paper format only and thus not easily accessible (Myrent, 2019). Reform efforts underway in many states to automate record expungement and sealing of records can affect the information available for research on recidivism. At least 10 states introduced record expungement bills during 2021 (Hernandez, 2021). The scope of records that could be expunged varies considerably among states, with arrests that did not result in a conviction or acquittal among a common focus of expungement and sealing.

In the next sections, we review some of the strengths and limitations of specific measures derived from administrative data.

Rearrest

Rearrest is defined as an arrest that occurs after a criminal conviction or post-conviction event such as release from prison. Summons and citations are not, by definition, arrests. Sources of arrest data are generally state and local law enforcement agencies, federal law enforcement agencies, or state criminal history repositories. The repositories work with the FBI to identify unique persons arrested and contain either a state ID number (a unique number assigned to each new arrestee in a state) or the FBI number (a unique number assigned to persons regardless of where they were arrested). These allow for linking records of persons as their cases move through the legal process.

Arrest records contain details of charges and generally contain information about their dispositions. Recidivism studies typically aggregate detailed charge information into standard offense categories (typically violent, property, drug, and public order) and report rearrest rates by category of offense type, even though details about the number and types of charges are usually available. The detailed charging information provides for the capacity to measure some aspects of the severity of arrests, although the analysis of charges within categories of crimes is often complicated. Rearrest as a measure of recidivism is commonly used in national-level recidivism studies (such as the BJS studies) and program evaluations.

The strength of rearrest measures lies in the official nature of the records representing local law enforcement agencies' records of events. The records contain rich details about arrests, although such details are often not used in recidivism studies. The weaknesses of arrest data derive in part from the local-agency origination of the data. Jurisdictions vary in statutory classifications of criminal events, including designations of felony and misdemeanor statutes, which may present challenges in cross-site comparisons. State requirements on the non-felonious arrests to report to the criminal history repositories differ, so the scope of what is included in non-felonious arrest records also varies. Dispositions of arrests are incomplete. At the local level, arrest records may be linked to clearances of offenses, including exceptional clearances, but they do not include the disposition of all arrests. In the state repositories, final dispositions of arrests are missing in about 30 percent of all arrests; in the states with the highest disposition-reporting rate, this drops to 20 percent (Goggins and DeBacco, 2020). This means that arrest charges that are dropped either because a person did not commit the crime or the evidence was insufficient to move forward with a prosecution may be counted among rearrests.

State-level variation in what must be reported to repositories can add difficulties to making cross-state comparisons. And like all criminal legal system measures, arrests reflect a combination of a person's behavior (e.g., criminal activity) and the response of law enforcement to that behavior. This cuts both ways, as some offenses do not result in arrests and some persons are arrested even though they have not committed a crime. Despite these weaknesses, efforts to reconcile self-report and arrest records as summarized by the National Research Council (2003) suggest that there is a high level of agreement between self-reports on having been arrested or having a police contact and having an official record. For more serious offenses and events, such as conviction, there is an even higher concordance between self-report and official records (Maxfield, Weller, and Widom, 2000; National Research Council, 2003).

Reconviction

Reconviction is a judicially determined event that occurs when an individual is found guilty of a criminal offense either by trial or by plea. Convictions are well measured in terms of the dates of event and the statutory charges and their dispositions. An administrative office aggregates data from local courts in some states so that a single source can be accessed to obtain statewide data. This varies by state, and some states do not aggregate misdemeanor offenses. Court dispositions are reported to the states' criminal history repositories, although complete disposition data may not exist in the repositories. Court records include information about each charge in a case when a defendant is charged with multiple offenses. This charge-specific information can be used in measuring the severity of the convicted offense. Some variations occur for how states handle misdemeanor offenses.

Reconviction measures exclude arrests that were not prosecuted. A conviction offense reflects the "bargained" or convicted offense behavior and not necessarily the behaviors that an individual engaged in. This bargained offense may be more or less serious than the underlying offense behavior. The determination of the convicted offenses reflects decisions of prosecutors, defense attorneys, and judges or juries, and the records of offense behaviors are based on criminal statutes, not offense-specific behaviors. Exceptions to this may exist under sentencing guidelines if the guidelines are based upon "real offense" behaviors, but in this case the real offense behaviors are applied at the sentencing and not the conviction stage. The distinction between the statutory classification of convictions and offense behaviors presents challenges in making inferences about offending behavior(s) when using conviction records. Reviews of self-report and official conviction records, however, have shown a high level of concurrent validity (Auty, Farrington, and Coid, 2015).

There are trade-offs in using reconviction and rearrest data in measuring recidivism. Using rearrests presents the risk of counting events in which a crime did not occur or that did not result in a conviction. Maltz ([1984] 2001) pointed to this concern by distinguishing any arrest from arrests that lead to conviction, and argued that when the latter is desired, it is incumbent on a user of administrative records to ensure that there is a conviction record for an arrest. Using arrests without disposition information presents a problem of false positives, because the measures then include as recidivism events acts that were not proven to be criminal.

Conversely, sole reliance on reconviction to measure recidivism presents the potential error of failing to capture data on an offense that did occur but for which charges were dropped or a conviction could not be obtained, for lack of evidence, witness cooperation, or prosecutor decisions not to move forward with a charge. This false-negative problem may understate the true level of criminal behavior. We do not know the extent to which the false-positive or false-negative errors present larger problems for recidivism estimates that are drawn from official records. Addressing this issue requires high-quality criminal history data (improvements to criminal history data are discussed below).

Reincarceration

Reincarceration is the recommitment of a person to custody, which generally includes either prison or jail but may also include halfway houses or community correctional facilities. These data typically come from local (mostly county) jails or state prison departments; supervising agencies may maintain data on community corrections. Data may be accessed by agreement with agencies that require evidence of a benefit to the agency, and limits on the use and release of information are imposed. Dates of entry, exit, and movements within a system are recorded, along with reasons for entry and exit. Prison and jail records include person-level identifiers that pertain to the jurisdiction (e.g., a unique ID that identifies persons incarcerated in a state or county), limiting their utility to within-jurisdiction comparisons of persons over time. Prison system administrative data record information about conduct while in custody, such as misconduct, participation in programs or treatment, or work assignments.

Depending upon the data source used to measure reincarceration rates, the events may be undercounted. For example, if prison systems provide the data, their data may exclude persons who are reincarcerated to jail (as may occur with parole violators awaiting hearings). Alternatively, if the data from state criminal history repositories are used, the jail incarceration information would be more likely to be included, but the reason for the incarceration (e.g., a technical violation) may not be reported. Like all of the measures derived from administrative record systems, a return-to-prison measure captures a wide range of behaviors, some of them new criminal offenses and others violations of conditions of supervision (Gaes et al., 2016).

Technical Violations-Revocations

Technical violations resulting in revocations involve the commitment of a person to custody for violating terms of probation, parole, or pretrial diversion, and not necessarily for committing a new crime while under supervision. The data on technical violations are maintained by supervising agencies or courts, although prison departments may also record technical violations as a reason for entry. Supervising agencies' record systems include information about contacts between officers and the persons they supervise. The extent of what is recorded varies and may include information about each interaction, outcomes of drug tests, and engagement in reintegration activities such as employment. Theoretically, the records of interactions can be reviewed to understand patterns leading to technical violations.

Pure technical violations do not involve a crime, but a new crime or arrest may be the reason for a technical violation. The extent to which technical violations occur as a result of new crimes is not well understood, but the evidence suggests that most events recorded as technical violations include new crimes as the cause of the technical violation. We previously cited the study by Grattet, Petersilia, and Lin (2008) who evaluated technical violations in California and concluded that 65 percent involved behaviors alleged to violate the California Penal Code, and that about 10 percent of these were serious penal code violations. The BJS *Annual Survey on Probation and Annual Survey on Parole* reports that 6.5 percent of individuals exiting probation are incarcerated without a new sentence and 4.9 percent are incarcerated with a new sentence. The respective rates for those exiting parole are 11.2 percent and 5.3 percent (Oudekerk and Kaeble, 2021). The establishment surveys that BJS uses to obtain these data do not ask respondents to distinguish between individuals returned without a new sentence who committed a new crime versus those who committed a technical violation such as a drug test failure. Lattimore and colleagues (2016; 2018) report that technical violations are commonplace when individuals are being supervised, whereas arrests tend to be rarer.

As revocation for a technical violation requires either a judicial or executive (e.g., paroling authority) decision, records of dates of events and decisions are available. Information to link data on persons over time within jurisdictions is generally available, but in states where probation is organized at the county level, linkages of person-level records across places may be more challenging.

Consistent with other sources of administrative data, data definitions are not standard across supervising agencies, which increases difficulties in making comparisons across jurisdictions. From a practice perspective, supervising agencies and courts also differ with respect to their standards for revocable behaviors. Within jurisdictions, judges differ in deciding outcomes of probation revocation hearings. While variation across places and within jurisdictions has value for research purposes, for statistical purposes it presents challenges when the same event is treated differently by legal actors, agencies, and jurisdictions.

Graduated Sanctions

Graduated sanctions are also used by supervision agencies to manage noncompliance with requirements of probation or parole. Graduated sanctions involve increasing sanctions or requirements as a result of noncompliance with the supervision conditions of release. The completeness and accuracy of supervision agencies' records of graduated sanctions are unknown. Local jails and state prisons will record entries into custody when ordered, but it is not clear that corrections departments' data systems can distinguish between a commitment under a graduated sanctions regime or another regime such as the imposition of a suspended custody sentence, technical violation, or new event. There is some question regarding whether the imposition of a graduated sanction is in fact a recidivism event, simply part of a sentencing package, or a management tool. Graduated sanctions policies are often not specified or uniformly applied (Rudes, 2012; Turner et al., 2012); consequently, their use reflects decisions by criminal legal system officials that may not systematically reflect the behaviors of the individuals on whom graduated sanctions were imposed. For example, Rudes (2012) found that parole officers resisted a rehabilitation-focused reform in California that discouraged the use of technical violations except in the most egregious cases through collaboration with police, the use of paperwork enhancement to encourage significant revocations, and by "piling" charges. Turner and colleagues (2012) similarly found that the implementation of a structured decisions-making tool for responding to violations of parole did not increase consistency in parole agent responses to violations.

Measurement Error

Earlier we described, in general terms, the sources of measurement error in both administrative and self-report data that measure recidivism events. All recidivism measures derived from administrative data reflect decisions by criminal legal system actors to take action and to record the actions taken in specific ways, as dictated by their roles in the criminal legal system and administrative records systems. As noted, these sources of measurement error present challenges for understanding the extent of recidivism events and in making comparisons across jurisdictions or over time. The issue is not whether administrative records will be used but how well they are used.

When recidivism measures derived from administrative data appear as dependent variables (e.g., what is the recidivism rate?), a general aim may be to make inferences about the true or underlying offending behavior. Measurement error can be additive or nonadditive. In the classic formulation of measurement error in a dependent variable, the measurement error is additive and is expressed as follows:

$$Y^* = Y + e,$$

where Y^* is the true, offense-based recidivism rate, Y is the observed arrest rate used to measure recidivism, and e is the random error, which is assumed to be normally distributed with zero mean and variance of one. Under these conditions, the expected value of Y^* equals the expected value of Y, and the arrest rate yields an unbiased estimate of the true recidivism rate.

Some sources of measurement error in administrative data may be random when, for example, certain types of criminal behavior or certain groups are both over- and under-arrested relative to the underlying offense; or when the choice of reporting an event as a technical violation (or not) depends on the discretion of an officer or judge, some of whom may report some events as technical violations while others may not; or when the other circumstances surrounding an event may (or may not) result in the events being tabulated as technical violations. Under these conditions, the arrest rate could result in an unbiased estimate of the underlying offense rate. Of course, simply assuming that the error in arrests is counterbalancing or random is not sufficient to warrant making this inference.

If the dependent variable is a binary (0/1) indicator of an event, then the misclassification of events arising from the use of administrative data can result in inconsistent estimates of recidivism when the probability of misclassification is very high (Hausman, 2001). Studies of more serious offenses, such as felonies, using administrative and self-report data on arrests and convictions tend to align with each other, suggesting that the probability of misclassification for serious offenses may be comparatively low (e.g., Auty, Farrington, and Coid, 2015). If so, then the binary estimates of the probability of a recidivism event derived from administrative data for felony offenses may not be biased. On the other hand, less is known about misclassification of less serious offenses (e.g., misdemeanor arrests for drug law violations and other public order offenses); these could be a major source of measurement error.

The more challenging measurement error problem is systematic error in the dependent variable, where the error is non-additive. Administrative data measures that reflect the intersection between behavior and criminal legal system responses are subject to systematic, non-additive error. This may result in an offset effect that reflects constant level differences among law enforcement departments in responding to different types of offenses, or it may result in a scale effect where the measurement error is proportionate to the true value (e.g., as recidivism rates increase the measured recidivism rates increase by a constant proportion). As non-additive error can lead to upward or downward bias in recidivism estimates, it is important to understand how systematic measurement error affects the direction of bias. Empirical solutions to these problems are available. Based on their analysis of measurement error in investor-related ticker searches, deHaan and colleagues (2019) recommend thoughtful consideration of the extent and form of noise in dependent variables and how the noise may bias inferences.

A more complete understanding of the nature of measurement error can improve the use of administrative data for measuring recidivism events.

We think it incumbent on the research community to examine the nature and effects of measurement error in administrative data. This may entail:

- conducting investigations of the processes that lead to the recording of events (such as arrests);
- designing studies that take into account differences among or within agencies in responses to offenses and how this affects the recording of recidivism events;
- further work on self-report and administrative data to better understand, in particular, how relatively minor offenses find their way into administrative data; and
- other research designs that improve our understanding of the effects of measurement error on recidivism estimates.

The sources and types of measurement error in recidivism measures require greater attention by researchers.

Efforts to Improve Administrative Data

We have shown that multiple and different measures of recidivism present challenges and opportunities for understanding. Used uncritically, multiple measures can cause confusion or misrepresent outcomes. Used critically, multiple measures can be analyzed and compared to generate conclusions about the impacts of incarceration on future offending and about the stages of the criminal legal system process responsible for outcomes. However, a challenge associated with multiple measures arises when the content of the data underlying a common term (e.g., percent rearrested) differ. Several efforts to improve administrative data focus on establishing common definitions of data elements.[6] The value of commonly defined data elements across places and over time lies in facilitating making comparisons. We have argued that recidivism rates are commonly used to measure the performance of state corrections systems, and this naturally leads to questions of whether recidivism rates increase or decrease over time within states. If a state changes how it measures recidivism because new data are introduced, this presents problems for measuring change over time.

Analogously, states and other units of government are apt to compare themselves with other states. One reason they compare themselves is to learn if one entity is doing better and if so to find out why. While differences in what states measure may occur, when states use common outcomes but measure them differently, the comparison they desire will be unreliable. For example, if one state can distinguish between types of technical violations

---

[6]See in this regard the Justice Counts initiative https://justicecounts.csgjusticecenter.org/.

and another cannot, but both report returns to prison for technical violations, the comparison will not be reliable. Hence, our primary concern is less with the measures and more with how the data elements used to create the measures are defined across places. We review several efforts to improve the measurement of violations of criminal law.

Efforts to develop national standards for criminal offenses as part of law enforcement statistics through the Uniform Crime Reporting (UCR) Program's National Incident-Based Reporting System (NIBRS) are a step toward achieving some uniformity in the information local law enforcement agencies capture about crimes and arrests. NIBRS provides an incident-based data model for capturing detailed data on each crime incident and multiple attributes of arrests, victimization, and individuals involved in the criminal legal system. In 2019 (the latest year of data available at the time of the writing of this report), nearly 8,500 law enforcement agencies submitted NIBRS data to the FBI. The participating agencies were disproportionately smaller agencies. Collectively they represent 51 percent of the agencies that submitted data to the UCR program, but they covered less than 45 percent of the U.S. resident population. The reliability of NIBRS data across participating jurisdictions has yet to be fully assessed.

Efforts to develop standards for state courts include those promoted by the National Center for State Courts through its National Open Court Data Standards. Through the latter, the National Center for State Courts aims to develop business and technical court data standards to support the creation, sharing, and integration of court data by developing the rules by which data are described and recorded.[7] Under this effort, states may still define events differently, but at a minimum the differences would be documented. The National Open Court Data Standards is not yet at an implementation stage, and the variability in record keeping continues to affect the use of court records in comparative studies of reconviction rates. To the committee's knowledge, no such efforts are underway to document sentencing decisions.

Within states, the state criminal history record repositories collect and integrate records of arrests and prosecutions. These repositories provide informational services to the National Instant Criminal Background Check System, respond to requests for background checks on persons applying for jobs, and report data to sex offender registries, among other activities. While the repositories may provide a mechanism for achieving some uniformity in reporting arrests and prosecutions within states, the national criminal records exchange system faces well-documented shortcomings despite substantial investments by the federal government. The repositories'

---

[7]See https://www.ncsc.org/services-and-experts/areas-of-expertise/court-statistics/national-open-court-data-standards-nods.

data integrate arrests with their prosecution and adjudication outcomes, but wide variation exists among states in the completeness of records that indicate the outcome of an arrest and in definitions of what records must be submitted to a state's repository.

For example, some repositories obtain data on misdemeanors that others do not. The repositories have a program for enhancing data quality, known as the State Repository Records and Reporting Quality Assurance Program, which offers voluntary standards for information maintenance and reporting requirements. Promising efforts are currently underway by SEARCH and Rand to systematically assess data quality issues (Roberts, 2021), but they still have a long way to go.[8] In the interim, the absence of uniform standards for criminal legal events results in measurement error, the full extent of which is unknown, that hinders comparisons within and across jurisdictions in the rearrest, reconviction, and reincarceration of persons released from prison.

RECIDIVISM AS BINARY: LIMITATIONS

Reporting recidivism in a binary way—sorting people into those who *are* and those who *are not* rearrested, reconvicted, or reincarcerated during the period of time being measured—gives an incomplete picture of a person's post-release experiences. When a person's re-engagement with the criminal legal system in any of these ways occurs, recidivism measures are interpreted to mean that person has failed, at least up to the point of the measured event. When it does not occur, the person has succeeded, as shown in studies of successful outcomes (Anderson, Schumacker, and Anderson, 1991; Peters et al., 2015). The same is true for criminal legal system programs: If the program reduces recidivism among its participants, it is considered promising or successful; if not, a naïve interpretation of the data implies that the program failed, whereas more sophisticated interpretations seek to find the reasons why a program that promised to reduce recidivism did not achieve the promised reductions.

When return to crime is measured simply by whether a person had a recidivism event or not, it limits efforts to understand post-release outcomes in the criminal legal system. An enhanced understanding of post-release outcomes occurs when recidivism studies address the seriousness, frequency, and trajectory of events (Lattimore, 2021). Breaking down recidivism rates by offense type (e.g., violent, property, public order) often represents an

---

[8]Personal communication between committee member William Sabol and David Roberts, Executive Director of SEARCH, September 16, 2021. SEARCH is a national nonprofit organization of the States that provides resources for collecting, sharing, and analyzing justice information.

attempt to better capture seriousness, but there are also significant differences in seriousness even within offense categories. Reincarceration measures that do not distinguish between re-commitments for new convictions and those for technical violations of conditions of supervision conflate distinct behaviors. This conflation occurs even if technical violations are a signal that persons under supervision are failing to adjust their behaviors to community norms, portending a return to crime (Bushway and Apel, 2012), or if sanctioning technical violations is done to prevent more crime through incapacitation, specific deterrence, and general deterrence (Piehl and LoBuglio, 2005).

Dealing with the many events that are recorded in arrest and other records of criminal legal system actors is not easy. For example, NIBRS data report on 52 offenses in 23 categories. Criminal history records contain even more detailed offense information. Processing and reporting on this level of detail is not straightforward, and any classification system introduces heterogeneity within broader classes. Some guidance does exist for classifying offenses by severity, such as the attribute-based classification systems recommended by the Committee on National Statistics (Lauritsen and Cork (eds.), 2016). A major challenge associated with using attribute-based classification systems is that statutory charges do not capture all the elements of offenses. Nonetheless, attribute-based systems can provide guidance on thinking about measuring the severity of recidivism events.

Using official records to study recidivism trajectories has moved beyond the simple "yes/no" question of whether a person has a recidivism event. The redemption work of Blumstein and Nakamura (2009; 2010) illustrates this. Using official data to measure the arrest trajectories of individuals, Blumstein and Nakamura compared the trajectories of persons who had arrest records to the risk of arrest for same-aged people in the general population and to the risk of arrest for people who had never been arrested. Depending on the type of offense and age of first arrest, they found that the arrestee population had similar risks as the general population after 4.4 to 8.5 years. In other words, after a period of time the recidivism rates as measured by rearrest fell to the level of risk of arrest in the general population.

Similarly, the recent efforts by Bushway and colleagues (2022) on resetting risk illustrate the use of conviction records to demonstrate that most people with a conviction do not have a subsequent conviction. As the authors point out, current methods of measuring recidivism risk are based on the time of a person's last conviction (or release from prison). Using this baseline, the measures do not adjust recidivism risk for the time a person has lived in the community without a new conviction. They find not only that most people with a conviction do not have a subsequent conviction, but that their risk of recidivism (measured by reconviction) declines considerably over the period from the last interaction with the criminal legal system.

Additional areas of recidivism research include those that focus on the contexts of criminal behavior. One such feature is the risk environment (community) into which a person is released. The risk environment includes community crime rates, socioeconomic conditions, and the availability of services and supports that facilitate access to affordable housing, health care, and other basic necessities. Kubrin and Stewart (2006) and Mears and colleagues (2008) find that neighborhood context and the social ecology of places matter. Accounting for both individual-level characteristics and characteristics of the ecological units in their studies, both find that the ecological units account for significant variation in recidivism. Persons released into disadvantaged, resource-deprived, and racially segregated places had higher recidivism rates. Both of these studies were of single jurisdictions.

The supervision environment is another key research area. Persons released from prison into community supervision face different risks of detection of noncompliant or criminal behavior than those released without supervision. Similarly, individuals face different recidivism risks depending on local policing practices and the extent of cooperation between law enforcement and probation and parole officials. These multiple and overlapping risk contexts play an important role in shaping post-release outcomes and future criminal activity.

Absent from binary measurements of recidivism are important features that contextualize involvement in criminal behavior, better define a trajectory of behavior, and would permit more thorough assessment of effects of various policy or programmatic interventions on the health, prosocial commitments, and overall well-being, as well as criminal behavior, of persons released from prison. (See Chapter 3 for additional discussion).

CONCLUSION

Measures of recidivism need to be tied to the intended purposes of a research project, an annual report, and other assessments. If the general purpose is to measure offending behavior(s) of individuals, then all sources of data and measures fall short. Self-report data may over- or under-state criminal behavior and are typically costly to collect. Administrative data and their associated measures reflect some combination of individual behavior and criminal legal system actors' responses and decisions. This does not mean that the definitions and data are not useful for some statistical and research purposes. For example, the redemption work of Blumstein and Nakamura (2009; 2010) illustrates the use of arrest records to measure the arrest trajectories of individuals compared to estimated probabilities of arrest for persons who do not have an arrest record. Similarly, the recent efforts by Bushway and colleagues (2022) on resetting risk illustrate the use of conviction records to demonstrate that most people with a conviction do not have a subsequent conviction.

Both examples show that future contact with the criminal legal system is not inevitable for persons who have initial contact. These studies show the need for more in-depth analyses of criminal legal administrative data than typically appear in many recidivism studies. They also suggest that lapses in time between events need to be acknowledged and considered, as is common in the medical literature, which refers to such events as relapses. Blumstein and Nakamura (2009) also emphasize that remission periods may vary depending on the nature of the offense (e.g., violent, drug, property), which is a major advancement in defining recidivism as specific to a certain type of behavior instead of being generic. These are examples of studies that are starting to reshape the concept of recidivism to mirror event outcomes such as remission, reoccurrence, and relapse in the substance abuse and medical literature.

Given these limitations and the potential for misuse of recidivism data, we highlight the following opportunities for improving measurement:

1. Broad generalizations about "the recidivism rate" need to be avoided. Rather, recidivism rates should be connected to their study populations and to the purpose of each inquiry. Because there are many recidivism events that can be measured, the general term "recidivism" needs to be accompanied by explicit reference to the recidivism events under study (recidivism as rearrest, as reconviction, etc.).

2. Cross-jurisdictional comparisons of recidivism rates are subject to misinterpretation if inadequate attention is given to the purposes of studies, definitions and measures used, and analyses conducted to generate the results. When done with care, cross-jurisdiction comparisons can inform an understanding of what contributes to post-prison recidivism.

3. When measuring the overall performance of corrections systems, event-based samples may be misinterpreted as applying to samples of all persons who have been to prison over time and are likely to overstate recidivism rates for this population.

4. Analogously, longitudinal studies of persons over time yield valuable information about how post-release outcomes change and generally show that individuals' recidivism rates fall over time.

5. Binary measures of recidivism that lump distinct behaviors into the same categories do not account for the seriousness and frequency of post-release criminal behavior, nor for the length of time between release and criminal behavior. Multiple measures of recidivism provide opportunities for learning about the events contributing to recidivism rates.

6. Explanations of recidivism rates that do not take into account the risk environments into which persons released from prison return may lead to misleading inferences about what affects the rates.

7. Recidivism measures yield information on the presence or absence of negative outcomes and by themselves do not reflect the multivalent nature of post-release success, including employment, housing, health, family and community attachment, and personal well-being, which may be either associated with or independent of recidivism.

The existing literature on recidivism is a stepping stone to improve our measures of outcomes for persons released from prison. Our review signals precautions for future efforts to improve the data used to measure post-release outcomes and clearly and accurately communicate research findings. We offer the following guiding principles for future research and policy analysis:

1. The goals of the inquiry need to be clearly articulated, including how post-release success is linked to the research aims and how it is measured.
2. The samples used in studies need to be tied to the purpose of the studies. Studies of interventions or impacts of incarceration are good candidates for event-based samples. Studies that examine sentencing policy are good candidates for person-based samples. Studies of correctional performance that use event-based samples should consider how well the sample reflects the population of persons incarcerated who do not appear in an event sample taken in a given period.
3. Limiting analyses to simple, binary outcomes (whether someone did or did not engage in criminal behavior following release) without disaggregating by measures of severity or other salient correlates is an approach that should be avoided. Where data allow, time-dependent measures that track experiences of persons over time and allow for analyses of trajectories of behavior are preferred. Analyses of within-person outcomes over time place greater demands on the data, and efforts to create or facilitate access to these data are warranted.
4. The use of multiple measures of recidivism has utility for understanding how different recidivism events occur, both in studies conducted within a jurisdiction and in studies conducted between jurisdictions. The use of multiple carefully constructed and documented measures is warranted to help improve understanding of recidivism.
5. Improvements are warranted in administrative data and criminal history records to enable them to focus on distinguishing events, such as pure technical violations vs. new crimes or arrests that are reported as violations.

6. Generic recidivism measures that treat dissimilar behaviors or criminal legal system actions (e.g., felonies, misdemeanors, technical violations) the same way are best avoided. Researchers are best served by drawing on recent reports on modernizing crime statistics for ideas about taxonomies and classification of the many types of criminal legal system actions so that greater emphasis can be placed on offense-specific measures to assess the impact of a policy or program on criminal behavior.

As this chapter has demonstrated, there is a great deal of work to be done to improve the measurement of post-release criminal behavior. Addressing the limitations identified in this chapter will require coordinated effort between funders, researchers, and policy makers. Chapter 5 offers specific recommendations in this area, including for the development of more uniform standards for the measurement of success.

REFERENCES

Agan, A., and Starr, S. (2018). Ban the box, criminal records, and racial discrimination: A field experiment. *Quarterly Journal of Economics* 133, 191–235.

Agnew, R. (1992). Foundations for a general strain theory of crime and delinquency. *Criminology* 30, 47–87.

Agnew, R. (2001). Building on the foundation of general strain theory: Specifying the types of strain most likely to lead to crime and delinquency. *Journal of Research in Crime and Delinquency* 38, 319–361.

Agnew, R. (2006). *Pressured into Crime: An Overview of General Strain Theory*. New York: Oxford University Press.

Aizer, A., and Doyle Jr., J.J. (2015). Juvenile incarceration, human capital, and future crime: Evidence from randomly assigned judges. *Quarterly Journal of Economics* 130, 759–803.

Akers, R.L. (1985). *Deviant Behavior: A Social Learning Approach* (3rd Ed.). Belmont, CA: Wadsworth.

Akers, R.L. (1998). *Social Learning and Social Structure: A Social Cognitive Theory*. Boston: Northeastern University Press.

Alper, M., Durose, M.R., and Markman, J. (2018). *2018 Update on Prisoner Recidivism: A 9-Year Follow-up Period (2005–2014)*. Report NCJ 250975. Washington, DC: Bureau of Justice Statistics.

Anderson, D.B., Schumacker, R.E., and Anderson, S.L. (1991). Release characteristics and parole success. *Journal of Offender Rehabilitation* 17, 1–2, 133–145.

Andersen, S.N., and Skardhamar, T. (2015). Pick a number: Mapping recidivism measures and their consequences. *Crime and Delinquency* 63, 5, 613–635.

Andrews, D.A., and Bonta, J. (2010). *The Psychology of Criminal Conduct* (5th ed.). New Providence, NJ: Lexis Nexis, Anderson Pub.

Antenangeli, L., and Durose, M.R. (2021). *Recidivism of Prisoners Released in 24 States in 2008: A 10-Year Follow-Up Period (2008–2018)*. Report NCJ 256094. Washington, DC: Bureau of Justice Statistics.

Austin, J. and McVey, A. D. (1989). The 1989 NCCD Prison Population Forecast. NCCD Focus. San Francisco, CA: National Council on Crime and Delinquency.

Auty, K.M., Farrington, D.P., and Coid, J.W. (2015). The validity of self-reported convictions in a community sample: Findings from the Cambridge study in delinquent development. *European Journal of Criminology* 12, 562–580.

Baird, C. (2009). *A Question of Evidence: A Critique of Risk Assessment Models Used in the Justice System*. Madison, WI: National Council on Crime and Delinquency.

Bales, W.D., and Mears, D.P. (2008). Inmate social ties and the transition to society: Does visitation reduce recidivism? *Journal of Research in Crime and Delinquency* 45, 287–321.

Bandura, A. (1977). *Social Learning Theory*. Englewood Cliffs, NJ: Prentice-Hall.

Bayer, P., Hjalmarsson, R., and Pozen, D. (2009). Building criminal capital behind bars: Peer effects in juvenile corrections. *Quarterly Journal of Economics* 124, 105–147.

Beatty, L.G. and Snell, T.L. (2021). Profile of Prison Inmates, 2016. Washington DC: Bureau of Justice Statistics. NCJ255037.

Beccaria, C. (1963 [1764]). *On Crimes and Punishments*. Translated by Henry Paolucci. New York: Macmillan Publishing Company.

Beck, A.J., and Blumstein, A. (2018). Racial disproportionality in US state prisons: Accounting for the effects of racial and ethnic differences in criminal involvement, arrests, sentencing, and time served. *Journal of Quantitative Criminology* 34, 3, 853–883.

Beck, A.J., and Shipley, B.E. (1989). *Recidivism of Prisoners Released in 1983*. Report, NCJ 116261. Washington, DC: Bureau of Justice Statistics.

Becker, G.S. (1968). Crime and punishment: An economic approach. *Journal of Political Economy* 76, 169–217.

Becker, H.S. (1963). *Outsiders: Studies in the Sociology of Deviance*. New York: Free Press.

Bell, N., Bucklen, K.B., Nakamura, K., Tomkiel, J., Santore, A., Russell, L., and Orth, R. (2013). Recidivism Report 2013. Harrisburg, PA: Pennsylvania Department of Corrections.

Bellair, P.E., and Kowalski, B.R. (2011). Low-skill employment opportunity and African American–white difference in recidivism. *Journal of Research in Crime and Delinquency* 48, 176–208.

Benecchi, L. (2021). Recidivism Imprisons American Progress. *Harvard Political Review* https://harvardpolitics.com/recidivism-american-progress/.

Benedict, W.R., and Huff-Corzine, L. (1997). Return to the scene of the punishment: Recidivism of adult male property offenders on felony probation, 1986–1989. *Journal of Research in Crime and Delinquency* 34, 237–252.

Bentham, J. (1988 [1789]). *The Principles of Morals and Legislation*. Amherst, MA: Prometheus Books.

Berg, M.T., and Huebner, B.M. (2011). Reentry and the ties that bind: An examination of social ties, employment, and recidivism. *Justice Quarterly* 28, 382–410.

Berk, R.A., and Rauma, D. (1983). Capitalizing on nonrandom assignment to treatments: A regression-discontinuity evaluation of a crime-control program. *Journal of the American Statistical Association* 78, 21–27.

Binswanger, I.A., Stern, M.F., Deyo, R.A., Heagerty, P.J., Cheadle, A., Elmore, J.G., and Koepsell, T.D. (2007). Release from prison—A high risk of death for former inmates. *New England Journal of Medicine* 356, 157–165.

Bird, M., Nguyen, V., and Grattet, R. (2021). Realignment and Recidivism Revisited: A Closer Look at the Effects of California's Historic Correctional Reform on Recidivism Outcomes. Criminal Justice Policy Review.

Blasko, B.L., Friedmann, P.D., Rhodes, A.G., and Taxman, F.S. (2015). The parolee–parole officer relationship as a mediator of criminal justice outcomes. *Criminal Justice and Behavior* 42, 722–740.

Blasko, B.L., and Taxman, F.S. (2018). Are supervision practices procedurally fair? Development and predictive utility of a procedural justice measure for use in community corrections settings. *Criminal Justice and Behavior* 45, 3, 402–420.

Blumstein, A., and Nakamura, K. (2009). Redemption in the presence of widespread background checks. *Criminology* 47, 327–359.

Blumstein, A., and Nakamura, K. (2010). *Potential of Redemption in Criminal Background Checks*. Final Report to the National Institute of Justice. Pittsburgh, PA: Carnegie Mellon University.

Boman IV, J.H., and Mowen, T.J. (2017). Building the ties that bind, breaking the ties that don't: Family support, criminal peers, and reentry success. *Criminology and Public Policy* 16, 753–774.

Braithwaite, J. (1989). *Crime, Shame and Reintegration*. Cambridge University Press.

Brame, R., Bushway, S.D., and Paternoster, R. (2003). Examining the prevalence of criminal desistance. *Criminology* 41, 423–448.

Bucklen, K.B., Duwe, G., and Taxman, F.S. (2021). *Guidelines for Post-Sentencing Risk Assessment*. NCJ Report 300654. Washington, DC: National Institute of Justice. Available: https://nij.ojp.gov/library/publications/guidelines-post-sentencing-risk-assessment.

Bureau of Justice Statistics. (1989). *Redesign of the National Crime Victimization Survey*. NCJ Report 111457. Washington, DC. https://bjs.ojp.gov/content/pub/pdf/rncs.pdf.

Bureau of Justice Statistics. (1994). *Technical Background on the Redesigned National Crime Victimization Survey*. NCJ Report 15112. Washington, DC.

Bureau of Justice Statistics. (2021). National Prisoner Statistics, [United States], 1978–2020. Inter-university Consortium for Political and Social Research. Available: https://doi.org/10.3886/ICPSR38249.v1.

Burgess, R., and Akers, R.L. (1966). A differential association-reinforcement theory of criminal behavior. *Social Problems* 14, 128–147.

Bursik Jr., R.J., and Grasmick, H.G. (1993). *Neighborhoods and Crime: The Dimensions of Effective Community Control*. New York: Lexington Books.

Burton Jr., V.S., Cullen, F.T., and Travis, III, L.F. (1987). The collateral consequences of a felony conviction: A national study of state statutes. *Federal Probation* 51, 52–60.

Bushway, S., and Apel, R. (2012). A signaling perspective on employment-based reentry programming: Training completion as a desistance signal. *Criminology and Public Policy* 11, 17–20.

Bushway, S., Vegetabile, B.G., Kalra, N., and Baumann, G. (2022). *Providing Another Chance: Resetting Recidivism in Criminal Background Checks*. Santa Monica, CA: The Rand Corporation.

Cantor, D., Miller, D., Townsend, R., Hartge, J.Y., Fay, R.E., Warren, A. and Heaton, L. (2021). *Methodological Research to Support the National Crime Victimization Survey: Self-Report Data on Rape and Sexual Assault—Pilot Test*. Washington, DC: Bureau of Justice Statistics.

Carson, E.A. (2020). *Prisoners in 2019*. NCJ Report 255115. Washington, DC: Bureau of Justice Statistics.

Chadwick, N., Dewolf, A., and Serin, R. (2015). Effectively training community supervision officers: A meta-analytic review of the impact on offender outcome. *Criminal Justice and Behavior* 42, 10, 977–989.

Chamberlain, A.W. (2018). From prison to community: Assessing the direct, reciprocal, and indirect effects of parolees on neighborhoods and crime. *Crime and Delinquency* 64, 166–200.

Chamberlain, A.W., and Wallace, D. (2016). Mass reentry, neighborhood context and recidivism: Examining how the distribution of parolees within and across neighborhoods impacts recidivism. *Justice Quarterly* 33, 912–941.

Chen, E.Y., and Meyer, S. (2020). Beyond recidivism: Towards accurate, meaningful, and comprehensive data collection on the progress of individuals reentering society. In A. Leverentz, E.Y. Chen, and J. Christian (Eds.), *Beyond Recidivism: New Approaches to Research on Prisoner Reentry and Reintegration*, 13–38. NYU Press.

Chen, M.K., and Shapiro, J.M. (2007). Do harsher prison conditions reduce recidivism? A discontinuity-based approach. *American Law and Economics Review* 9, 1–29.

Clear, T.R. (2007). *Imprisoning Communities: How Mass Incarceration Makes Disadvantaged Neighborhoods Worse*. New York: Oxford University Press.

Cloward, R.A., and Ohlin, L.E. (1960). *Delinquency and Opportunity: A Theory of Delinquent Gangs*. New York: Free Press.

Cloyes, K.G., Wong, B., Latimer, S., and Abarca, J. (2010). Time to prison return for offenders with serious mental illness released from prison: A survival analysis. *Criminal Justice and Behavior* 37, 175–187.

Cobbina, J.E., Huebner, B.M., and Berg, M.T. (2012). Men, women, and post-release offending: An examination of the nature of the link between relational ties and recidivism. *Crime and Delinquency* 58, 331–361.

Cohen, A.K. (1955). *Delinquent Boys: The Culture of the Gang*. New York: Free Press.

Cook, P.J. (1975). The correctional carrot: Better jobs for parolees. *Policy Analysis* 1, 11–54.

Cotter, R., Semisch, C., and Rutter, D. (2021). Recidivism of Federal Offenders Released in 2010. Washington, DC: United States Sentencing Commission. Available: https://www.ussc.gov/sites/default/files/pdf/research-and-publications/research-publications/2021/20210930_Recidivism.pdf.

Cotter, R. (2020). *Length of Incarceration and Recidivism*. Washington, DC: United States Sentencing Commission. Available: https://www.ussc.gov/research/research-reports/length-incarceration-and-recidivism.

Council of State Governments Justice Center. (2014). *Reducing Recidivism: States Deliver Results*. New York: Council of State Governments Justice Center. Available: https://csgjusticecenter.org/publications/reducing-recidivism-states-deliver-results/.

Cullen, F.T. (1994). Social support as an organizing concept for criminology. *Justice Quarterly* 11, 527–559.

deHaan, E., Lawrence, A., and Litjens, R. (2019). *Measurement Error in Google Ticker Search* (May 1, 2019). Available at SSRN: https://ssrn.com/abstract=3398287 or http://dx.doi.org/10.2139/ssrn.3398287.

Dooley, B.D., Seals, A., and Skarbek, D. (2014). The effect of prison gang membership on recidivism. *Journal of Criminal Justice* 42, 267–275.

Drakulich, K.M., Crutchfield, R.D., Matsueda, R.L., and Rose, K. (2012). Instability, informal control, and criminogenic situations: Community effects of returning prisoners. *Crime, Law and Social Change* 57, 493–519.

Durose, M.R. and Antenangeli, L. (2021). *Recidivism of Prisoners Released in 34 States in 2012: A 5-Year Follow-Up Period (2012–2017)*. Report NCJ 255947. Washington, DC: Bureau of Justice Statistics.Durose, M.R., and Antenangeli, L. (2021). *Recidivism of Prisoners Released in 34 States in 2012: A 5-Year Follow-Up Period (2012–2017)*. Report NCJ 255947. Washington, DC: Bureau of Justice Statistics.

Durose, M.R., Cooper, A.D., and Snyder, H.N. (2014). *Recidivism of Prisoners Released in 30 States in 2005: Patterns from 2005 to 2010*. Report NCJ 244205. Washington, DC: Bureau of Justice Statistics.

Durose, M.R., Snyder, H.N., and Cooper, A.D. (2015). *Multistate Criminal History Patterns of Prisoners Released in 30 States*. NCJ Report 248942. Washington DC: U.S. Department of Justice, Bureau of Justice Statistics, Special Report.

Eren, O., and Mocan, N. (2021). Juvenile punishment, high school graduation and adult crime: Evidence from idiosyncratic judge harshness. *Review of Economics and Statistics* 103, 34–47.

Estelle, S.M., and Phillips, D.C. (2018). Smart sentencing guidelines: The effect of marginal policy changes on recidivism. *Journal of Public Economics* 164, 270–293.

Evans Jr., R. (1968). The labor market and parole success. *Journal of Human Resources* 3, 201–212.

Farrington, D.P. (2000). Explaining and preventing crime: The globalization of knowledge. *Criminology* 38, 1–24.

Ford, L., and Rector, R. (2020). *Pay-for-Outcomes: Transforming Federal Social Programs to Expand Individual Well-Being*. Heritage Foundation Backgrounder 3550: 2020–11.

Gaes, G.G., and Camp, S.D. (2009). Unintended consequences: Experimental evidence for the criminogenic effect of prison security level placement on post-release recidivism. *Journal of Experimental Criminology 5*, 139–162.

Gaes, G.G., Luallen, J., Rhodes, W., and Edgerton, J. (2016). Classifying prisoner returns: A research note. *Justice Research and Policy 17*, 1, 48–70.

Garfinkel, H. (1956). Conditions of successful status degradation ceremonies. *American Journal of Sociology 61*, 420–424.

Garland, D. (Ed.). (2001). *Mass Imprisonment: Social Causes and Consequences*. Thousand Oaks, CA: Sage.

Gelb, A. (2018). *You Get What You Measure: New Performance Indicators Needed to Gauge Progress of Criminal Justice Reform*. NCJ Report 254650. Washington, D.C: U.S. Department of Justice, Office of Justice Programs.

Gelb, A. and Velazquez, T. (2018). The Changing State of Recidivism: Fewer People Going Back to Prison. Washington DC: Pew Public Safety Performance. https://www.pewtrusts.org/en/research-and-analysis/articles/2018/08/01/the-changing-state-of-recidivism-fewer-people-going-back-to-prison.

Gendreau, P., Little, T., and Goggin, C. (1996). A meta-analysis of the predictors of adult offender recidivism: What works! *Criminology 34*, 575–608.

Goffman, E. (1963). *Stigma: Notes on the Management of Spoiled Identity*. New York: Simon and Schuster.

Goggins, B.R., and DeBacco, D.A. (2020). *Survey of State Criminal History Information Systems, 2018*. Washington DC: Bureau of Justice Statistics.

Gomes, H.S., Farrington, D.P., Maia, A., and Krohn, M.D. (2019). Measurement bias in self-reports of offending: A systematic review of experiments. *Journal of Experimental Criminology 15*, 313–339. Available: https://doi.org/10.1007/s11292-019-09379-w.

Good-Collins, D. (2021, July 28). Remarks before the Committee. Committee on Evaluating Success Among People Released from Prison Meeting #2: Public Information Gathering Session. Washington, DC: National Academies of Sciences, Engineering, and Medicine.

Gottfredson, M.R., and Hirschi, T. (1990). *A General Theory of Crime*. Stanford, CA: Stanford University Press.

Grattet, R., Petersilia, J., and Lin, J. (2008). *Parole Violations and Revocations in California: Final Report*. Washington, D.C: National Institute of Justice.

Green, D., and Winik, D. (2010). Using random judge assignments to estimate the effects of incarceration and probation on recidivism among drug offenders. *Criminology 48*, 10–23.

Griffin, M.L., and Armstrong, G.S. (2003). The effect of local life circumstances on female probationers' offending. *Justice Quarterly 20*, 213–240.

Hagan, J. (1993). The social embeddedness of crime and unemployment. *Criminology 31*, 465–491.

Harding, D.J., Morenoff, J.D., Nguyen, A.P., and Bushway, S.D. (2017). Short- and long-term effects of imprisonment on future felony convictions and prison admissions. *Proceedings of the National Academies of Sciences 114*, 11103–08.

Harrell, A., Cavanagh, S. and Roman, J. (1998). *Findings from the Evaluation of the D.C. Superior Court Drug Intervention Program: Final Report*. Washington, DC: The Urban Institute.

Harris, H.M., Nakamura, K., and Bucklen, K.B. (2018). Do cellmates matter? A causal test of the schools of crime hypothesis with implications for differential association and deterrence theories. *Criminology 56*, 37–122.

Harrison, L. (2021). Colorado Division of Criminal Justice Adult and Juvenile Correctional Populations Forecasts: Pursuant to 24-33.5-503 (m), C.R.S. Denver, CO: Office of Research and Statistics, Division of Criminal Justice Colorado Department of Public Safety.

Hausman, J. (2001). Mismeasured variables in econometric analysis: Problems from the right and problems from the left. *Journal of Economic Perspectives* 15, 4, 57–67.

Hernandez, K. (2021). More States Consider Automatic Criminal Record Expungement. PEW Stateline. https://www.pewtrusts.org/en/research-and-analysis/blogs/stateline/2021/05/25/more-states-consider-automatic-criminal-record-expungement, accessed October 2021.

Hester, R. (2019). Prior record and recidivism risk. *American Journal of Criminal Justice* 44, 353–375.

Hipp, J.R., Petersilia, J., and Turner, S. (2010). Parolee recidivism in California: The effect of neighborhood context and social service agency characteristics. *Criminology* 48, 947–79.

Hipp, J.R., and Yates, D.K. (2009). Do returning parolees affect neighborhood crime? A case study of Sacramento. *Criminology* 47, 619–56.

Hirschi, T. (1969). *Causes of Delinquency*. Berkeley, CA: University of California Press.

Hirschi, T., and Gottfredson, M. (1983). Age and the explanation of crime. *American Journal of Sociology* 89, 552–584.

Hoffman, P.B., and Beck, J.L. (1984). Burnout—Age at release from prison and recidivism. *Journal of Criminal Justice* 12, 617–623.

Holtfreter, K., Reisig, M.D., and Morash, M. (2004). Poverty, state capital, and recidivism among women offenders. *Criminology and Public Policy* 3, 185–208.

Hooks, E. A. (2021). Fiscal Year 2019–2020 Annual Statistical Report. Raleigh, NC: North Carolina Department of Public Safety.

Horney, J.D., Osgood, W., and Marshall, I.H. (1995). Criminal careers in the short term: Intra-individual variability in crime and its relation to local life circumstances. *American Sociological Review* 60, 655–673.

Huebner, B.M., and Berg, M.T. (2011). Examining the sources of variation in risk for recidivism. *Justice Quarterly* 28, 146–173.

Huebner, B.M., and Cobbina, J. (2007). The effect of drug use, drug treatment participation, and treatment completion on probationer recidivism. *Journal of Drug Issues* 37, 619–641.

Huebner, B.M., DeJong, C., and Cobbina, J. (2010). Women coming home: Long-term patterns of recidivism. *Justice Quarterly* 27, 225–254.

Huebner, B.M., and Pleggenkuhle, B. (2015). Residential location, household composition, and recidivism: An analysis by gender. *Justice Quarterly* 32, 818–844.

Huebner, B.M., Varano, S.P., and Bynum, T.S. (2007). Gangs, guns, and drugs: Recidivism among serious, young offenders. *Criminology and Public Policy* 6, 187–221.

Hunt, K.S., and Dumville, R. (2016). *Recidivism Among Federal Offenders: A Comprehensive Overview*. Washington, DC: United States Sentencing Commission.

James, D.J., and Glaze, L.E. (2006). *Mental Health Problems of Prison and Jail Inmates*. Report NCJ 213600. Washington, DC: Bureau of Justice Statistics.

Jones-Tapia, N. (2021, July 28). Remarks before the Committee. Committee on Evaluating Success Among People Released from Prison Meeting #2: Public Information Gathering Session. Washington, DC: National Academies of Sciences, Engineering, and Medicine.

King, R.S., and Elderbroom, B. (2014). *Improving Recidivism as a Performance Measure*. Washington, DC: Urban Institute.

Kirk, D.S. (2015). A natural experiment of the consequences of concentrating former prisoners in the same neighborhoods. *Proceedings of the National Academy of Sciences* 112, 6943–6948.

Kirk, D.S. (2016). Prisoner reentry and the reproduction of legal cynicism. *Social Problems* 63, 222–243.

Kirk, D.S., and Wakefield, S. (2018). Collateral consequences of punishment: A critical review and path forward. *Annual Review of Criminology* 1, 171–194.

Kornhauser, R.R. (1978). *Social Sources of Delinquency: An Appraisal of Analytic Models.* Chicago: University of Chicago Press.

Kreager, D.A., Schaefer, D.R., Bouchard, M., Haynie, D.L., Wakefield, S., Young, J., and Zajac, G. (2016). Toward a criminology of inmate networks. *Justice Quarterly* 33, 1000–1028.

Kreager, D.A., Young, J.T.N, Haynie, D.L., Bouchard, M., Schaefer, D.R., and Zajac, G. (2017). Where "old heads" prevail: Inmate hierarchy in a men's prison unit. *American Sociological Review* 82, 685–718.

Kubrin, C., and Stewart, E.A. (2006). Predicting who reoffends: The neglected role of neighborhood context in recidivism studies. *Criminology* 44, 165–197.

Kurlychek, M.C., Brame, R., and Bushway, S.D. (2006). Scarlet letters and recidivism: Does an old criminal record predict future offending? *Criminology and Public Policy* 5, 483–504.

Kurlychek, M.C., Brame, R., and Bushway, S.D. (2007). Enduring risk: Old criminal records and prediction of future criminal involvement. *Crime and Delinquency* 53, 64–83.

Lageson, S.E. (2020). *Digital Punishment: Privacy, Stigma, and the Harms of Data-Driven Criminal Justice.* New York: Oxford.

Langan, P.A., and Levin, D.J. (2002). *Recidivism of Prisoners Released in 1994.* Report NCJ 193427. Washington, DC: Bureau of Justice Statistics.

Lattimore, P. (2021, July 27). Presentation to Committee on Evaluating Success Among People Released from Prison Meeting #2: Public Information Gathering Session. Washington, DC.

Lattimore, P.K, Dawes, D., MacKenzie, D.L., and Zajac, G. (2018). *Evaluation of the Honest Opportunity Probation with Enforcement Demonstration Field Experiment (HOPE DFE).* Washington, DC: National Institute of Justice. Available: https://www.ojp.gov/pdffiles1/nij/grants/251758.pdf.

Lattimore, P.K., MacKenzie, D.L., Zajac, G., Dawes, D., Arsenault, E., and Tueller, S. (2016). Outcome findings from the HOPE demonstration field experiment. *Criminology and Public Policy* 15, 1103–1141.

Lattimore, P.K., and Visher, C.A. (2010). *The Multi-Site Evaluation of SVORI: Summary and Synthesis.* Research Triangle Park, NC: RTI International.

Laub, J.H., and Sampson, R.J. (2001). Understanding desistance from crime. In M. Tonry (Ed.), *Crime and Justice: A Review of Research* 28, 1–69. Chicago: University of Chicago Press.

Lauritsen, J.L. and Cork, D.L. (2016). *Modernizing Crime Statistics Report 1: Defining and Classifying Crime.* Washington, DC: The National Academies Press.

Leasure, P., and Andersen, T.S. (2016). The effectiveness of certificates of relief as collateral consequence relief mechanisms: An experimental study. *Yale Law and Policy Review* 35, 11–22.

Lemert, E.M. (1951). *Social Pathology: A Systematic Approach to the Theory of Sociopathic Behavior.* New York: McGraw-Hill.

Lemert, E.M. (1972). *Human Deviance, Social Problems, and Social Control* (2nd Ed.). Englewood Cliffs, NJ: Prentice-Hall.

Li, S.D., Priú, H.D., and Mackenzie, D.L. (2000). Drug involvement, lifestyles, and criminal activities among probationers. *Journal of Drug Issues* 30, 593–619.

Li, S.D., and MacKenzie, D.L. (2003). The gendered effects of adult social bonds on the criminal activities of probationers. *Criminal Justice Review* 28, 278–298.

Link, N.W., and Hamilton, L.K. (2017). The reciprocal lagged effects of substance use and recidivism in a prisoner reentry context. *Health Justice* 5, 8.

Link, N.W., Ward, J.T., and Stansfield, J. (2019). Consequences of mental and physical health for reentry and recidivism: Toward a health-based model of desistance. *Criminology* 57, 544–573.

Listwan, S.J., Sullivan, C.J., Agnew, R., Cullen, F.T., and Colvin, M. (2013). The pains of imprisonment revisited: The impact of strain on inmate recidivism. *Justice Quarterly* 30, 144–168.

Liu, L., and Visher, C.A. (2019). The crossover of negative emotions between former prisoners and their family members during reunion: A test of general strain theory. *Journal of Offender Rehabilitation* 58, 567–591.

Liu, L, and Visher, C.A. (2021). Decomposition of the role of family in reentry: Family support, tension, gender, and reentry outcomes. *Crime and Delinquency* 67, 970–996.

Liu, L., Visher, C.A., and O'Connell, D.J. (2020). The strain from procedural injustice on parolees: Bridging procedural justice theory and general strain theory. *Crime and Delinquency* 66, 250–276.

Loeffler, C.E., and Nagin, D.S. (2022). The impact of incarceration on recidivism. *Annual Review of Criminology*, 5.

Loughran, T.A., Mulvey, E.P, Schubert, C.A., Fagan, J., Piquero, A.R., and Losoya, S.H. (2009). Estimating a dose-response relationship between length of stay and future recidivism in serious juvenile offenders. *Criminology* 47, 699–740.

MacKenzie, D.L. (2006). *What Works in Corrections: Reducing the Criminal Activities of Offenders and Delinquents*. Cambridge: Cambridge University Press. Available: https://doi.org/10.1017/CBO9780511499470.

Mackenzie, D.L., and Li, S.D. (2002). The impact of formal and informal social controls on the criminal activities of probationers. *Journal of Research in Crime and Delinquency* 39, 243–276.

Maltz, M.D. ([1984] 2001). *Recidivism*. Originally published by Academic Press, Inc., Orlando, Florida.

Marquis, K.H., and Ebner, P.A. (1981). *Quality of Prisoner Self-Reports: Arrest and Conviction Response Errors*. Santa Monica, CA: The Rand Corporation, R-2637.

Massey, D.S., and Denton, N.A. (1993). *American Apartheid: Segregation and the Making of the Underclass*. Cambridge, MA: Harvard University Press.

Maxfield, M.G., Weller, B.L., and Widom, C.S. (2000). Comparing self-reports and official records of arrests. *Journal of Quantitative Criminology* 16, 87–110.

McNeeley, S. (2018). Do ecological effects on recidivism vary by gender, race, or housing type? *Crime and Delinquency*, 64, 782–806.

McShane, M.D., Williams III, F.P., and Dolny, H.M. (2003). The effect of gang membership on parole outcome. *Journal of Gang Research* 10, 25–38.

Meade, B., Steiner, B., Makarios, M., and Travis, L. (2013). Estimating a dose-response relationship between time served in prison and recidivism. *Journal of Research in Crime and Delinquency* 50, 525–550.

Mears, D.P., Cochran, J.C., Bales, W.D., and Bhati, A.S. (2016). Recidivism and time served in prison. *Journal of Criminal Law and Criminology* 106, 81–122.

Mears, D.P., Wang, A., Hay, C., and Bales, W.D. (2008). Social ecology and recidivism: Implications for prisoner reentry. *Criminology* 46, 301–340.

Mellow, J., Schlager, M.D., and Caplan, J.M. (2008). Using GIS to evaluate post-release prisoner services in Newark, New Jersey. *Journal of Criminal Justice* 36, 416–425.

Miller, J., Caplan, J.M, and Ostermann, M. (2016). Home nodes, criminogenic places, and parolee failure: Testing an environmental model of offender risk. *Crime and Delinquency* 62, 169–199.

Mowen, T.J., Stansfield, R., and Boman IV, J.H. (2019). Family matters: Moving beyond "if" family support matters to "why" family support matters during reentry from prison. *Journal of Research in Crime and Delinquency* 56, 483–523.

Mowen, T.J., and Visher, C.A. (2015). Drug use and crime after incarceration: The role of family support and family conflict. *Justice Quarterly* 32, 337–359.

Mowen, T.J., Wodahl, E., Brent, J.J., and Garland, B. (2018). The role of sanctions and incentives in promoting successful reentry: Evidence from the SVORI data. *Criminal Justice and Behavior* 45, 8, 1288–1307.

Myrent, M. (2019). *Using State Criminal History Records for Research and Evaluation.* Washington, DC: Justice Research and Statistics Association.

Nagin, D.S., Cullen, F.T., and Johnson, C.L. (2009). Imprisonment and reoffending. *Crime and Justice* 38, 115–200.

Nagin, D.S., and Paternoster, R. (1991). On the relationship of past and future participation in delinquency. *Criminology* 29, 163–190.

Nagin, D.S., and Paternoster, R. (2000). Population heterogeneity and state dependence: State of the evidence and directions for future research. *Journal of Quantitative Criminology* 16, 117–144.

Naser, R.L., and LaVigne, N.G. (2006). Family support in the prisoner reentry process. *Journal of Offender Rehabilitation* 43, 93–106.

Naser, R.L., and Visher, C.A. (2006). Family members' experiences with incarceration and reentry. *Western Criminology Review* 7, 20–31.

National Academies of Sciences, Engineering, and Medicine. (2020). *Decarcerating Correctional Facilities during COVID-19: Advancing Health, Equity, and Safety.* Washington, DC: The National Academies Press. https://doi.org/10.17226/25945.

National Research Council. (2003). *Measurement Problems in Criminal Justice Research: Workshop Summary.* Washington, DC: The National Academies Press.

National Research Council. (2014). *The Growth of Incarceration in the United States: Exploring Causes and Consequences.* Washington, DC: The National Academies Press. https://doi.org/10.17226/18613.

Olson, D.E., and Lurigio, A.J. (2000). Predicting probation outcomes: Factors associated with probation rearrest, revocations, and technical violations during supervision. *Justice Research and Policy* 2, 73–86.

O'Neil, C. and Koushmaro, L. (2020). The 2021–22 Budget: State Correctional Population Outlook. Sacramento, CA: State Legislative Analyst Office.

Oudekerk, B., and Kaeble, D. (2021). *Probation and Parole in the United States, 2019.* Washington, DC: US Department of Justice. Available: https://bjs.ojp.gov/library/publications/probation-and-parole-united-states-2019.

Pager, D. (2003). The mark of a criminal record. *American Journal of Sociology* 108, 937–975.

Paternoster, R., and Iovanni, L. (1989). The labeling perspective and delinquency: An elaboration of the theory and an assessment of the evidence. *Justice Quarterly* 6, 359–394.

Patterson, E.J., and Preston, S.H. (2008). Estimating mean length of stay in prison: Methods and applications. *Journal of Quantitative Criminology* 28, 33–49.

Peters, D.J., Hochstetler, A., DeLisi, M., and Kuo, H.J. (2015). Parolee recidivism and successful treatment completion: Comparing hazard models across propensity methods. *Journal of Quantitative Criminology* 31, 1, 149–181.

Petersilia, J., and Turner, S. (1993). Intensive probation and parole. *Crime and Justice* 17, 281–335.

Peterson, M.A., Braiker, H.B., and Polich, S.M. (1980). *Doing Crime: A Survey of California Prison Inmates.* Santa Monica, CA: The Rand Corporation. R-2200-DOJ.

Peterson, M., Chaiken, J., Ebner, P., and Honig, P. (1982). *Survey of Prison and Jail Inmates: Background and Method.* Santa Monica, CA: The Rand Corporation, N-1635-NIJ.

Petrich, D.M., Pratt, T.C., Jonson, C.L., and Cullen, F.T. (2021). Custodial sanctions and reoffending: A meta-analytic review. *Crime and Justice* 50, 1.

Pew Center on the States (2011). *State of Recidivism: The Revolving Door of America's Prisons.* Washington, DC: The Pew Charitable Trusts.

Pfaff, J.F. (2015). The war on drugs and prison growth: limited importance, limited legislative options. *Harvard Journal on Legislation*, 52, 173–220.

Phelps, M.S. (2017). Mass probation: Toward a more robust theory of state variation in punishment. *Punishment and Society* 19, 53–73.

Piehl, A.M., and LoBuglio, S.F. (2005). Does supervision matter? In Travis, J.J., and Visher, C.C. (Eds.) *Prisoner Reentry and Crime in America*, 105–138. New York: Cambridge University Press.

President's Commission on Law Enforcement and Administration of Justice. (1967). *The Challenge of Crime in a Free Society*. Washington, DC: U.S. Government Printing Office.

Pyrooz, D.C., Clark, K.J., Tostlebe, J.J., Decker, S.H., and Orrick, E. (2021). Gang affiliation and prisoner reentry: Discrete-time variation in recidivism by current, former, and non-gang status. *Journal of Research in Crime and Delinquency* 58, 192–234.

Rand, M., and Catalano, S. (2007). *Criminal Victimization, 2006*. NCJ Report 219413. Washington, DC: Bureau of Justice Statistics.

Reisig, M.D., Bales, W.D., Hay, C., and Wang, X. (2007). The effect of racial inequality on black male recidivism. *Justice Quarterly* 24, 408–434.

Rhodes, W., Gaes, G.G., Kling, R., and Cutler, C. (2018). Relationship between prison length of stay and recidivism: A study using regression discontinuity and instrumental variables with multiple break points. *Criminology and Public Policy* 17, 731–769.

Rhodes, W., Gaes, G.G., Luallen, J., Kling, R., Rich, T., and Shively, M. (2014). Following incarceration, most released offenders never return to prison. *Crime and Delinquency* 63, 1003–1025.

Roodman, D. (2017). *The Impacts of Incarceration on Crime*. San Francisco, CA: Open Philanthropy.

Rose, D.R., and Clear, T.R. (1998). Incarceration, social capital, and crime: Implications for social disorganization theory. *Criminology* 36, 441–479.

Rose, D.R., Clear, T.R., and Ryder, J.A. (2001). Addressing the unintended consequences of incarceration through community-oriented services at the neighborhood. *Corrections Management Quarterly* 5, 62–71.

Rudes, D.S. (2012). Getting technical: Parole officers' continued use of technical violations under California's parole reform agenda. *Journal of Crime and Justice* 35, 2, 249–268.

Rydberg, J., and Clark, K. (2016). Variation in the incarceration length-recidivism dose-response relationship. *Journal of Criminal Justice* 46, 118–128.

Sabol, W., and Baumann, M. (2020). Justice reinvestment: Vision and practice. *Annual Review of Criminology* 3, 1, 317–339.

Sampson, R.J., and Laub, J.H. (1993). *Crime in the Making: Pathways and Turning Points through Life*. Cambridge, MA: Harvard University Press.

Sampson, R.J., and Laub, J.H. (1997). A life-course theory of cumulative disadvantage and the stability of delinquency. In T.P. Thornberry (Ed.), *Advances in Criminological Theory, Volume 7: Developmental Theories of Crime and Delinquency*, 133–161. New Brunswick, NJ: Transaction.

Sampson, R.J., and Loeffler, C. (2010). Punishment's place: The local concentration of mass incarceration. *Daedalus* 139, 20–31.

Sampson, R.J., Raudenbush, S.W., and Earls, F. (1997). Neighborhoods and violent crime: A multilevel study of collective efficacy. *Science* 277, 918–924.

Schaefer, D.R., Bouchard, M., Young, J.T.N., and Kreager, D.A. (2017). Friends in locked places: An investigation of prison inmate network structure. *Social Networks* 51, 88–103.

Schnell, P. (2021). Biennial Submission of Department of Corrections Performance Report, as Required by Minnesota Statutes, Section 241.016. St. Paul, MN: Minnesota Department of Corrections.

Schnepel, K.T. (2018). Good jobs and recidivism. *Economic Journal*, 128, 447–469.

Schur, E.M. (1971). *Labeling Deviant Behavior*. New York: Harper and Row.

Seigle, E., Walsh, N., and Weber, J. (2014). Core principles for reducing recidivism and improving other outcomes for youth in the juvenile justice system. New York: Council of State Governments Justice Center. Retrieved from: http://csgjusticecenter.org/wp-content/uploads/2014/07/Core-Principles-for-Reducing-Recidivism-and-Improving-Other-Outcomes-for-Youth-in-the-Juvenile-Justice-System.pdf.

Sharkey, P., Torrats-Espinosa, G., and Takyar, D. (2017). Community and the crime decline: The causal effect of local nonprofits on violent crime. *American Sociological Review* 82, 1214–1240.

Shaw, C.R., and McKay, H.D. (1942). *Juvenile Delinquency and Urban Areas*. Chicago: University of Chicago Press.

Sherman, L.W. (1993). Defiance, deterrence, and irrelevance: A theory of the criminal sanction. *Journal of Research in Crime and Delinquency* 30, 445–473.

Sherman, L.W., Gottfredson, D.C., MacKenzie, D.L., Eck, J., Reuter, P., and Bushway, S.D. (1998). *Preventing Crime: What Works, What Doesn't, What's Promising*. Research in Brief. National Institute of Justice: Washington, DC.

Sloas, L., Murphy, A., Wooditch, A., and Taxman, F.S. (2019). Assessing the use and impact of points and rewards across four federal probation districts: A contingency management approach. *Victims and Offenders* 14, 7, 811–831.

Stafford, M.C., and Warr, M. (1993). A reconceptualization of general and specific deterrence. *Journal of Research in Crime and Delinquency* 30, 123–135.

Steadman, H.J., Osher, F.C., Robbins P.C., Case, B., and Samuels, S. (2009). Prevalence of serious mental illness among jail inmates. *Psychiatric Services* 60, 761–765.

Sugie, N.F., and Lens, M.C. (2017). Daytime locations in spatial mismatch: Job accessibility and employment at reentry from prison. *Demography* 54, 775–800.

Sutherland, E.H. (1947). *Principles of Criminology* (4th Ed.). Philadelphia: Lippincott.

Taxman, F.S. (2002). Supervision-exploring the dimensions of effectiveness. *Federal Probation* 66, 14.

Taxman, F.S., and Ainsworth, S. (2009). Correctional milieu: The key to quality outcomes. *Victims and Offenders* 4, 4, 334–340.

Taxman, F.S., Smith, L., and Rudes, D. (2020). From mean to meaningful probation: The legacy of intensive supervision programs. In P. Lattimore, B. Huebner, and F.S. Taxman (Eds.), *Handbook on Moving Corrections and Sentencing Forward: Building on the Record*. New York: Routledge Press.

Taxman, F.S., and Thanner, M. (2004). Probation from a therapeutic perspective: Results from the field. *Contemporary Issues in Law* 7, 1, 39–63.

Taylor, C.J. (2016). The family's role in the reintegration of formerly incarcerated individuals: The direct effects of emotional support. *Prison Journal* 96, 331–354.

Tiedt, A.D., and Sabol, W.J. (2015). Sentence length and recidivism among prisoners released across 30 states in 2005: Accounting for individual histories and state clustering effects. *Justice Research and Policy* 16, 50–64.

Tillyer, M.S., and Vose, B. (2011). Social ecology, individual risk, and recidivism: A multilevel examination of main and moderating influences. *Journal of Criminal Justice* 39, 452–459.

Tonry, M. (2010). The social, psychological, and political causes of racial disparities in the American criminal justice system. *Crime and Justice* 39, 1, 273–312.

Turner, S., Braithwaite, H., Kearney, L., Murphy, A., and Haerle, D. (2012). Evaluation of the California parole violation decision-making instrument (PVDMI). *Journal of Crime and Justice* 35, 2, 269–295.

Uggen, C. (1999). Ex-offenders and the conformist alternative: A job quality model of work and crime. *Social Problems* 46, 127–151.

Uggen, C. (2000). Work as a turning point in the life course of criminals: A duration model of age, employment, and recidivism. *American Sociological Review* 65, 529–546.

Uggen, C., Wakefield, S., and Western, B. (2005). Work and family perspectives on reentry. In J. Travis and C. Visher (Eds.), *Prisoner Reentry and Crime in America*, 209–243. Cambridge, MA: Cambridge University Press.

Villettaz, P., Killias, M., and Zoder, I. (2006). The Effects of Custodial vs. Non-Custodial Sentences on Re-Offending: A Systematic Review of the State of Knowledge. *Campbell Systematic Reviews* 2, 1, 1–69.

Virginia Department of Corrections Research – Evaluation Unit. (2021). *Re-Incarceration and Re-Arrest Rates of VADOC FY2016 SR Releases*. Available: https://vadoc.virginia.gov /media/1681/vadoc-recidivism-re-arrest-rates-report-2016.pdf.

Visher, C.A., and Travis, J. (2003). Transitions from prison to community: Understanding individual pathways. *Annual Review of Sociology* 29, 81–113.

Wakefield, S., and Uggen, C. (2010). Incarceration and stratification. *Annual Review of Sociology* 36, 387–406.

Walker, S.C., and Bishop, A.S. (2016). Length of stay, therapeutic change, and recidivism for incarcerated juvenile offenders. *Journal of Offender Rehabilitation* 55, 355–376.

Wallace, D. (2015). Do neighborhood organizational resources impact recidivism? *Sociological Inquiry* 85, 285–308.

Wallace, D., and Papachristos, A.V. (2014). Recidivism and the availability of health care organizations. *Justice Quarterly* 31, 588–608.

Wallace, D., and Wang, X. (2020). Does in-prison physical and mental health impact recidivism? *Social Sciences and Medicine, Population Health* 11, 100569.

Wehrman, M.M. (2010). Race, concentrated disadvantage, and recidivism: A test of interaction effects. *Journal of Criminal Justice* 38, 538–544.

Weisberg, R. (2014). Meanings and measures of recidivism. *Southern California Law Review* 87, 785.

Western, B. (2018). *Homeward: Life in the Year after Prison*. New York: Russell Sage Foundation.

Western, B., and Simes, J. (2019). Drug use in the year after prison. *Social Science & Medicine* 235, 112357.

Wilson, W.J. (1987). *The Truly Disadvantaged: The Inner City, the Underclass, and Public Policy*. Chicago: University of Chicago Press.

Wodahl, E.J., Garland, B., Culhane, S.E., and McCarty, W.P. (2011). Utilizing behavioral interventions to improve supervision outcomes in community-based corrections. *Criminal Justice and Behavior* 38, 4, 386–405.

Woods, V. (2021, July 28). Remarks made before the Committee. Committee on Evaluating Success Among People Released from Prison Meeting #2: Public Information Gathering Session. Washington, DC: National Academies of Sciences, Engineering, and Medicine.

Yang, C.S. (2017). Local labor markets and criminal recidivism. *Journal of Public Economics* 147, 16–29.

Zweig, J.M., Yahner, J., Visher, C.A., and Lattimore, P.K. (2015). Using general strain theory to explore the effects of prison victimization experiences on later offending and substance use. *Prison Journal* 95, 84–113.

3

Beyond Recidivism: Toward a More Comprehensive Understanding of Reentry Challenges and Successes

As Chapter 2 details, current measurements of post-release success largely focus on recidivism—whether an individual ceases criminal activity upon release. However, current measurements often have tenuous links to theories of criminal behavior. In addition to understanding the extent to which criminal behavior persists after release from incarceration, it is important to understand *why* changes do or do not occur. These explanations are most robust when they are grounded in theory and supported with empirical evidence. Further, the focus on recidivism as the key post-release measure of success tells us little about outcomes in other key domains of well-being.

The first section of this chapter reviews theoretical frameworks that attempt to explain why people reoffend and to understand the reintegration process more broadly. Next, the chapter considers the reentry experience itself and the systemic barriers and obstacles people face after release from prison. This discussion directs attention toward interpersonal relationships and the community and macro-level processes and social environments that foster or inhibit successful reentry. The final section highlights how often-intersecting factors, such as race and ethnicity, gender, sexual orientation, economic status, and geographic location, shape individual reentry experiences, often layering additional needs and challenges onto those associated with prior imprisonment. In outlining alternative visions of success and the barriers to realizing them, this chapter sets the stage for the discussion of specific measurement strategies, which follows in Chapter 4.

69

THEORETICAL FRAMEWORKS FOR
RECIDIVISM AND CRIMINAL OFFENDING

Much of the existing scholarly work on criminal offending among released individuals adopts a risk paradigm (see Andrews et al., 1986; 1990; Farrington, 2000). This approach has a pragmatic focus on prediction and prevention of criminal offending rather than explanation per se, although risk factors and protective factors frequently have theoretical resonance.[1] An explicitly theoretical framework for the explanation of post-release offending would be informed by common theories of criminal offending, with those theories adapted to understanding repeat offending following legal sanction (acknowledging that most administrative measures of recidivism are indicators of system responses that may not reflect repeat offending). Theoretical explanations for why individuals return to crime after release from incarceration are broad and often overlapping. However, they tend to differ in the core mechanism they identify to explain post-release offending. Below, we review theories that explain post-release offending in terms of:

- Personal risk factors
- Confinement experiences
- Societal attachments
- Reentry stressors
- Ecological influences, and
- Supervision regimes.

The discussion below weaves together empirical findings with theoretical interpretation for each of these domains. The intent is to be expansive but not necessarily exhaustive.

The following section first focuses on research findings and theories related to post-release criminal offending, before proceeding to measures of desistance from crime and alternative conceptions of reentry success. We do not distinguish between different methods of measuring post-release offending, although readers are encouraged to bear in mind that studies are highly variable with respect to whether post-release offending is measured from self-report instruments or criminal history repositories; whether it is defined

---

[1]The risk paradigm is prominent among scholars and practitioners in the correctional field, where risk instruments are commonly used to match returning individuals to particular supervision conditions or to particular treatment services, based on their predicted likelihood of recidivism. This classification process is known as risk assessment (or risk/needs assessment). One popular and well-validated risk assessment tool is the trademarked Level of Service Inventory-Revised and Ohio Risk Assessment System.

as reoffending, rearrest, reconviction, or return to prison; and whether it includes revocations due to violation of technical conditions.

The focus in this chapter is also heavily tilted toward research on return to the community following prison incarceration, which may or may not coincide with a period of parole supervision, although research on criminal offending while on probation is included when it is relevant to the discussion. Finally, much of the extant research cited below combines study designs that are correlational as well as experimental or quasi-experimental, which limits our ability to make strong empirical generalizations about the causal status of the theories and the reported findings. More generally, the evidence for the correlates of recidivism and many "evidence-based" reentry/rehabilitation interventions is based on correlational or quasi-experimental research. To more firmly establish the causal linkages specified by theories linking human well-being and criminal behavior, stronger designs, including randomized controlled trials (RCTs), are needed. And even where experimental evidence is available, as in the case of prison work and vocational programs, such generalizations often depend on the choice of outcomes, treatment heterogeneity and treatment effect heterogeneity, program "stacking" or participation in multiple programs, and ambiguity in defining programs of different types (Nur and Nguyen, 2022).

Personal Risk Factors

Among the so-called "static" risk factors—static because they are either not subject to change or are not amenable to intervention—age and criminal history are among the most salient correlates of post-release criminal behavior (Andrews et al., 1990; Gendreau et al., 1996). Age has a robust correlation with criminal offending in general, so much so that some scholars claim it cannot (and should not) be explained theoretically because it is due merely to the "inexorable aging of the organism" (Gottfredson and Hirschi, 1990, p. 141; see also Hirschi and Gottfredson, 1983). Although many theories challenge this claim and offer their own explanation of the fact that crime declines with age (following late adolescence), there is no dispute about the existence of the age-crime correlation, and post-release offending is no exception.

Past behavior is also a reliable predictor of future behavior, and this continuity has been the subject of research seeking to untangle the degree to which it represents "population heterogeneity," which emphasizes relatively stable differences across people, "state dependence," which emphasizes change in response to life events and experiences, or some combination of the two (Nagin and Paternoster, 1991; 2000). Irrespective of the mechanism, this implies that individuals with more extensive prior criminal records have higher risk of post-release offending.[2] However, there are two dimensions to criminal history that are not easily distinguished: the number and type of prior offenses at the time of sentencing, and the nature of the commitment offense.

Most studies of returning individuals include both age and criminal history as predictors of post-release criminal offending, and they confirm that these static risk factors reliably predict outcomes. Namely, post-release offending declines monotonically (always decreasing or remaining constant, and never increasing) with age at release, and lengthier criminal history is positively correlated with repeat offending.[3,4]

There are also important "dynamic" risk factors—so-called because they are mutable and frequently the target of intervention efforts—or what are sometimes described as "criminogenic needs" (Andrews et al., 1990; Gendreau et al., 1996). Two examples of dynamic risk factors include substance use or abuse and serious mental illness, both of which have been the subject of studies of post-release criminal offending.[5] Substance use is a major correlate of criminal offending in general (see Tonry and Wilson, 1990, and

---

[2]A complication is that criminal history is also correlated with sentencing—individuals with more extensive or more serious prior records are sentenced to longer lengths of confinement, other things equal. As a result, it is a persistent challenge to untangle the nature of the relationship between criminal history and post-release criminal behavior (see Hester, 2019). There is an additional challenge presented by the length of time that has elapsed within a risk window, as the predictive ability of criminal history appears to degrade with time at risk (Kurlychek, Brame, and Bushway, 2006; 2007).

[3]Studies that find no correlation of age with post-release crime tend to measure the former from age at arrest or age at commitment, or else include measures of in-prison behavior (e.g., misconduct) or post-prison statuses (e.g., supervision level) which arguably mediate the relationship between age and repeat offending (Benedict and Huff-Corzine, 1997; Huebner Varano, and Bynum, 2007). On the other hand, studies that measure age of onset (e.g., age at first contact with the criminal legal system) find that age is inversely correlated with post-release criminal offending (Bellair and Kowalski, 2011). However, many of these same studies indicate that when criminal history is measured by the commitment offense, it is frequently uncorrelated with post-release criminal offending, and in fact, some studies find that commitments for violent crime correspond with lower rates of post-release offending than commitments for other types of offenses (see Bales and Mears, 2008). Despite these complicating factors, age and criminal history remain reliable predictors of repeat offending behavior.

[4]For references see Bales and Mears, 2008; Bellair and Kowalski, 2011; Berg and Huebner, 2011; Berk and Rauma, 1983; Boman and Mowen, 2017; Chamberlain and Wallace, 2016; Cobbina, Huebner, and Berg, 2012; Hester, 2019; Hoffman and Beck, 1984; Huebner and Berg, 2011; Huebner and Cobbina, 2007; Huebner, DeJong, and Cobbina, 2010; Huebner and Pleggenkuhle, 2015; Kubrin and Stewart, 2006; Listwan et al., 2013; Liu and Visher, 2021; Liu et al., 2020; MacKenzie and Li, 2002; Miller, Caplan, and Ostermann, 2016; Mowen and Visher, 2015; Olson and Lurigio, 2000; Zweig et al., 2015.

[5]Other dynamic factors in the criminogenic needs model relate to peer and family relationships, employment, leisure and recreational activities, and antisocial cognition (Andrews and Bonta, 2010).

the authors therein).[6] A large share of individuals in prison and jail report being under the influence at the time they committed the offense for which they were incarcerated (Maruschak, Bronson, and Alper, 2021a; Mumola, 1999; Wilson, 2000), and roughly 60 percent of individuals sentenced to prison and jail meet the diagnostic criteria for drug dependence or abuse (Bronson et al., 2017). Studies of released individuals confirm those with a drug use or drug abuse history have a higher likelihood of post-release offending (Benedict and Huff-Corzine, 1997; Boman and Mowen, 2017; Huebner and Cobbina, 2007; Olson and Lurigio, 2000; Zweig et al., 2015), and those identified as drug dependent at the time of release from prison are more likely to be involved in post-release offending (Berk and Rauma, 1983; Huebner and Berg, 2011; Huebner, DeJong, and Cobbina, 2010; Huebner and Pleggenkuhle, 2015; for evidence of a null relationship, see Berg and Huebner, 2011). When investigators are able to measure it, post-release drug use is also positively correlated with post-release offending (Griffin and Armstrong, 2003; Li et al., 2000; Link and Hamilton, 2017; MacKenzie and Li, 2002).

Serious mental illness is another commonly studied dynamic risk factor.[7] A substantial share of confined individuals meet the criteria for serious mental illness, defined as a mental, behavioral, or emotional disorder that impairs functioning and fits established diagnostic criteria (Bronson et al., 2017; James and Glaze, 2006; Steadman et al., 2009).[8] This has been linked with a higher risk of post-release criminal behavior (Berg and Huebner, 2011; Cloyes et al., 2010; Listwan et al., 2013; Wallace and Wang, 2020).

In summary, existing research finds that both static and dynamic risk factors are reliable correlates of post-release criminal behavior.

Confinement Experiences

The experience of incarceration itself provides the basis for another set of theories explaining the continuation of criminal offending post-release. Theories of deterrence speak directly to incarceration, emphasizing how

---

[6]Goldstein (1985) describes the drugs-crime relationship as stemming from psychopharmacological effects (e.g., intoxication or withdrawal), economic-compulsive effects (e.g., crime to support a drug habit), and systemic effects (e.g., drug market violence).

[7]Mental illness has been viewed as both a dynamic risk factor and a "responsivity factor" (a response to) incarceration (Andrews and Bonta, 2010).

[8]Bronson and colleagues (2017) estimate that 58 percent of people in state prisons and 63 percent of those serving sentences in local jails meet the diagnostic criteria for drug dependence or abuse. Earlier, James and Glaze (2006) estimated that 56 percent of people in state prisons, 45 percent of those in federal prisons, and 64 percent of those in local jails have had a mental health problem (the corresponding figures for those with a recent history of such problems are 24 percent in state prisons, 14 percent in federal prisons, and 21 percent in local jails). With regard to jail populations, Steadman et al. (2009) estimate the prevalence of current serious mental illness at 14.5 percent for males and 31.0 percent for females.

being sentenced to prison affects the likelihood of post-release criminal behavior (Beccaria, 1764; Bentham, 1789). Known as *specific deterrence*, a longer length of stay is predicted to lower the expected utility of continued offending (Becker, 1968). This arises because the direct experience of prison contributes to experiential learning about the unpleasant consequences of crime, or to updating of the perceived risk of sanction in the event of a return to crime (Stafford and Warr, 1993).

The assumption that longer prison stays discourage future criminal offending is the basis for a great deal of carceral policy. Yet research on this relationship has produced highly variable findings for reasons that are not yet well understood. There is evidence that longer length of stay is not correlated with recidivism (Walker and Bishop, 2016), is weakly correlated with less recidivism (Cotter, 2020; Estelle and Phillips, 2018; Loughran et al., 2009; Meade et al., 2013; Rhodes et al., 2018), or is weakly correlated with more recidivism (Aizer and Doyle, 2015; Eren and Mocan, 2021; Green and Winik, 2010; Tiedt and Sabol, 2015). In still other studies longer sentences are correlated with both more and less recidivism at different points in the distribution of length of stay or for individuals with different commitment offenses (Mears et al., 2016; Rydberg and Clark, 2016).

It is thus not possible to say with confidence that longer length of stay has a deterrent effect, as longer sentences might actually worsen post-release criminal offending. These findings run contrary to expectations from the specific deterrence doctrine (for reviews of research on length of stay, see Loeffler and Nagin, 2021; Nagin, Cullen, and Jonson, 2009).[9] A quasi-experimental study found that when Georgia eliminated parole for some incarcerated people, they accumulated more disciplinary infractions, completed fewer prison rehabilitative programs, and returned to prison at higher rates than those whose sentences were unaffected by the reform (Kuziemko, 2013). These results suggest some degree of responsiveness to the incentives of early release.

An opposing theoretical narrative drawn from the labelling tradition suggests that confinement experiences can result in increased likelihood of post-release criminal offending. Theories of *secondary deviance* seek in part to explain why people who experience prison or longer length of stay might be more rather than less likely to continue offending. According to this view, some post-release criminal offending results from societal reactions to the incarcerated individual. The act of the criminal legal system

---

[9]Evidence related to the confinement experience is also available from studies comparing the use of custodial sanctions versus probation or some other form of diversion on post-release criminal offending (for informative reviews, see Nagin, Cullen, and Jonson, 2009; Petrich et al., 2021). These studies differ from those described in this paragraph because they consider the impact of incarceration on repeat offending along the "extensive" margin (incarceration vs. diversion) as opposed to the "intensive" margin (i.e., longer length of stay among those who are incarcerated).

officially labeling someone as an "offender" and the formal exclusionary processes and stigmas associated with this label can amplify criminal offending (Becker, 1963; Garfinkel, 1956; Goffman, 1963; Lemert, 1951, 1972; Schur, 1971). These labeling processes can contribute to institutional exclusion, identity transformation, subculture formation, or outright defiance by labeled individuals (Braithwaite, 1989; Paternoster and Iovanni, 1989; Sampson and Laub, 1997; Sherman, 1993).

Studies of confinement experiences are also informed by social learning principles (see Bandura, 1977), which often emphasize some degree of *prison enculturation* that can harden criminal offending after release. Hagan (1993) refers to this as the development of "criminal capital" that might not be easily shed by returning individuals.[10] Research on the prison environment supports the possibility that prisons can be "schools of crime." For example, there is some suggestion that individuals who have committed the same type of criminal offense experience reinforcing peer effects, thus increasing the chance of post-release criminal offending with that offense type after release (Bayer, Hjalmarsson, and Pozen, 2009; for null peer effects, see Harris et al., 2018). Research on security level also finds that assignment to a more secure prison environment is correlated with more post-release offending (Chen and Shapiro, 2007; Gaes and Camp, 2009), with some indication the effect is at least partly due to peer influences.[11] Scholars have only recently begun to probe the network structure of incarcerated individuals, both inside and outside of prison, and to explore the consequences of these networks for in-prison behavior as well as post-release behavior (see Kreager et al., 2016; 2017; Schaefer et al., 2017).

Societal Attachments and Reentry Stressors

Social institutions such as the family, school, and workplace attract a great deal of criminological interest, and studies of post-release criminal offending are no exception. Theories tend to view social ties as sources of *informal social control*, because they constitute an enduring social bond (Hirschi, 1969), a fount of social capital (Sampson and Laub, 1993), a source of social support (Cullen, 1994), or a set of "local life circumstances" (Horney, Osgood, and Marshall, 1995) that would be jeopardized

---

[10]Such explanatory mechanisms include differential associations with patterns and definitions favorable to criminal behavior (Sutherland, 1947), coupled with imitation and differential reinforcements (Akers, 1985; 1998; Burgess and Akers, 1966).

[11]There is a positive correlation between gang affiliation and post-release offending (Dooley, Seals, and Skarbek, 2014; Huebner, Varano, and Bynum, 2007; McShane et al., 2003; Pyrooz et al., 2021), although it has been difficult in this literature to isolate the unique influence of prison gang exposure from community gang exposure.

by a return to criminal behavior. Conversely, returning individuals for whom social ties have eroded face a higher likelihood of returning to crime.

Individuals who have been released from prison are uniquely vulnerable to strained relationships, financial hardship, homelessness, and even victimization, particularly during the early period of their return to the community (Binswanger et al., 2007; Comfort et al., 2018; Miller, 2021). The period following release can be thought of as having the potential for crisis (e.g., Western, 2018), especially if individuals return with little more than what they brought with them to prison. Some strain is more or less chronic and a byproduct of the disproportionately lower-class status of incarcerated individuals that reduces access to legitimate opportunities for upward mobility (Cohen, 1955; Cloward and Ohlin, 1960; Merton, 1938). The more acute features of strain can motivate post-release criminal offending by inducing *negative emotional states*, including anger, frustration, and feelings of injustice, consistent with expectations from general strain theory (Agnew, 1992; 2001; 2006). Individuals who experience these strains are theorized to be vulnerable to using crime as a coping mechanism, especially when they lack the resources and supports for more conventional coping.

Ecological Influences

Ecological frameworks for explaining post-release criminal behavior focus attention on characteristics of communities to which individuals return. Individuals reentering the community from prison concentrate in neighborhoods characterized by higher-than-average levels of economic disadvantage, residential instability, and racial heterogeneity.[12] And just as crime rates are correlated with these indicators of local ecology, criminal offending of formerly incarcerated individuals tends to correlate with neighborhood context. In particular, with exceptions, prior studies document a positive correlation between concentrated disadvantage and post-release offending in a variety of states (Hipp, Petersilia, and Turner, 2010; Huebner and Pleggenkuhle, 2015; Kirk, 2015; Kubrin and Stewart, 2006; McNeeley, 2018; Mears et al., 2008; for exceptions, see Chamberlain and Wallace, 2016; Miller, Caplan, and Ostermann, 2016; Tillyer and Vose, 2011; Wehrman, 2010).[13]

---

[12]This pattern has been described as concentrated reentry or mass reentry (Chamberlain and Wallace, 2016), the latter of which unites it with scholarship on mass incarceration (Garland, 2001) and mass probation (Phelps, 2017). Concentrated reentry has a more explicit geographical emphasis, similar to concentrated disadvantage.

[13]Some evidence suggests the correlation between concentrated disadvantage and post-release offending is strongest for formerly incarcerated African Americans (Mears et al., 2008). There are also unexpected findings from some jurisdictions that concentrated disadvantage is inversely correlated with post-release offending for at least certain groups of returning individuals (Huebner and Berg, 2011; Huebner, DeJong, and Cobbina, 2010; Reisig et al., 2007).

Many ecological perspectives have interpreted the relationship between post-release criminal behavior and concentrated disadvantage through the theoretical lens of *social disorganization* and its variants (see Bursik and Grasmick, 1993; Kornhauser, 1978; Peterson and Krivo, 2010; Sampson, Raudenbush, and Earls, 1997; Shaw and McKay, 1942; Shaw et al., 1929). Briefly, structural disadvantages erode interpersonal and institutional ties among residents and thus weaken the capacity of neighborhoods to act collectively and to regulate behavior in public spaces. If some returning individuals settle in neighborhoods with high rates of concentrated disadvantage, then their repeat offending is partly a consequence of a setting that lacks the capacity to exert informal social control over unwanted behavior. A less obvious facet of social disorganization is rooted in *coercive mobility*, the idea that the regular removal of residents from a community results in instability. Coercive mobility thus implicates the criminal legal system itself in the perpetuation of structural disadvantages facing individuals returning from prison (Clear, 2007; Rose and Clear, 1998; Sampson and Loeffler, 2010). For example, studies document the complex way in which the concentration of a large number of formerly incarcerated individuals can contribute to erosion in neighborhood structure and culture, both through the housing market (Chamberlain, 2018; Drakulich et al., 2012) and through collective legal cynicism (Kirk, 2016) and legal estrangement (Bell, 2017).

Explanations inspired by ecological perspectives also assign high theoretical priority to the density of opportunities available for returning individuals. Consider employment opportunities. A unifying theme of this research is spatial mismatch between the demand for jobs that do not require advanced training or degrees and their supply (for general perspectives on spatial mismatch, see Massey and Denton, 1993; Wilson, 1987). Sugie and Lens (2017), for example, find that individuals on parole exposed to a higher density of accessible, low-wage job openings in proximity to their residence have higher employment likelihood. This suggests facilitating access to low-skill jobs, such as through commuting subsidies, can be a meaningful form of support during reentry (see Bohmert, 2016). Research on so-called "willing industries" also provides evidence for the importance of access to jobs, for which formerly incarcerated individuals are likely to be eligible given their educational level and work experience. These industries tend to be in construction and manufacturing, and occasionally the retail and service sector. Individuals released on parole to areas with more abundant jobs in willing industries have a lower likelihood of post-release criminal offending.[14]

---

[14]Bellair and Kowalski (2011) found individuals released on parole to areas with more abundant jobs in willing industries have lower likelihood of post-release criminal offending in Ohio. Similar results were found in California (Schnepel, 2018) and a multistate study (Yang, 2017).

Research on concentrated reentry also points to the salience of residents' attitudes toward crime and reentry (Leverentz, 2011) and organizational capacity and resource availability for returning individuals. For example, neighborhoods that absorb large concentrations of returning individuals benefit from close proximity to service providers (Hipp, Petersilia, and Turner, 2010; Mellow et al., 2008; Rose, Clear, and Ryder, 2001). But high numbers of returning individuals often impose costs on these neighborhoods (Miller, 2014). Service concentration need not be limited to parole services, however; the density of other community organizations is also linked with lower post-release offending (Hipp and Yates, 2009; Wallace, 2015; Wallace and Papachristos, 2014; for complexity in these findings, see Wo and Park, 2019). Organizational density is also correlated with lower crime rates (Rosenfeld, Messner, and Baumer, 2001; Sharkey, Torrats-Espinosa, and Takyar, 2017; Slocum et al., 2013; Wo, Hipp, and Boessen, 2016).

Broadly, the communities and local "activity spaces" (Leverentz, 2020) to which individuals return play an important role in shaping their lives, including their likelihood of engaging in further criminal behavior.

Supervision Regimes

The theoretical discussion to this point emphasizes forces that act on returning individuals in ways that affect their risk of engaging in criminal behavior, with different theoretical traditions pointing to different facets of the reentry experience. It is important to bear in mind that measures of post-release offending partially and imperfectly measure actual behavior. As described in Chapter 2, existing measures of post-release offending typically use official criminal records as a proxy for all criminal activity. These administrative records reflect the interaction between individual behavior and the criminal legal system—including what different jurisdictions label as criminal and which communities are exposed to greater police presence. Thus any theoretical account of post-release offending that overlooks the actions of the criminal legal system itself is fundamentally incomplete.

Policies and practices at the local and state levels are implicated in explanations of post-release criminal offending (see Visher and Travis, 2003). For example, some variation in recorded levels of repeat offending is an artifact of the degree of surveillance; more intensive and punitive supervision in the community by probation and parole agencies will expose more disallowed behaviors. At the extreme, wraparound support services can beget "wraparound incarceration" (Flores, 2016). Indeed, supervision regimes that merely emphasize intensive surveillance through frequent contacts and drug tests have no impact on new arrests, but do increase the likelihood of technical violations and thus reincarceration due to revocation (Petersilia and Turner, 1993; Schiraldi and Arzu, 2018). This is generally true of the enhancement of technical conditions of probation or parole supervision through the use of control- and sanction-oriented technologies (e.g., house arrest, electronic monitoring, curfews) (see MacKenzie, 2006; Sherman et al., 1998; Taxman, 2002; Taxman, Smith, and Rudes, 2020).

The training of community supervision officers also seems to be correlated with post-release reoffending (Andrews and Bonta, 2010; Chadwick, Dewolf, and Serin, 2015; Dowden and Andrews, 2004). The use of incentives to reward positive post-release behavior, as opposed to the use of sanctions to punish negative post-release behavior, also has a growing evidence base in its favor (Mowen et al., 2018; Sloas, Murphy, and Taxman, 2019; Wodahl et al., 2011). Moreover, when individuals on supervision feel they can trust their officer and that the officer is fair, their outcomes include less post-release offending and fewer technical violations (Skeem et al., 2007; Taxman and Ainsworth, 2009; Taxman and Thanner, 2004).

MODELS OF REENTRY SUCCESS

The historical emphasis on recidivism among policy analysts, practitioners, and scholars reflects, in part, a desire by researchers and institutions to establish a common "success rate" indicator. But it is quickly apparent that success and failure are relative concepts—and that crude dichotomies fail to capture the real changes that people returning from incarceration experience. Recidivism is therefore limited as a performance measure or metric for success (King and Elderbroom, 2014). Today, many analysts are calling for "a paradigmatic shift" in criminal justice practices that would better align with contemporary theories of desistance from crime (Bersani and Doherty, 2018; Bushway and Uggen, 2021). For our purposes, we can think of these models in terms of two broad conceptions of "success": (1) desistance from crime and (2) social integration and well-being.

Desistance from Crime

Desistance refers to why and how people stop committing crime. The key distinction between recidivism and desistance approaches is that the former focuses on a negative outcome (i.e., crime at a discrete point in time), whereas the latter seeks to track positive outcomes that may result in reduced involvement in offending over time, ultimately leading to the complete cessation of criminal behavior. Early models of desistance focused on the relationship between age and crime and the natural process of aging or maturation (Glueck and Glueck, 1940). In recent decades, theories have emerged that explain desistance as the product of social and developmental processes (Bersani and Doherty, 2018; Maruna, 2001; Sampson and Laub, 1993; Uggen and Piliavin, 1998; Weaver, 2019). These models conceptualize desistance as a process marked by a decline in the rate or severity of offending that is closely linked to other life-course processes, such as work and family transitions (Bushway et al., 2001; Laub and Sampson, 2001). The study of desistance represents an important refinement, as it explicitly recognizes that changes in criminal behavior rarely map neatly onto a recidivist versus non-recidivist dichotomy.

Some desistance researchers explain these shifts in crime over time as a consequence of the development of adult social bonds and informal social controls (e.g., Sampson and Laub, 1993). A long line of research establishes associations between adult employment and recidivism, although the evidence is mixed regarding causality (Uggen, 2000; Visher, Winterfield, and Coggeshall, 2005). Similarly, strong family ties are consistently associated with both employment and reduced recidivism (Berg and Huebner, 2011), although some studies suggest that such effects may depend on the criminal history of the partner (Andersen, Andersen, and Skov, 2015).

In contrast to social control–based models, identity-based models of desistance emphasize the social-psychological processes that link these adult role behaviors to changes in self-concept, identity, and behavior (Giordano, Cernkovich, and Rudolph, 2002; Maruna, 2001; Matsueda and Heimer, 1997; Paternoster and Bushway, 2009). By this logic, desistance is partly a process of "de-labeling" (Maruna, 2001) or nullifying the effects of a criminal label. For Giordano, Cernkovich, and Rudolph (2002), employment and marriage are less predictive of desistance than an individual's cognitive shifts and development of a "replacement self" (e.g., as the good wife or involved mother). Qualitative research suggests that the process of desistance from crime is a "fragile project," frequently subject to derailment, setbacks, and recovery (Halsey, Armstrong, and Wright, 2017).

In both control-based and identity-based models, however, desistance theory and research typically link particular roles and statuses of life course development—such as education, employment, housing, family transitions, and civic participation—to subsequent criminal behavior. Shifts in activity patterns, social networks, and underlying identities appear to be key mechanisms in both desistance from crime and recovery from substance dependence (Best and Savic, 2014). Incarceration represents another important life experience that likely shapes desistance patterns (Maruna and Toch, 2005). A recent review of the effects of incarceration on subsequent conviction and reincarceration observed reductions in settings with rehabilitative programming and criminogenic effects in settings without such programming (Loeffler and Nagin, 2021).

In addition to concrete success markers such as employment and housing, formerly incarcerated people who participated in the committee's information-gathering sessions emphasized social-psychological processes. These include the importance of self-efficacy, feelings of worthiness, healing from trauma, self-compassion, confidence, and a sense of personal responsibility in the process of successful reintegration into society. Several participants discussed identity transformations that took place in prison or afterwards, often facilitated by participation in therapeutic, educational, and vocational programs. At the same time, they shared accounts of obstacles they encountered during reentry, such as the denial of jobs and housing because they had to "check the box" and other experiences of discrimination related to their criminal record, gender or racial identity, social class, or other characteristics. Regardless of their intrinsic feelings of self-worth, formerly incarcerated persons are burdened by stigma attached to them by society. These experiences are consistent with the conclusions of some scholars that feelings of self-efficacy and the acceptance of a prosocial identity are necessary precursors to successful desistance; however, they may not be sufficient (LeBel et al., 2008).

Social Reintegration and Well-Being

Although facilitating desistance from crime is a key goal of prison reentry programs, people with criminal records are, of course, human beings who are more than the sum of their recidivism risks. It is the view of this committee, particularly informed by those committee members who have been incarcerated, that a myopic focus on recidivism or desistance as the sole indicator of post-release success is problematic. Social integration and reintegration constitute success markers in their own right, irrespective of their effect on crime and desistance (Harding, Morenoff, and Wyse, 2019; Western, 2018).

This conception of success emphasizes flourishing and well-being, often in work, family, and civic roles that benefit families and communities as well as the reentering individual. By this logic, programs that improve post-release education and employability, family functioning, or civic participation may be considered successful and socially beneficial. Research in this tradition often emphasizes economic costs and benefits, as well as reintegration across varied social domains, such as socioeconomic reintegration, familial reintegration, and civic reintegration (Drake et al., 2009; Uggen, Manza, and Behrens, 2004).

In contrast to a recidivism framework organized around a risk paradigm, the committee views post-release success through the lens of flourishing and well-being. Such an approach is consonant with recent scholarship on the social determinants of health, which emphasizes "the environments in which people are born, grow, work, live, learn, play, worship, and age" that affect health and quality of life (U.S. Department of Health and Human Services, 2021). Hastening desistance from crime is an important aspect of post-release success, but social reintegration is a success marker in its own right. This conception of success emphasizes flourishing and healthy adult development, often in work, family, and civic roles that directly benefit families and communities as well as the reentering individual.

Of course, the experience of criminal punishment and resulting "carceral citizenship" (Lerman and Weaver, 2014; Miller and Stuart, 2017) can directly undermine social reintegration (Brayne, 2014) and well-being. That is, incarceration, monetary sanctions, and other civil disabilities actually impede successful reintegration. Formerly incarcerated people and those with felony-level criminal records face severe restrictions on their work, family, and civic participation due in part to the "invisible punishment" (Travis, 2002) of collateral sanctions. Imposing sanctions such as welfare restrictions or disenfranchisement does little to support victims or improve public safety (see Box 3-1 for further discussion of collateral sanctions).

BOX 3-1
Collateral Sanctions of Incarceration

Collateral sanctions are typically set outside of the penal code, implemented by non-criminal legal institutions, and interpreted by courts as civil regulations rather than criminal penalties. Among other limitations, these include restrictions on occupational licensure (Aukerman, 2005), parental rights, housing, education, public benefits, and voting rights (Manza and Uggen, 2006). Today, approximately 5.2 million U.S. adults remain disenfranchised due to a felony conviction, representing about 2.3 percent of the total U.S. voting eligible population and 6.2 percent of the Black voting eligible population (Uggen et al., 2020). Although these legal and informal restrictions are separable for analytic purposes, people experience them in combination, as compounding challenges (Uggen and Stewart, 2014).

People who have been released from prison are also required to navigate the stigma and negative reactions of those in their community. This arises in both immediate face-to-face interaction and in what sociologist Sarah Lageson calls "digital punishment," a product of the widespread public availability of criminal records in the information age, which can further restrict opportunities and enhance the stigma of a criminal record (Lageson, 2016; Lageson, 2020). Efforts to remove such barriers and reduce stigma, however, pose their own challenges. For example, some research finds that "ban the box" laws that inhibit employers' access to criminal record information may result in greater discrimination against Black men without criminal records (Agan and Starr, 2018). Nevertheless, other collateral consequences may be reduced or eliminated with little to no threat to public safety or negative consequences for other groups. For example, more U.S. states are now paring back restrictions on voting (Uggen et al., 2020), an important gesture of civic inclusion.

Ineligibility for certain welfare benefits also adds to the financial insecurity of formerly incarcerated individuals. Some states restrict or completely ban those with a felony drug conviction from accessing food assistance through SNAP

KEY DOMAINS OF SUCCESSFUL REINTEGRATION

Models of social integration and well-being offer an important supplement and alternative to standard measures of recidivism and account for the general tasks associated with adult citizenship: completing school, establishing independent residency, and entering into adult work and family roles. This conception of success emphasizes flourishing and well-being, often in work, family, and civic roles that benefit families, victims, and communities as well as the reentering individual. In this view, programs that improve post-release education and employability, family functioning, or civic participation can be considered socially beneficial. To the extent that such measures of success help end the cycle of criminal behavior, they

(Supplemental Nutrition Assistance Program, formerly food stamps), cash assistance through TANF (Temporary Assistance for Needy Families), or both. Reductions in assistance to the poor began with the 1996 federal reform bill, which primarily affected female-headed families with dependent children (Bloom, Owen, and Covington, 2004; U.S. Government Accountability Office, 2005). The reform bill restricted access to monetary support through TANF by establishing time limits for receipt of aid and requiring a minimum percentage of welfare recipients in each state to be involved in work preparation or employment. Moreover, the act permitted states to impose a lifetime ban on SNAP and TANF for those with a previous drug felony conviction, regardless of whether they have completed their sentence or received a lighter sentence due to the nonviolent or low-level nature of the offense (Center for Law and Social Policy, 2021). Since successful reentry into society requires being able to meet basic needs (i.e., food, health care, housing, employment, training services), denying access to programs that provide basic needs makes it difficult for people with a criminal record to successfully integrate into society.

Such exclusions are especially punitive to Black and Latinx communities due to the War on Drugs, which targets poor communities of color. Disproportionalities in drug law enforcement have led to disproportionate exclusion from public benefits for Black women and Latinas (Bloom, Owen, and Covington, 2004). In addition, due to federal policies and local practices that deny assistance to individuals convicted of a drug felony offense, many criminal legal system-involved individuals face unique barriers to obtaining housing assistance. For example, the law allows individuals who house relatives or friends engaged in criminal activity to be evicted even if the tenant "did not know of, could not foresee, or could not control the behavior of other occupants or guests" (Love, Roberts, and Klingele, 2013).

The committee heard from formerly incarcerated persons about how housing and contact restrictions can sometimes undermine supportive relationships. People returning from prison need greater access to effective reentry programming, including access to needed housing, labor force opportunities, and welfare support.

clearly impact public safety and the well-being of victims. Nevertheless, successful reintegration does not stop at public safety but also benefits communities by contributing to their economic vitality and family stability and by strengthening civil society. Criminal legal institutions, reentry programs, and other agencies that serve individuals returning from prison can thus be evaluated, in part, based on their success in improving participant and victim outcomes in a set of domains central to overall well-being.

The following section reviews existing research on key domains of support and strain in the reintegration process.[15] Effective programming and services support successful reentry in each of these domains by implementing validated assessments, effective cognitive-behavioral therapy and treatment, individually tailored case plans, behavioral incentives, and graduated sanctions. Success in domains such as education and employment is important in its own right, but may also support the cessation of criminal activity. Where that is the case, we note this relationship. However, a domain need not promote desistance from crime in order to be central to successful reintegration. Box 3-2 describes perspectives from correctional leaders on defining successful reentry and the key domains of the reintegration process.

Housing

One significant challenge facing individuals exiting prison is finding stable, affordable housing (Lattimore and Visher, 2021; Miller, 2021; Visher and La Vigne, 2021), which is particularly difficult for people convicted of sex crimes (Dum, 2016). Locating a place to live is one of the immediate concerns individuals exiting prison experience, yet it is often permeated with obstacles. Formerly incarcerated people are 10 times more likely than the general public to be homeless, with homelessness rates higher for women, African Americans, individuals over age 45, individuals who have been incarcerated multiple times, and people recently released from prison (Couloute, 2018). Individuals with sex offense convictions, substance abuse problems, and mental illness are especially susceptible to homelessness (Metraux, Hunt, and Yetvin, 2020). Many formerly incarcerated individuals face financial difficulties securing housing, as many are excluded from housing options (Greenberg and Rosenheck, 2008). Both public housing authorities and private landlords can use screening criteria, including criminal record checks, to exclude reentering individuals (Couloute, 2018). Moreover, a sizeable group of these individuals may have never lived on their own and require substantial support in finding suitable housing after release (Hyde et al., 2021).

---

[15]A recent study (Love, 2022), which appeared after the completion of this report, grades the 50 states on their effectiveness in reintegrating persons into civil society after arrest or conviction.

BOX 3-2
Correctional Perspectives on Measures of Success

In their information-gathering efforts, members of the committee met with correctional leaders, including directors of state departments of corrections, staff in county departments of community justice, and members of the Correctional Leaders Association and American Probation and Parole Association. Correctional leaders emphasized the need for broader measures of post-release outcomes and described the limitations of recidivism as an "all or nothing" approach to success.

One of the chief weaknesses of recidivism, according to the correctional leaders who provided their perspectives, is that it is free of context and hinders consideration of the supports that are available and being acted on as well as the positive impact of the work of correctional staff. Indeed, one correctional leader lamented that parole and probation offers can typically tell you their revocation rate, but lack the metrics to tell you anything about the success of their caseload. Multiple leaders suggested that the correctional system and the reentry process are too complex to be accurately measured by a single dominant metric. Correctional leaders also identified a need for nuance in tracking what types of crimes were associated with recidivism, and multiple leaders expressed a need to acknowledge and track incremental progress.

Multiple leaders noted that their offices are moving away from a sole emphasis on recidivism and focusing on measures of stability and progress in terms of stable housing, regular employment, educational attainments, prosocial involvement with family and community, and participation in drug treatment and other behavioral health services, to name a few metrics that were commonly highlighted. The individuals we spoke with also saw value in the inclusion of subjective assessments from individuals released from prison, such as how successful they believe they will be upon release, and how they feel they have been treated by program and service providers post-release. Some agencies noted challenges in obtaining this information, given limited infrastructure for the collection and sharing of such data.

SOURCE: Discussions with representatives of the committee, David Edwards, Travis Gramble, Anne Precythe, Erika Preuitt, Bryan Smith, Katie Roller, Glenn Tapia, and Heidi Washington, held February 15, 22, and 25, 2022.

As a result, most reside with family members (unless prohibited from staying with them due to their criminal records), while many others stay in transitional housing such as emergency shelters (LeBel, 2017; Metraux, Hunt, and Yetvin, 2020; Visher and La Vigne, 2021). Formerly incarcerated people who are housed often live in unstable, marginal housing situations, such as motels and rooming houses, and move frequently in the first year or two after release (Couloute, 2018; LeBel, 2017).

Housing instability and homelessness can compromise public safety and contribute to an increased likelihood of recidivism as measured in various ways, including return to prison, rearrest, and parole revocation (LeBel, 2017; Lutze, Rosky, and Hamilton, 2014; Metraux, Hunt, Yetvin, 2020). Housing options are often limited to neighborhoods with high rates of crime and poverty, limited employment opportunities, and a high concentration of other formerly incarcerated residents (Metraux, Hunt, Yetvin, 2020). When formerly incarcerated people manage to secure housing it is often less safe, as many face increased exposure to drugs and victimization (Harding, Morenoff, and Wyse, 2019). Stable, secure housing—particularly housing that includes access to supportive services such as mental health or substance use treatment, vocational and employment assistance, and health care—can not only reduce homelessness for returning individuals but also support reintegration and desistance, especially when provided during the first month after release (Fontaine and Biess, 2012; Metraux and Culhane, 2004; Metraux, Hunt, and Yetvin, 2020). Relatedly, state provision for short-term needs during the reentry period, including subsidized housing, serves as an important buffer that reduces repeat offending (Holtfreter et al., 2004).

Employment

Finding employment is another large concern reported by men and women before release from incarceration (Visher and La Vigne, 2021; Western, 2018), as many leave prison with economic obligations including debts associated with child support, fines, restitution costs, court costs, and supervision fees (Harris, 2016). Employment ties provide structure as well as an income stream for returning individuals, and a great deal of emphasis is thus devoted to job placement during reentry. Research indicates that formerly incarcerated individuals who are employed have a lower likelihood of post-release criminal offending (Berg and Huebner, 2011; Griffin and Armstrong, 2003; Huebner and Cobbina, 2007; Link, Ward, and Strassfield, 2019; Listwan et al., 2013; MacKenzie and Li, 2002). Some studies find a null or positive relationship (Boman and Mowen, 2017; Mowen et al., 2018), although this might only be true for men (Cobbina, Huebner, and Berg, 2012) and individuals in their late 20s or older (Uggen, 2000).[16] Reductions in criminal activity associated with employment may be attributable, in part, to the fact that employment eases financial pressures (Link, Ward, and Strassfield, 2019). Scholars have also observed that returning individuals benefit from higher-quality employment opportunities (Cook, 1975; Evans, 1968; Uggen, 1999), although their educational and

---

[16]Li and MacKenzie (2003) find that employment is inversely correlated with offending among males on probation, but positively correlated with criminal behavior among females.

prior work credentials pose a number of challenges, as do employment-based reentry programs and parole supervision practices that prioritize placement in any job as opposed to placement in jobs that inspire a high level of satisfaction.

Familial and Social Relationships and Support

Because of what they signify about a returning individual's societal attachments, familial relationships are central to studying and theorizing the reentry process (Uggen, Wakefield, and Western, 2005). Although it is difficult to disentangle the effects of incarceration from the preexisting characteristics of those who are incarcerated, the criminal legal system itself plays a part in disconnecting formerly incarcerated people from family and other social institutions (see reviews in Kirk and Wakefield, 2018; National Research Council, 2014; Wakefield and Uggen, 2010). Adult social bonds such as relationships with family members have been widely documented to be an important factor in successful transitions away from criminal activity and toward community engagement (Blokland and Nieuwbeerta, 2005; Laub and Sampson, 2006; Naser and Visher, 2006; Sampson and Laub, 2003; Warr, 1998). Family offers an important social network for men and women exiting prison, as many live with their family usually for several months (Visher and La Vigne, 2021). Research indicates that after release from prison people expect a high level of support from their family (La Vigne et al., 2004; Nelson, Deess, and Allen, 1999) and attach importance to commitment to family roles, including as parents (Uggen, Manza, and Behrens, 2004; Zamble and Quinsey, 1997). In addition to acting as a core domain for reintegration, social ties can also support desistance. For example, in a study of interviews with previously incarcerated fathers and mothers, interviewees attributed family connections and parent-child contact as key factors in their post-release success (Charles, Meuntner, and Kjellstrand, 2019).

People who are released from prison generally receive some level of emotional, social, and economic support from family (Martinez and Christian, 2009; Miller, 2021; Visher and Courtney, 2006). Such family support is associated with higher rates of employment, reductions in substance use, and fewer physical, mental, and emotional problems (Harding et al., 2014; Naser and LaVigne, 2006; Naser and Visher, 2006). Further research has suggested that the instrumental support provided by family (e.g., housing, employment, transportation) eclipses emotional and other forms of support in lowering the risk of post-release criminal behavior (Mowen et al., 2019; for a contrary finding, see Taylor, 2016). Familial ties with extended relatives, in particular, may affect repeat offending indirectly by facilitating access to employment for those with a history of employment difficulty (Berg and Huebner, 2011).

BOX 3-3
The Role of Social and Community Support

Formerly incarcerated individuals, policy practitioners, and scholarly experts who participated in the committee's information-gathering sessions highlighted the need for personal connections, relationships, a sense of belonging, and support systems during the reentry process.

Sam Lewis, Executive Director of the Anti-Recidivism Coalition, "when a person comes home from incarceration, you're trying to fit back into society and you need to feel like you're welcome. And often because of all of the stereotypes that go along with it, and the red scarlet letter, and the boxes you have to check—[it] make[s] you feel like you're not part of society. But if you have a community of people who have gone through the same thing you've gone through and overcome those things, then you know you can do it too. And not only that but should you stumble and fall you have a community that is going to reach down and lift you up and walk with you."

John Valverde, President and CEO of YouthBuild USA, "for me success is experiencing a sense of belonging and worthiness in society. . . . It's about the sense of belonging and feeling you can contribute to society, that you're accepted."

Some also discussed the need for these social support networks during and prior to incarceration. They emphasized how social and correctional structures and policies can constrain returning citizens' ability to actualize their prosocial self-identities.

Those with family supports, including supportive relationships with parents and romantic partners, also have a lower risk of post-release offending (Berg and Huebner, 2011; Boman and Mowen, 2017; Cobbina, Huebner, and Berg, 2012; Huebner and Pleggenkuhle, 2015; Link, Ward, and Stransfield, 2019; Liu and Visher, 2021). Even visitations by family members in the months leading up to release from prison are correlated with a lower probability of post-release criminal behavior (Bales and Mears, 2008).[17] In a 10-year follow-up study of 400 individuals released from South Carolina prisons, family members were often mentioned as factors that made respondents less likely to engage in criminal behavior. Rebuilding family relationships and being around people not involved in criminal

---

[17]This does not include marital status, which is generally uncorrelated with post-release offending (Bellair and Kowalski, 2011; Listwan et al., 2013). Li and MacKenzie (2003) report that living with a spouse is inversely correlated with offending among males on probation, but is positively correlated with offending among females. For evidence of an inverse relationship with post-release offending, see Boman and Mowen (2017).

Merry Morash, Professor of Criminal Justice at Michigan State University, "these obstacles include a lack of transportation, unavailability of jobs paying a living wage, lack of access to welfare and health benefits, housing discrimination, and monetary costs of supervision."

Such barriers place formerly incarcerated individuals at increased economic risk; if their needs continue to be unmet, this increases the odds that they will not only reoffend but also fail to successfully integrate into the community. Even if these impediments do not prevent progress during reentry, obstacles like these can cause delays and setbacks, and keep reentering individuals in a precarious state (Morash et al., 2015).

John Valverda, President and CEO of YouthBuild USA, "structural injustice exists and has done harm inter-generationally . . . barriers are real and can feel insurmountable."

Participants also emphasized that the mitigation of structural and cultural impediments such as economic marginalization and social exclusion can promote subjective changes that are associated with desistance. Likewise, successful reentry can be facilitated by allocating sufficient resources to appropriate community-based programming and support structures around employment, education, housing, and health care.

SOURCE: Committee on Evaluating Success Among People Released from Prison, Meeting #2. See Session 1: https://www.nationalacademies.org/event/07-27-2021/evaluating-success-among-people-released-from-prison-meeting-2-public-information-gathering-session-1. Session 2: https://www.nationalacademies.org/event/07-28-2021/evaluating-success-among-people-released-from-prison-meeting-2-public-information-gathering-session-2.

behavior have also been found to be factors in desistance trajectories (Lattimore, Dawes, and Berrick, 2018).

However, recent qualitative and quantitative research documents a decline in intimate partnerships, co-residence, and relationship happiness during the reentry period (Comfort et al. 2018). Family members also experience hardships during the reentry process from financial strain, increased anxiety, and trouble with familial and peer relationships (Naser and Visher, 2006; Visher and La Vigne, 2021). These hardships can lead to negative emotional states and maladaptive coping (Liu and Visher, 2019), and family conflict is correlated with higher risk of post-release criminal behavior and substance use (Mowen and Visher, 2015) (See Box 3-3).

Physical Health, Mental Health, and Substance Use

Health challenges facing people exiting prison are often overlooked amid the myriad array of other issues they face (Link et al., 2019; Visher and

Mallik-Kane, 2007; Western, 2018). Individuals report serious mental and physical health problems even at relatively young ages (under 40). In one study, almost half of men reported having a chronic physical health condition; the most commonly reported conditions were asthma, hepatitis, and high blood pressure (Visher and Mallik-Kane, 2007). Research based on the National Comorbidity Survey finds that incarceration is associated with the onset of major depressive disorder, bipolar disorder, and dysthymia (Schnittker, Massoglia, and Uggen, 2012). Among people with a history of incarceration, this study estimates the lifetime prevalence of major depression at 19.8 percent and the lifetime prevalence of post-traumatic stress disorder at 10.8 percent.

In general, incarcerated and formerly incarcerated individuals have an elevated risk of experiencing a diverse set of chronic health conditions compared with the general population (Massoglia and Pridemore, 2015). Consequently, elevated risk of poor health conditions increases mortality both immediately after and years after release from prison (Wang, Pletcher, and Lin, 2009). In general, compared with individuals who have never been imprisoned, incarceration is associated with worse health for formerly incarcerated persons (Massoglia and Pridemore, 2013).

Several studies have also explored mortality patterns following release from prison. One Washington State study found a mortality rate for formerly incarcerated individuals that was 3.5 times higher than for other residents of the state (Binswanger et al., 2007). This excess mortality was not distributed evenly over time, as the risk of death within two weeks of release was 13 times higher than for the general population. Other studies find significant variation in the risk depending on the amount of time the individual served in prison (Patterson, 2013).

In addition, the life domains discussed earlier negatively influence health. Unemployment, poverty, residential instability, and reduced social support are correlated with poor health outcomes (Massoglia and Remster, 2019). While formerly incarcerated people often find it challenging to secure employment, the jobs they do obtain are less likely to offer comprehensive healthcare benefits (Western, 2006). As a result, individuals exiting prison are less likely to have adequate means to treat their health conditions.[18]

People exiting prison also have extensive substance use histories. According to data from the Bureau of Justice Statistics, nearly half (47%) meet the criteria for drug dependence (Maruschak, Bronson, and Alper, 2021a). Returning individuals often identify drug use as the primary cause of many of their past and current problems including family, relationship, employment, legal, or financial problems (Lattimore, Dawes, and Berrick, 2018; Visher and

---

[18]As of December 1, 2021, the Build Back Better Act contained a provision that would allow people who are incarcerated to receive Medicaid benefits 30 days prior to release (Da Silva, 2021). Such a provision has the potential to improve care and the continuity of care at reentry.

La Vigne, 2021). Yet, many individuals report lower rates of substance use after release compared to pre-prison use. A recent systematic review reports that 18 of 31 studies assessing the effects of drug treatment (the primary modalities included cognitive-behavioral therapy and 12-step programming) found reduced recidivism for the treatment group on at least one indicator, though the pattern of results was somewhat inconsistent (Moore et al., 2020).

Here, as elsewhere, the criminal legal system enmeshes coercion and care, imposing punishment while also providing needed services, including health care (Miller, 2021; Phelps and Ruhland, 2021). The specific conditions of carceral care are likely to play an important part in shaping outcomes. Emerging qualitative studies suggest that reentry services and state-sponsored healthcare have been especially important during the COVID-19 pandemic. For example, a participant in a recent Ohio studied remarked, "I'd probably be in the dirt" without the "good insurance" that accompanied his parole (Vuolo, Schneider, and Laplant 2022, p. 12).

Participation in Peer Support and Help-Giving Roles

Another emerging form of important social support after release is the role of formerly incarcerated people who serve as peer mentors. The employment of formerly incarcerated people to provide peer support, assistance, and advocacy in rehabilitation and reentry programs provides benefits not only to the program participants, but also to those providing the peer support. Applying differential association theory to rehabilitation programming, Cressey (1965, p. 50) proposed that people with criminal histories "can be highly effective agents of change and, further, as they act as *agents* of change they themselves become the *targets* of change, thus insuring their own rehabilitation." The ability of formerly incarcerated program personnel to understand the lived experiences and thought patterns of reentering individuals, and to offer options to manage and overcome circumstantial and psychological obstacles, allows them to be especially effective mentors and guides (Cressey, 1965; Riessman, 1965). These ideas have been the basis for many self-help and mutual assistance groups, including Alcoholics Anonymous and other substance treatment programs (Katz, 1981; Zemore, Kaskutas, and Ammon, 2004).

In turn, individuals serving as peer mentors develop and reinforce new, prosocial identities, hone leadership skills, and often benefit socially and financially from this work while acknowledging their past behaviors (Brown, 1991; Riessman, 1965). Help-giving and mentoring roles can strengthen formerly incarcerated individuals' active coping strategies, self-esteem, life satisfaction, and sense of self-agency (Aresti, Eatough, and Brooks-Gordon, 2010; LeBel, 2007; LeBel, Richie, and Maruna, 2015; Maruna, 2001). While all of these benefits can help formerly incarcerated people pursue prosocial lifestyles and reintegrate into society (LeBel, Richie, and Maruna, 2015), Sharp and Hope (2001) note that engagement as a "professional ex-" does not necessarily lead to desistance from all drug use or criminal behavior. Furthermore, work as a "professional ex-" does not necessarily fully mitigate the stigma associated with the label of "ex-offender" (Aresti, Eatough, and Brooks-Gordon, 2010).

Despite these caveats, the value of peer support in reentry was consistently reaffirmed by formerly incarcerated individuals and practitioners who participated in the committee's information-gathering sessions. They emphasized the value of formerly incarcerated individuals' perspectives in the creation of appropriate and effective programs grounded in mutual respect, trust, and cultural sensitivity (see Box 3-4).

Voting and Civic Engagement

As noted above, approximately 5.2 million U.S. adults remain disenfranchised due to a felony conviction (Uggen et al., 2020). However, a number of states have recently restored the franchise for this population, wholly or

---

BOX 3-4
The Value of Lived Experience in Reentry Programming

During a public information-gathering session held by the committee, practitioners and those with lived experience spoke to the value of peer support in reentry programming.

George Braucht, who heads a peer recovery program consultancy called Brauchtworks in Georgia, noted, "fundamentally what's missing from most reentry programs are people with lived experience who meet with the staff and the returning citizens," whom he called "peer-roes."

Jai Diamond, a formerly incarcerated transgender woman working at the New York City Criminal Justice Agency, explained why it is valuable to have program providers from diverse backgrounds: "We need to get the people that work in these institutions to look more like the communities that they're serving. There is too much of a cultural difference between the two to build any trust."

Kara Nelson, Director of Public Relations and Development at True North Recovery in Alaska, explained, "those with lived experience need to [be able to] share their stories so people can identify and know that they can too." Nelson added, "We have to be at the table. We're not just redemption stories. We're leaders who have something to say and something to offer. We will be the ones with the solutions to make that change."

SOURCE: Committee on Evaluating Success Among People Released from Prison, Meeting #2. See: https://www.nationalacademies.org/event/07-27-2021/evaluating-success-among-people-released-from-prison-meeting-2-public-information-gathering-session-1.

after a certain period of time. Civic engagement involves more than voting, of course, extending to volunteer experiences, coaching and mentoring, participation in service learning experiences, and attendance at rallies and demonstrations. When they are not formally barred from participating, people with a history of incarceration often lack the resources, ability to mobilize, and in some cases the motivation to be civically engaged. Those who are incarcerated in jails often retain the right to vote, though jail administrators do not often facilitate the voting process for people housed in their facilities (Paikowsky, 2019). Moreover, many incarcerated and formerly incarcerated people may be uncertain about their voting eligibility or fear prosecution for illegal voting (Uggen, Manza, and Thompson, 2006). Although more rigorous studies are needed in this area, some research finds that voting and other forms of civic participation by incarcerated people may enhance public safety (Uggen and Manza, 2004) and willingness to cooperate with law enforcement (Shineman, 2018). When people have resources, motivation, and are able to mobilize and exercise the right to participate in their communities, they may be more strongly tied to these communities and less likely to engage in behaviors that would harm them (Bazemore and Stinchcomb, 2004; Fox, 2010; Miller, 2021; Uggen, Manza, and Behrens, 2004; Weaver and Lerman, 2010).

In addition to holding promise as a marker of broader reintegration and well-being, civic engagement may also support cessation of criminal behavior. Researchers find clear negative correlations between voting and recontact with the criminal legal system, with one study finding approximately 16 percent of nonvoters in 1996 were rearrested during the subsequent three years, relative to five percent of 1996 voters (Manza and Uggen, 2006). A 2012 investigation reports that individuals released in states that permanently disenfranchise are approximately ten percent more likely to reoffend than those released in states that restore the right to vote following release (Hamilton-Smith and Vogel, 2012; for similar findings see Hoover, 2021). This relationship holds when analysis accounts for prior criminal history and when self-report crime data is used in place of official arrest records (Larson and Uggen, 2017). Although some of the association between voting and recontact with the criminal legal system is likely due to preexisting differences between voters and nonvoters, the results suggest a link between political participation and desistance from crime. Other studies show similar patterns for probation and parole (Uggen and Inderbitzin, 2010). It may be the case that voting is tapping a desire to participate as a law-abiding stakeholder in one's community. Practicing citizenship may, in turn, help to reinforce an identity as a law-abiding citizen.

It stands to reason that the more civically engaged people are, when they have resources, motivation, and the ability to mobilize and exercise the right to vote, the less likely they might be to utilize their power to harm the community by engaging in criminal acts. In particular, symbolic interactionist and social control theories link desistance from crime to age-graded transitions in work and family life. More broadly, writers such as Alexis de Tocqueville and John Stuart Mill have pointed to the potentially educative and constitutive impact of political participation. Voting may thus engender some degree of identification with the polity and its norms and values. Others point to the expressive impact of voting and its potential to mold "virtuous" citizens. As Winkler (1993, p. 331) put it, "Voting is a meaningful participatory act through which individuals create and affirm their membership in the community and thereby transform their identities both as individuals and as part of a greater collectivity."

Civic engagement may also take the form of participation in criminal legal system reform and advocacy efforts. While there has been no compre-hensive review of the considerable policy and legislative efforts that have been orchestrated and championed *by* formerly incarcerated individuals and their supporters, people with histories of incarceration have been intimately involved in advocating for criminal legal system reform initia-tives, such as police body cameras, alternatives to incarceration, expanding access to health care and therapeutic services for people in correctional custody, and eliminating parole revocations for technical parole violations (Felsenthal, 2018; Rafei, 2021; Sonnenberg, 2017).

This work has often been accomplished within grass-roots organiza-tions or through aligning with broader social justice and legal organizations (Goddard, Myers, and Robison, 2015; Jones and Sayegh, 2021; Ziegelheim, 2018). Formerly incarcerated individuals have established political capital, in spite of the collateral consequences associated with a criminal conviction and wide-ranging attempts to relegate them to the margins (Alexander, 2010; Chesney-Lind and Mauer, 2003; Western, 2018). The voices of indi-viduals who have experienced incarceration have made key contributions to prominent legislative and policy efforts in this area (e.g., the First Step Act, Fair Chance employment laws, the restoration of voting rights, and reductions in the use of solitary confinement). These efforts necessitate an expansion of the framework for what is classified as success for people with criminal legal system involvement to include civic engagement of this type.

Education

Educational opportunities upon reentry (and in prison) can offer poten-tial catalysts for personal transformation and desistance. Education in prison can provide needed credentials, as well as space to achieve personal growth, develop new interests, and increase mutual support, prosocial modeling, and positive socialization (Casey et al., 2013; Waller, 2000). The Bard Prison Ini-tiative, for example, has helped provide college degrees to over 500 incarcer-ated persons in six New York correctional facilities (Fullilove et al., 2020).

Other models, such as the Inside-Out Prison Exchange Program, offer semester-long academic courses that bring college students together with incarcerated individuals to study as peers in a seminar behind prison walls (Pompa, 2013). Although some students may initially enroll in an Inside-Out course for extrinsic reasons, many who graduate from the Inside-Out class are intrinsically motivated and realize that they are enthusiastic about learning (Wright, 2020). Individuals who have participated in Inside-Out have gone on to create programs, pursue post-secondary education in and out of prison, and engage in scholarship to improve the system and enhance the lives of people involved in the criminal legal system by informing policy makers (Wright, 2020). Recent work by Pelletier and Evans (2019) found that participants in higher education programs within prisons identified numerous positive outcomes beyond avoidance of recidivism, including the development of personal skills, prosocial networks, and bonds with social institutions. In this vein, education can provide a space for people in prison to develop new identities and roles (Søgaard et al., 2016), as they take on the role of "learner." As Szifris, Fox, and Bradbury (2018, p. 57) state:

> Education can, under the right circumstances, and with careful facilitation by appropriate staff, cultivate an environment for the development of positive pro-social identities. When achieved, this promotes an identity that is focused on growth and development as opposed to preoccupied with survival.

Other "hooks" for change can include membership in therapeutic or religious communities or prosocial romantic or family relationships, which allow a reentering individual to embrace a new identity (Giordano, Cernkovich, and Rudolph, 2002).

COMMUNITY AND MACRO-LEVEL
IMPACTS ON REENTRY SUCCESS

Much work to support post-release success has been focused on individual-level processes and phenomena, for example by providing vocational training for people in prison. Yet structural contexts, such as the demand for labor, necessarily shape the opportunities for such people or programs to be successful (Hagan, 1997). Similarly, returning from prison with an advanced degree and work skills is likely to provide far more opportunities in a full-employment economy than in the midst of a deep recession or a pandemic. As Farrall (2021) has recently argued, most research on criminal careers and desistance has neglected such macro-level social, economic, and political structures, often as a result of studying single cohorts within limited geographic areas.

A large literature on "neighborhood effects" stresses that residing in a community characterized by poverty, inequality, and socioeconomic disadvantage can increase the risk of several negative outcomes, including reinvolvement with the criminal legal system. Conversely, living in a neighborhood with ample resources, services, and amenities may mitigate negative outcomes. The immediate environment may help or hinder reintegration after release from prison or successful completion of community supervision (Kubrin and Weitzer, 2003; Simes, 2019; Visher and Travis, 2003).

Neighborhood disadvantage and affluence explained significant variation in arrest for a new crime in a study of individuals in Portland and surrounding areas (Kubrin, Squires, and Stewart, 2007). Other research has expanded on this path-breaking study in a number of ways. Using longitudinal data from the Returning Home project in three states (see Visher and La Vigne, 2021), several studies have identified a variety of neighborhood-level factors that affect reentry outcomes. In one study community cohesion, measured using individual perceptions of networks and ties in community by those returning to the community after incarceration, was protective against returning to prison. However, the impact of community cohesion was dependent on neighborhood-level reentry resources (Liu, 2020). This suggests that communities with low cohesion also suffer from resource depletion and that neighborhood-level deprivation helps to explain why people released from prison fail when they return to impoverished, resource-depleted communities. Another study using the Returning Home data (Liu, 2020) found that parole officers provided more support and spent more time communicating with individuals on parole in more cohesive communities, whereas people returning to disorganized communities received a significantly lower level of support from parole officers and experienced higher rates of return to prison and resumption of drug use. Thus, community and neighborhood factors, specifically community cohesion and material resources, appear to play an outsized role in the success of individuals following release from incarceration.

In addition to surmounting their individual barriers, people leaving prison in recent years have had to contend with widening inequality, declining real wages, lack of access to quality education, rising student debt, a deepening housing crisis, and the enduring effects of structural racism (Bushway and Uggen, 2021). Crime rates fluctuate dramatically over time and across space, which suggests that community context as well as individual factors play a large role in driving criminal behavior and opportunities. While much of the work on reentry generally focuses on changing individual attitudes and behaviors, it is limited by ignoring the constraints imposed by social structure and policies.

A lack of reentry success is not only a criminal justice problem, it is also an employment problem, housing problem, and mental health problem (Wright, Morse, and Sutton, 2021). This has implications for the agencies charged with crime control, but responsibility for reentry success cannot rest solely upon their shoulders. Such responsibility also extends to institutions charged with higher education, health care, workforce development, housing, public assistance, and the full complement of government and nongovernment organizations charged with public health and well-being. Each organization must be evaluated, in part, based on how well it fulfills its primary mission for persons reentering society after release from incarceration. The research literature on the effects of structural interventions suggests that expanding opportunities and paring back restrictions can make a tangible difference in well-being and socioeconomic attainment. Sampson and Laub (1996), for example, found that the benefits of training provided as part of the GI Bill were significantly larger for veterans stigmatized with an official delinquent past. Moreover, replicating programs that have been successful outside the U.S. context may also help us understand the role of institutional and social context in supporting or undermining the individual drivers of desistance and reintegration (for more on international reentry programs and social contexts see Kazemian, 2021).

Structural Inequality

A new wave of critical reentry research focuses on the systems and practices that contribute to reentry difficulties (Henson, 2020; Middlemass and Smiley, 2019). As a consequence of oppression, marginalization, or isolation associated with characteristics such as poverty, race, ethnicity, gender, and LGBTQ+ status, certain subpopulations enter prison with greater disadvantage, experience disproportionate harm from incarceration, and encounter more obstacles upon release from prison. This section offers several examples of barriers to reentry that are disproportionately experienced by particular segments of the population. These identities are intersectional, and the combined effects of any given individual's race, ethnicity, gender, class, sexual orientation, and other characteristics can create unique advantages, disadvantages, challenges, and needs. That said, it is important for scholars, practitioners, and policymakers to be cognizant of how patterns of discrimination and disadvantage are perpetuated and sustained against certain groups, and to be responsive to challenges that disproportionately affect certain reentering subpopulations and shape their needs during reentry.

Given the limitations of existing research, the committee acknowledges that this discussion is far from exhaustive. Our objective here is to draw attention to the shortcomings of "one size fits all" approaches to the measurement of success in research, policy, and reentry programing, and to highlight why it is important to recognize and address reentering individuals' experiences, concerns, and needs in a culturally responsive manner to assess their success. In addition to being more accurate and informative, improved measurement of structural barriers to success has the potential to produce more effective reentry policies and programs including, potentially, programs targeting structural barriers themselves.

Reentry Challenges Facing People of Color

As discussed in Box 3-5, the development and expansion of the U.S. criminal legal system(s) are inexorably intertwined with the long history of slavery and subsequent civil rights suppression in America (Alexander, 2010; Wilkerson, 2020). Furthermore, racial, ethnic, and sexual minorities have historically experienced oppression and discrimination not only in the criminal

---

BOX 3-5
Slavery and the Origins of the Criminal Legal System

The effects of Black people enslavement transmitted through generations has been labeled by many scholars as the Residual Effects of Slavery (Akbar, 1996; Wilkins et al., 2013) or Post-Traumatic Slave Syndrome (Crawford, Nobles, and DeGruy, 2003). Throughout the 17th and 18th centuries, millions of people were forcibly removed from the African continent and forced into slavery in the American colonies. Enslaved people endured horrific conditions of physical, sexual, emotional, verbal, and psychological abuse (Baker, 2007). The enslavement of Africans stemmed from and reinforced White supremacy, a racist ideology pronouncing Whites as superior and Black people as inferior (Hooks, 1995). As a result of the racialized system of American slavery, Black people were relegated to subhuman status (Mills, 1997; Smith, 2011), and Slave Codes were established allowing slave owners complete power to govern their slaves as chattel or property. Given their status as property, enslaved Black people were subjected to different laws and more severe forms and durations of punishments than Whites, and had minimal legal rights (Kennedy, 1997). In Southern cities including New Orleans, Savannah, and Charleston, slave patrols emerged to monitor enslaved persons and prevent them from organizing revolts or escaping. These professionalized slave patrols were the precursor to police forces in these cities, as well as in small towns and rural areas (Vitale, 2017). In the North, law enforcement authorities as well as U.S. marshalls were expected and required to assist in the capture and return of "fugitive slaves" (Kennedy, 1997). Black people shouldered the burden of proof to prove they were free; this "linkage of blackness with suspiciousness" endures today in the form of racial profiling (Kennedy, 1997, p. 138).

In 1865, the 13th Amendment officially abolished the institution of slavery; however, states relied on legal systems to continue exploiting and controlling freed Black people (Stevenson, 2017). Early slave patrols were succeeded by the racial terror of the Ku Klux Klan (KKK) and systematic racialized patterns of law enforcement (Hadden, 2021). Black Codes, for instance, were established, which created new offenses for certain behaviors, such as loitering and vagrancy (Alexander, 2010). Anyone in violation would be punished by fines, imprisonment, or forced labor for up to one year. These laws were discriminatory in nature because they were applied selectively to Black people to restrict their freedom and force them to work

legal system, but throughout numerous interconnected and intersecting policy domains, including education, housing, health care, employment, and political rights. Structural racism and discrimination throughout numerous domains are fundamental sources of disparities in reentry outcomes. Structural racism refers to the normalization and legitimization of historical, cultural, institutional, and interpersonal dynamics that routinely advantage White people and simultaneously produce "cumulative and chronic adverse outcomes for people of color" (Lawrence and Keleher, 2004, p. 1). It is a system of hierarchy and inequity, primarily characterized by the preferential treatment, privilege, and power for White people at the expense of people of color (see Box 3-5).

based on cheap labor or debt. Black Codes opened the door to convict leasing, in which incarcerated individuals were contracted out to plantation owners and private companies but often paid wages too low to pay off their debts (Blackmon, 2008). Convict leasing adopted practices similar to those in slavery, as Black people were routinely starved and beaten by corporations, government officials, farmers, and businessmen who remained determined that Black people would be controlled and be subject to racially segregated conditions (Blackmon, 2008). Current-day prison labor practices, in which incarcerated people are paid far lower than minimum wage, while incurring fines and charges for expenses associated with their incarceration, bear strong resemblances to convict leasing practices of the past (Alexander, 2010).

During Reconstruction (1865–1876), Black people experienced a period of economic and political advancement. After 250 years, slavery had been abolished, Black individuals were recognized as full citizens, provided due process and "equal protection under the law," and given the right to vote and hold office (Alexander, 2010). Despite these gains, there was a strong backlash against the advancement of Black people. Support for Reconstruction policies tapered after they were undercut by the KKK, a white supremacist organization (Williams, 2015). Not only did the KKK fight against the Reconstruction government and its leaders, they also resorted to bombings, mob violence, and lynching (Durr, 2015). After "redemption" the federal government stopped enforcing federal civil rights legislation and federal troops withdrew from the South, abandoning even those Black people who had fought for racial equality (Alexander, 2010). This, in turn, led to the reestablishment of vagrancy laws and opened up a market for convict leasing. At the time, individuals who were convicted had few legal rights and no effective form of redress.

Between 1877 and the mid-1960s, Jim Crow—a system of legalized racism imposed and enforced by local, state, and national legislative bodies, law enforcement agencies, and courts—was established out of a state of economic crisis, racial fear, and political opportunism and represented the legitimization of anti-black racism (Woodward, 1955). Throughout this era, the police and the criminal legal system played an important part in enforcing Jim Crow laws and segregation (Jett, 2021). As a racial caste system that entailed a series of anti-Black laws, Jim Crow touched every aspect of daily life and Black people were relegated to second-class citizenship. Consequently, racial bias and oppression extended the trauma of enslavement, manifesting itself in social, psychological, and physical problems and outcomes (Akbar 1996; DeGruy, 2017).

Geographic environment has significant differential impacts on the success of Black and Latino/a individuals, who are more likely to return to neighborhoods that lack cohesion and material resources (Kubrin and Stewart, 2006; Visher and Travis, 2003). The Boston Reentry Study followed 122 returning citizens as they left prison and returned to the community (Western and Simes, 2019; Western, 2018). The findings indicate that Black and Hispanic respondents moved to significantly worse neighborhoods than White respondents and were more likely to live in unstable or temporary housing and in areas of concentrated disadvantage. Respondents who returned to their pre-prison neighborhood (25%) were exposed to more concentrated disadvantage than those who moved away. Older respondents were more vulnerable to returning to distressed neighborhoods. Importantly, in this study having a history of employment prior to their most recent arrest served as a buffer from the effects of distressed neighborhoods.

While individuals of all racial and ethnic backgrounds experience challenges after release from prison, reentry can be particularly challenging for Black individuals who face collateral consequences that limit their ability to successfully integrate back into the free world. As noted, typical challenges associated with reentry include disenfranchisement, restrictions pertaining to employment, housing, student loans, child custody, and public service ineligibility (Chesney-Lind and Mauer, 2003; Garretson, 2016). However, formerly incarcerated Black men also have limited social capital, as they are often "isolated from employers, health care services, and other institutions that can facilitate a law-abiding reentry into society" (Reisig et al., 2007, p. 413). Studies show that a criminal record serves as a major barrier to employment, as employers are less likely to hire someone with a felony record, especially Black males (Pager, 2003). Race plays a powerful role in directing employment decisions in ways that contribute to persistent racial inequality (Pager, 2003). This comes at a high cost, as Black men returning to communities with high levels of racial inequality face a higher likelihood of reengaging in crime (Reisig et al., 2007).[19]

Structural inequality and economic disparity have created conditions in urban areas that foster criminal involvement (Kubrin and Stewart, 2006). Challenges to securing legitimate employment can drive individuals who have been released from prison to turn to illicit means to support themselves and their families (Visher and Travis, 2003). Stigma, lack of employment, and lack of family support can serve as barriers to successful integration back into society for Black formerly incarcerated individuals (Williams, Wilson, and Bergeson, 2019). In contrast, connections to legitimate jobs, ownership, being

---

[19]After release from prison, White people are likely to live in significantly poorer neighborhoods than they did before prison, whereas Black and Latinx people are more likely to reside in significantly disadvantaged neighborhoods both before and after prison (Massoglia, Firebaugh, and Warner, 2012).

entrepreneurial, using one's past experience to assist others, and the achievement of heteronormative masculine expectations are factors that many incarcerated men define as being successful post-release (Andersen et al., 2020).

Latino men, as the fastest growing U.S. ethnic group of incarcerated individuals (Carson and Sabol, 2012; Harrison and Beck, 2002), face unique cultural and social needs during the reentry process. For example, they are often characterized by distinct circumstances associated with low educational attainment, limited language ability, and limited access to health care (Harlow, 2003; Schafhalter-Zoppoth, Walther, and Flattery, 2013). These characteristics place formerly incarcerated Latinos at a disadvantage for successful reentry, as many have difficulty securing housing and employment (Schafhalter-Zoppoth, Walther, and Flattery, 2013). Moreover, formerly incarcerated Latinos often return to disadvantaged communities, and remain vulnerable to poor outcomes post-incarceration, as they have complex psychosocial, health, and economic needs (Golembeski and Fullilove, 2005; Lee et al., 2016). However, evidence suggests that family mechanisms of social control and social support can influence the reentry process among Latino men (Lee et al., 2016), and ethnic pride can serve as a source of strength for young men of color transitioning from jail to the community (Upadhyayula et al., 2017).

While the issue of Latino criminalization has often been linked to the issue of immigration, research shows that immigrants reoffend at a much lower rate than native-born residents (Ramos and Wenger, 2019). Evidence suggests that concentrated immigration in a community can serve as a protective factor against reoffending among justice-involved youth (Wolff et al., 2015), including Latina girls (Wright and Rodriguez, 2014). Rather than a "culture of poverty" in which individuals residing in economically distressed neighborhoods adapt in ways that perpetuate their conditions (Lewis, 1965), immigration may contribute to a "culture of resilience" (Wright and Rodriguez, 2014).

Although Mexico is currently the top country of origin among U.S. immigrants today, it is important not to conflate ethnicity and immigration status. In general, recidivism rates are lower for immigrants compared to native-born U.S. residents (Ramos and Wenger, 2019; Light, He, and Robey, 2020), although reoffending rates for individuals who are convicted of illegal entry and reentry in the United States remain high. When incarcerated, deportable non-U.S. citizens housed in federal prisons are provided with fewer educational opportunities and minimal access to substance treatment, and they are ineligible for residential reentry centers (Kimpel, 2018). Moreover, a large number of deportees no longer have strong familial ties in their home countries. Reintegration is made more challenging for them, as they are told to establish roots in a country where they no longer have family (Kimpel, 2018).

Native Americans experience rates of jail and prison incarceration about double that for white Americans, as well as elevated rates of return to prison, mostly for technical violations (Daniel, 2020; Hansen, 2018). While 78 percent of Native Americans do not reside on reservations, many formerly incarcerated Native Americans return to rural communities, where poverty, drug and alcohol misuse, as well as geographic isolation pose challenges to reentry (Wodahl and Freng, 2017). Despite high rates of poverty, a recent study of fines, fees, and restitution in Minnesota found that Native Americans are subject to higher monetary sanctions than any other racial or ethnic group (Stewart et al., 2021). Kara Nelson from True North Recovery, a participant in the committee's information-gathering sessions, mentioned that the state of Alaska provides a vast array of services for reentry. But fellow participant Venus Woods from the Cook Inlet Tribal Council pointed out that Alaska natives need culturally competent programming. Conventional instruments for assessing risk and resiliency may not include culturally specific factors relevant to Native American populations (Hansen, 2018). Culturally responsive reentry programs could involve positive elements such as tribal "restorative or reparative" principles, approaches, values, and ceremonies (Melton et al., 2010). The involvement of tribal governments and justice systems, often alongside state and federal court systems, adds another layer of complexity to the coordination of reentry services for Native Americans (Melton et al., 2010).

Gender-specific Reentry Challenges

Although men greatly outnumber women among incarcerated populations, the growth in incarceration of women outpaced that of men from 1978 to 2015 (Sawyer, 2018). From 1990 to 2000, the proportion of women on probation and parole also increased, and in 2004, 85 percent of women under correctional supervision were under community supervision (Bloom, Owen, and Covington, 2004). Nearly two-thirds of women in prison or jail are Black or Hispanic, while nearly two-thirds of women on probation are White (Bloom, Owen, and Covington, 2004).

Criminal legal system (CLS)-involved women are more likely to have histories of childhood and adult abuse and have more serious health problems, higher rates of mental health problems, and substance dependencies than criminal legal system-involved men (Bronson et al., 2017; Harlow, 1999; National Institute on Drug Abuse, 2020; Wolff, Shi, and Siegel, 2009). Many women who suffer from abuse, either as children or as adults, develop mental illnesses (e.g., depression, anxiety, post traumatic stress disorder [PTSD]) (Lynch et al., 2012a; Lynch et al., 2012b). These mental illnesses, if not treated by a professional, may cause women to "self-medicate" through drugs as a coping mechanism to ease the physical, sexual, and psychological pain of abuse (Chesney-Lind, 1997; Daly, 1998; DeHart, 2004). Women are also more susceptible to sexual misconduct and abuse while incarcerated (Bloom, Owen, and Covington, 2004).

Although many incarcerated men also suffer from substance problems, women who enter and exit prison are more likely to have substance abuse problems (Maruschak, Bronson, and Alper, 2021a). According to one study, not all women had access to prison-based drug treatment programs, and some who did have access found them to be limited in duration and also found that community-based programs after release were scarce (Harm and Phillips, 2001). Certain conditions are associated with women's drug relapse after release from incarceration, including parole to homes where family members use drugs, reconnecting with drug-using friends, economic strain, crisis events, and negative emotions (Harm and Phillips, 2001). Convictions for drug offenses can have long-term consequences post-release. As noted above, welfare reform–era restrictions on public assistance for people convicted of felony drug crimes had a large effect on African-American and Latina mothers, who are disproportionately poor and need public assistance.

Benda (2005, p. 337) found that "childhood and recent sexual and physical abuse, adverse feelings, living with a criminal partner, and drug use are particularly powerful predictors of women's recidivism." For men, job satisfaction and education had particularly strong effects on reducing the risk of recidivism. For women, these factors also reduced recidivism, but were less important than close relationships with family, romantic partners, and friends, along with number of children. Adult social bonds have been found to inhibit criminal offending for both male and female probationers, but the effects are stronger for women (De Li and MacKenzie, 2003). Programming that can help women identify and strengthen prosocial networks during incarceration and during the transition from incarceration to the community can facilitate women's efforts to successfully reintegrate (Bui and Morash, 2010; McKay et al., 2016).

In addition, compared to men, women place a greater value and rely more heavily on social support following release from prison (Barrick, Lattimore, and Visher, 2014; Clone and DeHart, 2014; Cobbina, Huebner, and Berg, 2012). Once women are released to the community from prison, they are more likely than formerly incarcerated men to reconnect with family and seek out family ties (Cobbina et al., 2012). Positive social support, especially emotional and tangible support, has been shown to be critical to women's well-being following release from prison (Martinez and Christian, 2009). Most women who return home from prison to economically distressed neighborhoods, however, have small homogeneous networks that result in their marginalization, making successful reintegration more challenging. Since many of these women reside in unsafe, inaccessible, and car-dependent areas, they must often rely heavily on social support to get around (Bohmert, 2016).

In addition to family support, reunification with their children is often a primary goal for women following release from prison (Giordano, Cernkovich, and Rudolph, 2002; Richie, 2001); the possibility of reconnecting often remains a source of hope and inspiration (Bachman et al., 2016). 52 percent of individuals incarcerated in state prisons (51.2% of men and 61.7% of women), and 63 percent of those in federal facilities

(62.9% of men and 55.9% of women) are parents of minor children (Glaze and Maruschak, 2016). More imprisoned mothers than fathers were the primary caregivers for their children before their incarceration. As a result, their family networks are more severely disrupted, and the need to reestablish relations with children and other family members can be especially complex for women upon reentry. The termination of incarcerated mothers' parental rights can make it difficult or impossible to resume custody of their children (Michalsen, 2011). Moreover, the relationship between family demands and caretaking responsibilities is complicated. Mothers involved with the criminal legal system face particular maternal hardships and additional stigma and discrimination (Mitchell and Davis, 2019; Gurusami, 2019). While childbearing can serve as an impetus for maturation out of crime, children can serve as a source of parental stress, especially when coupled with other life responsibilities. Caring for children while maintaining steady employment may be challenging without reliable and affordable health care (Blitz, 2006). Gender caretaking roles create disproportionate economic constraints for women, which translate into higher rates of women engaging in criminal activity as a means for survival (Belknap, 2015; Wattanaporn and Holtfreter, 2014). When some women feel overwhelmed and unprepared with the obligations of motherhood it can impact their ability to successfully integrate back into the free world and desist from crime.

At the same time, the desire to regain custody can provide motivation to mothers to avoid recidivism. Incarceration of a custodial parent creates serious psychological, emotional, and economic problems for children as well. It also increases responsibilities and sometimes hardships for family members—who are usually women—who must step in as caregivers (Western et al., 2015). Contacts between formerly incarcerated parents and their children are weakly related to monthly income, but strongly associated with stable private housing, as opposed to transitional housing or homeless shelter beds (Western and Smith, 2018).

Due to the importance of relationships and community ties, formerly incarcerated women may be especially drawn toward caregiving both in their personal lives and as vocational options (Chen and Adams, 2019). Unfortunately, the disclosure of criminal records in background checks can eliminate otherwise-qualified candidates from applicant pools for positions in health care, child care, and elder care well after they have served their time in prison and desisted from criminal activity.

Intersecting Effects of Race and Gender on Reentry

Following their release from prison, most women, especially women of color, return to neighborhoods that are characterized by high levels of poverty, unemployment, inequality, segregation, and crime (Massey and

Denton, 1993; Wilson, 1996). Black people tend to be situated in communities with limited political and economic resources (Cobbina et al., 2014; Owen and Bloom, 1995) and reentering Black women report feeling "marginalized within the context of a disenfranchised community," such that their "needs as women are not a priority" (Richie, 2001, p. 383).

In an effort to avoid criminal activity, Black women on probation and parole often isolate themselves by avoiding everyone, including family members (Cobbina et al., 2014). This is problematic for several reasons. First, women's networks are smaller than those of men (Campbell and Rosenfeld, 1985), comprising more relatives (Marsden, 1987) and containing fewer ties to non-kin (Marsden, 1987; Moore, 1990), which suggests that women have less ability to use networks to secure employment. Second, compared to White people, Black people have smaller networks that contain a lower proportion of relatives (Marsden, 1987; McPherson, Smith-Lovin, and Brashears, 2006), and they have less frequent contact with others in their networks (Pugliesi and Shook, 1998). Thus, women involved with the criminal legal system who avoid everyone and stay at home to avoid criminal involvement weaken networks that are far from adequate.

Third, when Black women avoid their relatives who have a criminal record, they relinquish a central source of support that has been important to African American families, whose members typically rely on each other. Fourth, structural conditions, including joblessness, persistent poverty, and family disruption, can lead to African Americans traveling in small, isolated social networks that prevent the development of strong social supports (Reisig, Holtfreter, and Morash, 2002). Consequently, their strategies for avoiding offending may intensify this pattern. Overall, women who live in poor neighborhoods, who are disproportionately Black women, generally face unique challenges as they attempt to navigate their communities.

Reentry Challenges for Individuals Experiencing Trauma

High rates of lifetime trauma are common among many incarcerated men and women. There is a high prevalence of victimization and previous trauma among people involved in the criminal legal system, especially among women who bring past trauma into prison settings (Harlow, 1999; Yoon, Slade, and Fazel, 2017). According to the *Diagnostic and Statistical Manual of Mental Disorders* (American Psychiatric Association, 2013), trauma is a stressor in an individual's life that includes exposure to death, the threat of death, actual or threatened serious injury, or sexual violence. Individuals may experience these stresses through direct or indirect exposure. The Substance Abuse and Mental Health Services Administration (SAMHSA) defines trauma more broadly as "an event, series of events, or set of circumstances that is experienced by an individual as physically or emotionally harmful or life threatening and that has lasting adverse effects on the individual's functioning and mental, physical, social, emotional, or spiritual well-being" (SAMHSA, 2014). Notably, incarcerated women have histories of victimization and trauma at higher rates than incarcerated men (Swavola, Riley, and Subramanian, 2016). And many of these women have dealt with trauma exposure, interpersonal trauma, victimization, PTSD, and violence before incarceration (Lynch, Fritch, and Heath, 2012; Harner et al., 2015). Such histories are often linked to pathways that lead to women's imprisonment.

Many individuals involved in the criminal legal system have experienced high levels of violent victimization and undergone significant trauma before, during, and after their time behind bars (Atkinson and Warnken, 2016). Scholars have long underscored the victim-offender overlap, recognizing that "neither victimization nor offending can be understood without full consideration of the other" (Lauritsen and Laub, 2007, p. 56). Nevertheless, most people who have survived victimization do not receive the services they need to heal (Hastings and Kall, 2020). Many victims and survivors face barriers to services, including victim service providers who

---

BOX 3-6
Perspectives on Reentry: Service Providers for Victims

In information-gathering efforts, members of the committee met with service providers for crime victims and survivors, including staff with experience working for state-level Offices of Victims Services, the National Network for Victim Recovery, the National Organization for Victim Assistance, the National Center for Victims of Crime, and the federal Office for Victims of Crime. The service providers consistently drew attention to the overlap between incarcerated individuals and victims of crime. One service provider described facilitating dialogue between incarcerated individuals and crime victims, only to realize that nearly every incarcerated individual in dialogue had been victimized before their incarceration.

A number of service providers noted that existing methods for crime victims to engage in the criminal legal system are often not satisfying, and that even codified crime victims' rights are often not implemented. Facilitated dialogues and restorative justice practices were highlighted by several service providers, who emphasized their success in achieving accountability and healing. Multiple providers noted that the adversarial structure of the criminal legal system can undermine both of these aims. One service provider noted that they regularly hear that the opportunity to offer a victim impact statement is not enough. In fact, their office realized that victims were independently seeking out visitation with incarcerated individuals who had harmed them. The office brought those individuals in for professionally facilitated dialogue.

Service providers pointed to research suggesting that crime victims are most satisfied with the criminal legal system when they have meaningful opportunities to participate, regardless of the outcome. Factors that shape a survivor's satisfaction with the criminal legal system include the way they are treated throughout the process by the system, the amount of control they are given, as well as the

do not view them as crime victims (Hastings and Kall, 2020) and see them solely as perpetrators of harm rather than victims of harm, with many unaware that trauma is often a causal factor contributing to criminal activity.

This false dichotomy between criminal offending and victimization has also been formalized through policy and funding structures. For example, in a listening session with the committee, Michelle Garcia of the Washington, D.C., Office of Victims Services and Justice Grants reported that her office had historically been two separate offices referred to in shorthand as "victims" or "perpetrators." Before the offices were combined, victim service providers did not work with individuals with criminal legal system involvement—Garcia noted that they were not trained or equipped to do so. Similarly, reentry providers did not screen for victim or trauma histories. At the federal level, Victims of Crime Act grantees were for many years prohibited from using grant funds to support rehabilitation and counseling services for criminal legal system-involved individuals (this prohibition was removed in 2016) (Federal Register, 2016). The committee heard additional perspectives from service providers for victims of crime in its information gathering (see Box 3-6).

extent to which they are able to participate within the system (Bell et al., 2011; Campbell, 2005; Orth, 2002). Research has also found that interaction with the system can cause secondary victimization or secondary trauma, which has been associated with mental and physical distress and PTSD (Campbell and Raja, 2005; Herman, 2003). When people who have been harmed feel they have been unfairly treated (e.g., faced with disbelief, forced to experience unnecessary delays, left uninformed, prohibited from exercising their rights), they report more traumatic symptoms and are likely to report feeling as if they have been revictimized by the system (Herman, 2003; Orth, 2002).

Service providers emphasized that crime victims hold a broad range of perspectives on what successful reentry requires and that these perspectives often change over time. Needs might range from establishing a safety plan to pursuing restorative justice dialogues. Still other crime victims and survivors may prefer not to be informed of release dates or to have any further contact with correctional or probation officials. One service provider noted that individuals released from prison may also have fears around their own safety, as victims of crime themselves. Another suggested that public safety concerns in reentry cannot take a one-size-fits- all approach—the requirements for allowing victims to feel safe will vary based on the crime and the individuals involved. Multiple service providers identified a need to educate crime victims both about the services and rights available to them and about the complex roots of crime and recidivism. Because the needs of crime victims vary on a case-by-case basis, one service provider stressed that the key is providing people who have been harmed with timely information so that they can make decisions for themselves based on their own needs and priorities.

SOURCE: Discussion with committee representatives Michelle Garcia, Sarah Ohlsen, Bridgette Stumpf, Alejandro Palacio, and Heather Warnken, February 11, 15, and 18, 2022.

Because of the stigma of having been incarcerated, many justice-involved trauma survivors also internalize deep societal stigma of being an "offender" and believe that society cannot view them as victims since they have experienced imprisonment (Hastings and Kall, 2020). The false binary of populations viewed as either victims or criminal legal system-involved individuals, coupled with the stigma of having a criminal history, serves as a formidable barrier to healing. Not only can it cause trauma survivors who have previously been incarcerated to internalize beliefs of shame and unworthiness, but it can also keep survivors from seeking the help they need (Hastings and Kall, 2020). This presents a significant barrier to serving crime victims, given that many of the nearly 600,000 people returning home from prison and the 10 to 12 million who cycle in and out of local jails each year were once, if not many times, themselves victims of violence (Atkinson and Warnken, 2016). Consequently, many people with criminal records have unaddressed trauma. When trauma goes unaddressed, people who have survived victimization may be more likely to resort to substance abuse or other self-destructive behavior as a coping mechanism, which can lead to continued involvement in the legal system and fuel the cycle of violence and harm (Federal Interagency Reentry Council, 2016).

Individuals entering the carceral system typically bring higher-than-average levels of trauma and violent victimization. And prison itself is often a site where violence and trauma are experienced and exacerbated (Briere, Agee, and Dietrich, 2016; Cima, Smeets, and Jelicic, 2008; Courtney and Maschi, 2012; Meade, Wasileski, and Hunter, 2021). Physical and sexual violence is a real concern among individuals who are incarcerated, and disproportionately affects people with disabilities, LGBTQ+ people, and people who have experienced sexual victimization prior to imprisonment (Beck et al., 2013; Caravaca Sánchez and Wolff, 2016; Meyer et al., 2017). Criminal victimization in prison presents a significant threat to well-being (Johnson Listwan et al., 2010). The threat of violence coupled with the stress of prison (including the lack of privacy, crowds, fights, new rules to abide by, etc.), make it challenging to respond appropriately to the environment of a correctional facility (Pringer and Wagner, 2020). Moreover, the stress of prison is particularly acute for individuals who have experienced physical, sexual, and emotional abuse prior to their incarceration (Martin et al., 2015). Because many individuals in prison have experienced preexisting trauma, they face an increased likelihood of experiencing more triggers—the event, person, or thing that reminds individuals of their trauma—while having less privacy to deal with their emotional and behavioral reactions (Pringer and Wagner, 2020). And when people survive violence while imprisoned, they have little access to victim services (Hastings and Kall, 2020).

Trauma not only serves as a pathway to prison but shapes incarcerated people's lived experiences within carceral spaces and reentry (Williams,

Spencer, and Wilson, 2021). As noted previously, most survivors who have been previously incarcerated do not receive the services required to heal and experience unaddressed trauma stemming from victimization experienced at some point in their lives (Hastings and Kall, 2020). The failure to recognize individuals involved in the criminal legal system as victims discourages participation in many victim-oriented services. In addition, pressing material needs, including the needs to secure food, housing, employment, transportation, and medical care, create barriers to healing from trauma. Moreover, stigmatization remains a significant barrier to seeking mental health treatment, especially among African Americans and among men in general (Conner et al., 2010; Gary, 2005). Navigating the reentry experience with unaddressed trauma stemming from violence can result in serious negative outcomes for persons released from prison, including criminal involvement and technical violations that send them back to prison (Hastings and Kall, 2020) (see Box 3-7).

Numerous recent studies emphasize that individuals suffer from profound anxiety and feelings of isolation after release from prison (Hyde et al., 2021; Western et al., 2015). Nevertheless, correctional facilities can serve as a venue for people in prison to address the deeper emotional responses tied to trauma through trauma-informed care (Levenson and Willis, 2018). Trauma-informed care in corrections may contribute to successful reentry and reduced recidivism. Some incarcerated people obtain access to vocational, therapeutic, educational, and spiritual programming, as well as physical and mental health care, while in prison. Additionally, prison can serve as a venue where opportunities for self-improvement become available, and some U.S. prisons are actively implementing changes to facilitate these opportunities (Hyatt et al., 2021). More generally, however, formerly incarcerated individuals who participated in the committee's information-gathering sessions expressed a desire for preparation for reentry to begin at a much earlier stage in prison.

Reentry Challenges Associated with LGBTQ+ Status

Lesbian, gay, and bisexual people are imprisoned at a rate three times that of the general public (Meyer et al., 2017). The incarceration rate for transgender people is twice the general population rate; for Black transgender women, it is 10 times higher (National Center for Transgender Equality, 2018). Moreover, sexual minority adults are twice as likely as the general population to experience homelessness (Wilson et al., 2020).

LGBTQ+ individuals experience extensive social and economic marginalization in employment (Baumle and Poston Jr., 2011; Dilmaghani and Robinson, 2022; Flage, 2019; Mallory, Flores, and Sears, 2021), health care (Brummett and Campo-Engelstein, 2021; Casey et al., 2019), and housing

---

BOX 3-7
Trauma and Barriers to Success

Formerly incarcerated individuals, policy practitioners, and scholarly experts who participated in the committee's information-gathering sessions emphasized the ways in which experiences of incarceration can result in trauma and barriers to reentry success.

Sam Lewis Executive of the Anti-Recidivism Coalition cautioned that trauma can be debilitating. "Sometimes people are so broken," Mr. Lewis noted, "even if you provide every opportunity you can, they cannot succeed."

Jai Diamond, Peer Specialist with the New York City Criminal Justice Agency: "defining moment of stay in prison was being transferred to a women's facility after six years. It's a horrible thing to be a transgender woman in a men's facility. Those six years were a very dark time in which I learned to use my voice and to advocate and to speak up even if it didn't end me up in the best position."

Kara Nelson, Director of Public Relations and Development, True North Recovery: "this stigma and shame. . . . I believed that, I believed those things when I was inside, I believed those things when I got out. I believed what the probation officer said about me. I believed what the world said about me."

Susan Burton, founder of A New Way of Life Reentry Center: "one of the things people don't think or talk about is the condition people are returned to us in. . . . People need a place to heal from the effects of the time that they've spent incarcerated. I've almost called it like a detox period. The way people detox from drugs and alcohol they have to detox from the experience of incarceration."

SOURCE: Committee on Evaluating Success Among People Released from Prison Meeting #2: Public Information Gathering Session (July 27, 28, 2021). Session 1: https://www.nationalacademies.org/event/07-27-2021/evaluating-success-among-people-released-from-prison-meeting-2-public-information-gathering-session-1. Session 2: https://www.nationalacademies.org/event/07-28-2021/evaluating-success-among-people-released-from-prison-meeting-2-public-information-gathering-session-2.

(Schwegman, 2018), many of which are compounded for LGBTQ+ people of color (Wilson, Bouton, and Mallory, 2022). Given the challenges posed in these domains by incarceration histories, it is likely that formerly incarcerated LGBTQ+ individuals face compounded challenges in these areas. Like other reentering individuals, many LGBTQ+ people have histories of mental illness and substance abuse problems. They are more likely to face employment discrimination, experience bullying and harassment in educational settings, and to have strained, disrupted, or nonexistent family connections (Movement Advancement Project, 2016).

Barriers to legal employment can lead LGBTQ+ individuals with histories of sex work and drug-related offenses to reengage in those activities (Belenko, Hiller, and Hamilton, 2013; Roe-Sepowitz et al., 2011). Transgender individuals are often housed in jail, prison, and residential reentry facilities that do not match their gender identity, and they may experience harassment and violence in these settings (Movement Advancement Project, 2016). In prison, LGBTQ+ people disproportionately experience sexual victimization by fellow incarcerated persons as well as staff (Beck et al., 2013). They are also at risk of victimization in homeless shelters and halfway houses, where many reentering individuals temporarily reside (Santos, 2021, Movement Advancement Project, 2016). LGBTQ+ people are overrepresented in sex offender registries, in part due to the criminalization of certain sexual acts; this presents additional barriers to housing and employment (Santos, 2021). The need exists for culturally responsive reentry programs and services that are inclusive of diverse gender identities and sexual orientations.

Persons with Disabilities and Reentry

Approximately 40 percent of individuals in state prison and 30 percent of people in federal prison have a disability (Maruschak, Bronson, and Alper, 2021b). That translates to an estimated 760,000 people with disabilities living behind bars, dealing with cognitive, ambulatory (mobility), vision, hearing, or independent-living disabilities (Maruschak, Bronson, and Alper, 2021b). Individuals with disabilities, especially cognitive and intellectual, are at greater risk of serving longer, harder sentences, and they are vulnerable to exploitation, violence, and suicide, especially in solitary confinement (Fazio, Pietz, and Denney, 2012; Shlanger, 2017). Those with physical and cognitive disabilities may face exclusion from programs and services as well as isolation (Cowardin, 1997; Petersilia, 1997; Shlanger, 2017). According to 2011–2012 National Inmate Survey data, disability rates are even higher among incarcerated women and White individuals, compared with men and people of other racial backgrounds (Maruschak, Bronson, and Alper, 2021b). However, an analysis of 2002–2011 Rehabilitation Services Administration data also showed particularly high rates of mental disabilities among Black people in prison (Baloch and Jennings, 2019).

While discussions of mental health in prison generally focus on psychiatric disabilities like bipolar disorder, depression, and schizophrenia, the needs of incarcerated people with intellectual and developmental disabilities have largely been overlooked. As a result, there is little support for people with neurodevelopmental disorders in prison (Young et al., 2018), and there is limited research on this topic.

With nearly 600,000 adults released in 2019 from state and federal prisons (Carson, 2020), individuals with mental disabilities generally lack access to programs that would facilitate full integration into the free world. Only 20 percent of incarcerated people with mental illness receive access to discharge planning services (Dlugacz and Droubi, 2017). When individuals with mental disabilities leave prison without sufficient medication supplies, access to mental health and support services, and housing, they may struggle post-release, resulting in technical violations or commission of new crimes. One study of a supportive housing program for individuals with behavioral health disabilities in Ohio (Fontaine, 2013) found that access to the program was associated with a reduced probability of rearrest and reincarceration (participants were 61 percent less likely to be reincarcerated within one year of release compared with those who did not participate in the program).

Lack of stable housing is particularly acute among those with mental health disorders. In 2010, a SAMHSA study found that 15.3 percent of individuals in jail custody were homeless at some point in the year before incarceration, and that 20 percent of the incarcerated population with mental illness were homeless. Of the jail population who were homeless in the year prior to incarceration, 79 percent showed symptoms of drug/alcohol abuse or dependence, and 75 percent showed symptoms of mental illness. Research on homelessness conducted by Metraux and Culhane from 2004 to 2007 has shown that a history of shelter use prior to incarceration in prisons was a strong predictor of shelter use within two years of release, with the presence of mental illness and increasing age both linked to a substantial increase in the likelihood of shelter use on release. In studies of jail populations, the rate of mental disorder was 30 percent among those in jail who were previously homeless. A 2006 study of incarceration histories of homeless populations indicated that at least 20 percent of homeless populations were incarcerated at some point, with even higher rates among homeless populations with a diagnosis of mental illness (Metraux and Culhane, 2006).

Reentry Challenges and Socioeconomic Status

A number of post-incarceration policies have unintended consequences, including exacerbating problems of poverty and homelessness. For example, reentering prisoners often owe monetary sanctions or fines, fees, surcharges, and restitution associated with their conviction (Harris, 2016; Piquero and Jennings, 2017). As noted above, Section 115 of the Welfare Reform Act (Personal Responsibility and Work Opportunity Reconciliation Act, 1996) was originally enacted to discourage the use and sale of illicit drugs. However, this policy reduced the capacity of families to economically provide for their children upon returning home from prison prior to securing employment (Morgenstern and Blanchard, 2006), increasing financial strain on women and children residing in economically distressed neighborhoods (Patterson, 2013; Visher et al., 2004). Moreover, the inability of a large segment of the U.S. population to access housing, employment, education, and public assistance may increase the national poverty rate (Hall, Wooten, and Lundgren, 2016) and in turn increase levels of crime and imprisonment.

While poverty is a risk factor for criminal behavior and incarceration for men and women (Van Voorhis et al., 2010), many individuals returning home from prison will return to families and communities facing similar circumstances that resulted in their incarceration (Belknap, Lynch, and DeHart, 2015). Due to discrimination and low levels of human capital, formerly incarcerated individuals, Black people, and women are disproportionately represented among workers in the secondary labor market characterized by low paying, insecure, dead-end jobs (Martin, 2011). Evidence suggests that the burden of poverty falls heavily on women and children, as most women involved in the criminal legal system are mothers of minor children (Owen and Bloom, 1995). In their examination of 134 women convicted of a felony offense, Holtfreter, Reisig, and Morash (2004) found that poverty status increased the odds of rearrest and supervision violation; yet the odds of recidivism were reduced by 83 percent among those who received state-sponsored support.

Programs and criminal justice interventions providing services to persons released from prison are likely to be located within poor communities (Clear, 2007; Wacquant, 2010). Reuben Miller (2014) has argued that the community-based organizations that serve individuals involved in the criminal legal system manage more poor people and people of color than the correctional system itself. This arrangement provides needed services but contributes to the concentration of social disadvantage within blighted neighborhoods, with disproportionate impacts on the poor, Black, and brown residents in these areas (Miller, 2014). From this perspective, the dominance and proliferation of reentry services in low-income communities of color represents a longstanding collusion between social welfare and criminal justice actors in managing marginalized populations and demonstrates one way that the state has been reconfigured to manage the urban poor (Beckett and Western, 2001; Miller, 2014).

Reentry Barriers Facing Rural Populations

Studies of reentry have focused heavily on the experiences and needs of individuals returning to urban neighborhoods, with less attention to those returning to rural communities, whose circumstances may require different forms of support (Wodahl, 2006; Zajac et al., 2013). People in rural areas also have more difficulty accessing programs and services such as mental and physical health care, substance abuse treatment, subsidized or transitional housing, and food support (Huebner, Kras, and Pleggenkuhle, 2019; Zajac et al., 2013). The lack of public resources may be due, in part, to the more limited tax base in rural communities (Ethridge, et al., 2014).

Compared to urban areas, rural communities are less geographically dense. People on parole are often required to traverse great distances to check in with parole officers and participate in treatment programs (Huebner, et al., 2021). Reliable transportation is also a necessity for job-seekers and employed persons, but it is often unavailable (Wodahl, 2006; Zajac et al., 2013. Jobs that pay a living wage are also less prevalent in rural areas (Wodahl, 2006). For rural women, traditional notions of "women's work" may pose additional obstacles to adequately compensated employment (Beichner and Rabe-Hemp, 2014). Compared with people returning to urban areas, individuals reentering rural areas may be less prone to illicit drug use, but more likely to have problems with alcohol or sedatives (Wodahl, 2006). Individuals returning to rural communities may also experience more stigma, due to a relative lack of privacy and anonymity (Huebner, Kras, and Pleggenkuhle, 2019; Zajac et al., 2013).

Structural Reentry Barriers and the Measurement of Success

To summarize this section of the report, the limited research literature has identified reentry and reintegration needs that are particularly acute in particular communities. In many cases, these needs reflect specific manifestations of a general need, such as transportation or housing. In other cases, however, such needs are more localized, such as the need for translation assistance in non-English-speaking communities. This section makes clear that reentry needs and barriers are distributed unevenly in the population of individuals incarcerated and released. Post-release success, whether in terms of cessation of criminal activity or a broader conception of flourishing, is shaped by differential exposure to these barriers. Yet to date, standard methods of measuring success among those released from prison have not accounted for the varied, significant, and systemic differences in barriers to reintegration.

CONCLUSION

In outlining the theoretical rationale for looking beyond recidivism and identifying the barriers to success, the foregoing discussion raises a critical question: What do we know or need to learn about reentry success beyond recidivism? This chapter has illustrated how a singular or primary focus on recidivism ignores scholarly understanding of how the cessation of criminal activity actually occurs, and more broadly ignores the best available knowledge on the reentry process and needs. Further, an overreliance on recidivism can inhibit the design and delivery of effective, appropriate programs and services for formerly incarcerated individuals. Expanding our attention to the complex, iterative, and multidimensional processes of desistance and reintegration helps us apply and test theories regarding *why* and *how* reentering individuals persist in, or desist from, criminal activity.

In orienting to lasting success across a variety of domains, such a focus can also enhance public safety, protect victims, and promote the common good. Correspondingly, an emphasis on recidivism imposes unnecessary and unhelpful constraints on the range of outcomes of interest with regard to the success of people released from prison. This chapter builds on Chapter 2 in concluding that because cessation or reduction in criminal behavior often occurs as a part of a gradual process that may involve setbacks, measures of desistance from crime can offer a more accurate, complete, and nuanced account of an individual's reduction in criminal activity than do measures of recidivism.

As this chapter has demonstrated, advancing the measurement of success for individuals released from prison is far beyond a methodological issue. Improving our methods for evaluating success also requires theoretical and conceptual work—shifting from a recidivism frame to a desistance frame in measuring criminal legal system outcomes and expanding our understanding of success to encompass the life domains central to successful reintegration and overall well-being. Successful reintegration and post-release success require progress in a number of areas beyond the cessation of criminal activity. This chapter's analysis of reintegration, reentry barriers, and well-being supports the conclusion that post-release success involves multiple life domains (e.g., health, employment, housing, civic engagement) and not simply involvement in the criminal legal system. Success entails a heightened sense of personal well-being.

Finally, this chapter explores persistent patterns of disparities in reentry supports, and unique reentry needs facing historically marginalized groups. A review of the literature demonstrates that these disparities are both significant and under-studied. The existence of community-level and policy barriers to success is documented in studies that link data on post-release success and local socioeconomic conditions; policies that restrict access to employment, housing, and public benefits; and structural inequalities that disproportionately affect persons of color. Thus, meaningful measurement of success requires attention to systemic disparities in exposure to barriers and access to opportunities that shape post-release outcomes.

A more robust measurement of success could result in policies and programs that better support the needs of those returning from incarceration and more effectively support success. They could also help policy makers, criminal legal system actors, and service providers to recognize and address structural inequalities shaping post-release outcomes. The following chapter charts possible paths toward improving measures of success, including identifying key indicators of post-release well-being, and considers how we might measure these alternative indicators of success.

REFERENCES

Agan, A., and Starr, S. (2018). Ban the box, criminal records, and racial discrimination: A field experiment. *The Quarterly Journal of Economics* 133, 1, 191–235.

Agnew, R. (1992). Foundation for a general strain theory of crime and delinquency. *Criminology* 30, 1, 47–87.

Agnew, R. (2001). Building on the foundation of general strain theory: Specifying the types of strain most likely to lead to crime and delinquency. *Journal of Research in Crime and Delinquency* 38, 4, 319–361.

Agnew, R. (2006). *Pressured into Crime: An Overview of General Strain Theory*. Oxford University Press.

Aizer, A., and Doyle Jr., J.J. (2015). Juvenile incarceration, human capital and future crime: Evidence from randomly assigned judges. *The Quarterly Journal of Economics* 130, 2, 759–803.

Akbar, N. (1996). *Breaking the Chains of Psychological Slavery*. Tallahassee, FL: Mind Productions and Associates.

Akers, R.L. (1985). *Deviant Behavior: A Social Learning Approach* (3rd Ed.). Belmont, CA: Wadsworth.

Akers, R.L. (1998). *Social Learning and Social Structure: A Social Cognitive Theory*. Boston: Northeastern University Press.

Alexander, M. (2010). *The New Jim Crow: Mass Incarceration in the Age of Colorblindness*. New York, NY: New Press.

American Psychiatric Association. (2013). *Diagnostic and Statistical Manual of Mental Disorders: DSM-5* (5th Ed.). Arlington, VA.

Andersen, S.H., Andersen, L.H. and Skov, P.E. (2015), Effect of Marriage and Spousal Criminality on Recidivism. *Journal of Marriage and Family* 77, 2, 496–509. Available: https://doi.org/10.1111/jomf.12176.

Andersen, T.S., Scott, D.A.I., Boehme, H.M., King, S., and Mikell, T. (2020). What matters to formerly incarcerated men? Looking beyond recidivism as a measure of successful reintegration. *The Prison Journal* 100, 4, 488–509. Available: https://doi.org/10.1177/0032885520939295.

Andrews, D.A., and Bonta, J. (2010). *The Psychology of Criminal Conduct*. New Providence, NJ: Anderson.

Andrews, D.A., Kiessling, J.J., Robinson, D., and Mickus, S. (1986). The risk principle of case classification: An outcome evaluation with young adult probationers. *Canadian Journal of Criminology* 28, 377–384.

Andrews, D.A., Zinger, I., Hoge, R.D., Bonta, J., Gendreau, P., and Francis, T.C. (1990). Does correctional treatment work? A clinically relevant and psychologically informed meta-analysis. *Criminology* 28, 369–404.

Aresti, A., Eatough, V., and Brooks-Gordon, B. (2010). Doing time after time: An interpretative phenomenological analysis of reformed ex-prisoners' experiences of self-change, identity and career opportunities. *Psychology, Crime and Law* 16, 3, 169–190.

Atkinson, D., and Warnken, H. (2016). *Working Together to Prevent Cycles of Harm*. U.S. Department of Justice, Office of Justice Programs. https://www.justice.gov/opa/blog/working-together-prevent-cycles-harm.

Aukerman, M.J. (2005). The somewhat suspect class: Towards a constitutional framework for evaluating occupational restrictions affecting people with criminal records. *Journal of Law in Society* 7, 18.

Bachman, R., Kerrison, E.M., Paternoster, R., Smith, L., and O'Connell, D. (2016). The complex relationship between motherhood and desistance. *Women & Criminal Justice* 26, 3, 212–231.

Baker, D. (2007). Systematic White racism and the brutalization of executed Black women in the United States. In R. Muraskin (Ed.), *It's a Crime: Women and Justice* (4th Ed.), 398–443. Upper Saddle River: Pearson.

Bales, W.D., and Mears, D.P. (2008). Inmate social ties and the transition to society: Does visitation reduce recidivism? *Journal of Research in Crime and Delinquency,* 45, 3, 287–321.

Baloch, N.A., and Jennings, W.G. (2019). A preliminary investigation of the intersection of race and disabilities among inmates in the U.S. state prison system. *International Journal of Offender Therapy and Comparative Criminology* 63, 4, 597–609.

Bandura, A. (1977). *Social Learning Theory.* Englewood Cliffs, NJ: Prentice-Hall.

Barrick, K., Lattimore, P.K., and Visher, C.A. (2014). Reentering women: The impact of social ties on long-term recidivism. *The Prison Journal* 94, 3, 279–304.

Baumle, A.K., and Poston Jr., D.L. (2011). The economic cost of homosexuality: Multilevel analyses. *Social Forces* 89, 3, 1005–1031.

Bayer, P., Hjalmarsson, R., and Pozen, D. (2009). Building criminal capital behind bars: Peer effects in juvenile corrections. *The Quarterly Journal of Economics* 124, 1, 105–147.

Bazemore, G., and Stinchcomb, J. (2004). A civic engagement model of reentry: Involving community through service and restorative justice. *Federal Probation* 68, 2, 14.

Beccaria, C. (1963 [1764]). *On Crimes and Punishments.* Translated by Henry Paolucci. New York: Macmillan Publishing Company.

Beck, A.J., Berzofsky, M., Caspar, R., and Krebs, C. (2013). *Sexual Victimization in Prisons and Jails Reported by Inmates, 2011–2012.* Washington, DC: Bureau of Justice Statistics.

Becker, H.S. (1963). *Outsiders: Studies in the Sociology of Deviance.* New York: Free Press.

Becker, G.S. (1968). Crime and punishment: An economic approach. In *The Economic Dimensions of Crime,* 13–68. Palgrave Macmillan, London.

Beckett, K., and Western B. (2001). Governing social marginality: Welfare, incarceration, and the transformation of state policy. *Punishment and Society* 3, 1, 43–59.

Beichner, D., and Rabe-Hemp, C. (2014). "I don't want to go back to that town": Incarcerated mothers and their return home to rural communities. *Critical Criminology* 22, 527–543.

Belenko, S., Hiller, M., and Hamilton, L. (2013). Treating substance use disorders in the criminal justice system. *Current Psychiatry Reports* 15, 414.

Bell, M.E., Perez, S., Goodman, L.A., Dutton, M.A. (2011). Battered women's perceptions of civil and criminal court helpfulness: The role of court outcomes and processes. *Violence Against Women* 71, 72.

Bellair, P.E., and Kowalski, B.R. (2011). Low-skill employment opportunity and African American-White difference in recidivism. *Journal of Research in Crime and Delinquency* 48, 2, 176–208.

Belknap, J. (2015). *The Invisible Women: Gender, Crime, and Justice* (4th Ed.). Belmont, CA: Thomas Higher Education.

Belknap, J., Lynch, S., and DeHart, D. (2016). Jail staff members' views on jailed women's mental health, trauma, offending, rehabilitation, and reentry. *The Prison Journal* 96, 79–101.

Bell, M.C. (2017). Police reform and the dismantling of legal estrangement. *The Yale Law Journal* 126, 7, 2054–2150.

Benda, B.B. (2005). Gender differences in life-course theory of recidivism: A survival analysis. *International Journal of Offender Therapy and Comparative Criminology* 49, 3, 325–342.

Benedict, W.R., and Huff-Corzine, L. (1997). Return to the scene of the punishment: Recidivism of adult male property offenders on felony probation, 1986–1989. *Journal of Research in Crime and Delinquency* 34, 2, 237–252.

Bentham, J. (1988 [1789]). *The Principles of Morals and Legislation.* Amherst, MA: Prometheus Books.

Berg, M.T., and Huebner, B.M. (2011) Reentry and the ties that bind: An examination of social ties, employment, and recidivism. *Justice Quarterly* 28, 2, 382–410. DOI: 10.1080/07418825.2010.498383.

Berk, R.A., and Rauma, D. (1983). Capitalizing on nonrandom assignment to treatments: A regression-discontinuity evaluation of a crime-control program. *Journal of the American Statistical Association* 78, 381, 21–27.

Bersani, B.E., and Doherty, E.E. (2018). Desistance from offending in the twenty-first century. *Annual Review of Criminology* 1, 311–334.

Best, D., and Savic, M. (2014) Substance abuse and offending: Pathways to recovery. In R. Sheehan and J. Ogloff (Eds.), *Working within the Forensic Paradigm: Cross-discipline Approaches for Policy and Practice.* Abingdon: Routledge.

Binswanger, I.A., Stern, M.F., Deyo, R.A., Heagerty, P.J., Cheadle, A., Elmore, J.G., and Koepsell, T.D. (2007). Release from prison—a high risk of death for former inmates. *New England Journal of Medicine* 356, 2, 157–165.

Blackmon, D. (2008). *Slavery by Another Name: The Re-enslavement of Black People in America from the Civil War to World War II.* New York: Doubleday.

Blitz, C.L. (2006). Predictors of stable employment among female inmates in New Jersey: Implications for successful reintegration. *Journal of Offender Rehabilitation* 43, 1, 1–22.

Blokland, A.J., and Nieuwbeerta, P. (2005). The effects of life circumstances on longitudinal trajectories of offending. *Criminology* 43, 4, 1203–1240.

Bloom, B., Owen, B., and Covington, S. (2004). Women offenders and the gendered effects of public policy. *Review of Policy Research* 21, 1, 31–48.

Bohmert, M.N. (2016). The role of transportation disadvantage for women on community supervision. *Criminal Justice and Behavior* 43, 11, 1522–1540.

Boman IV, J.H., and Mowen, T.J. (2017). Building the ties that bind, breaking the ties that don't: Family support, criminal peers, and reentry success. *Criminology and Public Policy* 16, 3, 751–772.

Braithwaite, J. (1989). *Crime, Shame and Reintegration.* Cambridge University Press.

Brayne, S. (2014). Surveillance and system avoidance: Criminal justice contact and institutional attachment. *American Sociological Review* 79, 3, 367–391.

Briere, J., Agee, E., and Dietrich, A. (2016). Cumulative trauma and current posttraumatic stress disorder status in general population and inmate samples. *Psychological Trauma: Theory, Research, Practice, and Policy* 8, 4, 439–446.

Bronson, J., Stroop, J., Zimmer, S., and Berzofsky, M. (2017). *Drug Use, Dependence, and Abuse among State Prisoners and Jail Inmates, 2007–2009.* Washington, DC: Bureau of Justice Statistics. NCJ 250546.

Brown, J.D. (1991). The professional ex-: An alternative for exiting the deviant career. *Sociological Quarterly* 32, 2, 219–230.

Brummett, A., and Campo-Engelstein, L. (2021). Conscientious objection and LGBTQ discrimination in the United States. *Journal of Public Health Policy* 42, 322–330.

Bui, H.N., and Morash, M. (2010). The impact of network relationships, prison experiences, and internal transformation on women's success after prison release. *Journal of Offender Rehabilitation* 49, 1, 1–22.

Burgess, R.L., and Akers, R.L. (1966). A differential association-reinforcement theory of criminal behavior. *Social Problems* 14, 2, 128–147.

Burton, S. (2021, July 28). Remarks made before the Committee. Committee on Evaluating Success Among People Released from Prison Meeting #2: Public Information Gathering Session. Washington, D.C.: National Academies of Sciences, Engineering, and Medicine.

Bushway, S.D., Piquero, A.R., Broidy, L.M., Cauffman, E., and Mazerolle, P. (2001). An empirical framework for studying desistance as a process. *Criminology* 39, 2, 491–516.

Bushway, S., and Uggen, C. (2021). Fostering desistance. *Contexts* 20, 4, 34–39.

Bursik Jr., R.J., and Grasmick, H.G. (1993). Economic deprivation and neighborhood crime rates, 1960–1980. *Law and Society Review* 27, 2, 263–283.

Campbell, R. (2005). What really happened? A validation study of rape survivors' help-seeking experiences with the legal and medical systems. *Violence and Victims* 55, 56.

Campbell, R. and Raja, S. (2005). The Sexual Assault and Secondary Victimization of Female Veterans: Help-Seeking Experiences with Military and Civilian Social Systems. *Psychology of Women Quarterly* 97, 98.

Campbell, K.E., and Rosenfeld, R.A. (1985). Job search and job mobility: Sex and race differences. *Research in the Sociology of Work* 3, 14, 147–174.

Caravaca Sánchez, F., and Wolff, N., 2016. Self-report rates of physical and sexual violence among Spanish inmates by mental illness and gender. *The Journal of Forensic Psychiatry & Psychology* 27, 3, 443–458.

Carson, E.A. (2020). *Prisoners in 2019*. Washington, DC: U.S. Department of Justice, Bureau of Justice Statistics.

Carson, E.A., and Sabol, W.J. (2012). *Prisoners in 2011*. NCJ 255115. Washington, DC: U.S. Department of Justice, Bureau of Justice Statistics.

Casey, S., Day, A., Vess, J., and Ward, T. (2013). *Foundations of Offender Rehabilitation*. Oxfordshire: Routledge.

Casey, L.S., Reisner, S.L., Findling, M.G., Blendon, R.J., Sayde, J.M., Miller, C. (2019). Discrimination in the United States: Experiences of lesbian, gay, bisexual, transgender, and queer Americans. *Health Services Research: Special Issue: Experiences of Discrimination in America: Race, Ethnicity, Gender, and Sexuality* 54, 52, 1454–1466.

Chadwick, N., Dewolf, A., and Serin, R. (2015). Effectively training community supervision officers: A meta-analytic review of the impact on offender outcome. *Criminal Justice and Behavior* 42, 10, 977–989.

Chamberlain, A.W. (2018). From prison to the community: Assessing the direct, reciprocal, and indirect effects of parolees on neighborhood structure and crime. *Crime and Delinquency* 64, 2, 166–200.

Chamberlain, A.W., and Wallace, D. (2016). Mass reentry, neighborhood context and recidivism: Examining how the distribution of parolees within and across neighborhoods impacts recidivism. *Justice Quarterly* 33, 5, 912–941.

Charles, P., Muentner, L., and Kjellstrand, J. (2019). Parenting and incarceration: Perspectives on father-child involvement during reentry from prison. *Social Service Review,* 93(2), 218–261. https://doi.org/10.1086/703446.

Chen, E.Y., and Adams, E.B. (2019). "I've Risen Up from the Ashes That I Created": Record clearance and gendered narratives of self-reinvention and reintegration. *Feminist Criminology* 14, 2, 143–172.

Chen, M.K., and Shapiro, J.M. (2007). Do harsher prison conditions reduce recidivism? A discontinuity-based approach. *American Law and Economics Review* 9, 1, 1–30.

Chesney-Lind, M. (1997). *The Female Offender: Girls, Women, and Crime*. Thousand Oaks, CA: Sage.

Chesney-Lind, M., and Mauer, M. (2003). *Invisible Punishment: The Collateral Consequences of Mass Imprisonment*. New York, NY: New Press.

Cima, M., Smeets, T., and Jelicic, M. (2008). Self-reported trauma, cortisol levels, and aggression in psychopathic and non-psychopathic prison inmates. *Biological Psychology* 78, 1, 75–86.

Clear, T. (2007) *Imprisoning Communities: How Mass Incarceration makes Disadvantaged Neighborhoods Worse.* Oxford: Oxford University Press.

Clone, S., and DeHart, D. (2014). Social support networks of incarcerated women: Types of support, sources of support, and implications for reentry. *Journal of Offender Rehabilitation* 53, 7, 503–521.

Cloward, R., and Ohlin, L. (1960). *Delinquency and Opportunity: A Theory of Delinquent Gangs.* New York, NY: Free Press.

Cloyes, K.G., Wong, B., Latimer, S., and Abarca, J. (2010). Time to prison return for offenders with serious mental illness released from prison: A survival analysis. *Criminal Justice and Behavior* 37, 2, 175–187.

Cobbina, J.E., Huebner, B.M., and Berg, M.T. (2012). Men, women, and post-release offending: An examination of the nature of the link between relational ties and recidivism. *Crime and Delinquency* 58, 3, 331–361.

Cobbina, J.E., Morash, M., Kashy, D. A., and Smith, S.W. (2014). Race, neighborhood danger, and coping strategies among female probationers and parolees. *Race and Justice* 4, 1, 3–28.

Cohen, A.K. (1955). *Delinquent Boys; The Culture of the Gang.* Free Press.

Comfort, M., Krieger, K.E., Landwehr, J., McKay, T., Lindquist, C.H., Feinberg, R., Kennedy, E.K. and Bir, A. (2018). Partnership after prison: Couple relationships during reentry. *Journal of Offender Rehabilitation* 57, 2, 188–205.

Conner, K.O., Copeland, V.C.,Grote, N.K., Koeske, G., Rosen, D., Reynolds III, C.F., and Brown, C. (2010). Mental health treatment seeking among older adults with depression: The impact of stigma and race. *The American Journal of Geriatric Psychiatry* 18, 6, 531–543.

Cook, P.J. (1975). The correctional carrot: Better jobs for parolees. *Policy Analysis*, 1, 1, 11–54.

Cotter, R. (2020). *Length of Incarceration and Recidivism.* Washington, DC: United States Sentencing Commission. Available: https://www.ussc.gov/research/research-reports/length-incarceration-and-recidivism.

Couloute, L. (2018). *Nowhere To Go: Homelessness Among Formerly Incarcerated People.* Prison Policy Initiative.

Council of State Governments Justice Center. (2014). *Reducing Recidivism: States Deliver Results.* New York: Council of State Governments Justice Center. Available: https://csgjusticecenter.org/publications/reducing-recidivism-states-deliver-results/.

Courtney, D., and Maschi, T. (2012). Trauma and stress among older adults in prison: Breaking the cycle of silence. *Traumatology* 1–9.

Cowardin, N. (1997). Advocating for learning disability accommodation in prisons. *Wisconsin Defender* 5, 5, 1–14.

Crawford, J., Nobles, W.W., and DeGruy, J.D. (2003). Reparations and health care for African Americans: Repairing the damage from the legacy of slavery. In R. Windbush (Ed.), *Should America pay? Slavery and the Raging Debate on Reparations,* 251–281. New York, NY: Harper Collins.

Cressey, D.R. (1965). Social psychological foundations for using criminals in the rehabilitation of criminals. *Journal of Research in Crime and Delinquency* 2, 2, 49–59.

Cullen, F.T. (1994). Social support as an organizing concept for criminology: Presidential address to the Academy of Criminal Justice Sciences. *Justice Quarterly* 11, 4, 527–559.

Daly, K. (1998). Gender, crime, and criminology. *The Oxford Handbook of Crime and Justice.* Oxford, England: Oxford University Press, 85–108.

Daniel, R. (2020). *Since You Asked: What Data Exists About Native American People in the Criminal Justice System?* Prison Policy Initiative. Available: https://www.prisonpolicy. org/blog/2020/04/22/native/#:~:text=According%20to%20the%20American%20 Indian,of%20incarceration%20nationwide%20if%20multi%2D.

Da Silva, D.T. (2021). "Putting Medicaid behind bars." *The Hill.* Available: https://thehill.com/ opinion/healthcare/582772-putting-medicaid-behind-bars, accessed November 2021.

De Li, S., and MacKenzie, D.L. (2003). The gendered effects of adult social bonds on the criminal activities of probationers. *Criminal Justice Review* 28, 2, 278–298.

DeGruy, J.D. (2017). *Post-traumatic Slave Syndrome: America's Legacy of Enduring Injury and Healing.* Milwaukie, OR: Uptown Press.

DeHart, D.D. (2004). *Pathways to Prison: Impact of Victimization in the Lives of Incarcerated Women.* Washington, DC: National Institute of Justice.

Dilmaghani, M., and Robinson, M. (2022). The blue of the rainbow: Queerness and hiring discrimination in blue-collar occupations. *Review of Social Economy*, 1–29.

Dlugacz, H.A., and Droubi, L. (2017). The reach of the ADA and its integration mandate: Implications for the successful reentry of individuals with mental disabilities in a correctional population. *Behavioral Sciences and the Law* 35, 2, 135–161.

Dooley, B., Seals, A., and Skarbek, D. (2014). The effect of prison gang membership on recidivism. *Journal of Criminal Justice* 42, 3, 267–275.

Dowden, C., and Andrews, D.A. (2004). The importance of staff practice in delivering effective correctional treatment: A meta-analytic review of core correctional practices. *International Journal of Offender Therapy and Comparative Criminology* 48, 2, 203–214.

Drake, E.K., Aos, S., and Marna, G.M. (2009). Evidence-based public policy options to reduce crime and criminal justice costs: Implications in Washington State. *Victims and Offenders* 4, 170–196.

Drakulich, K.M., Crutchfield, R.D., Matsueda, R.L., and Rose, K. (2012). Instability, informal control, and criminogenic situations: Community effects of returning prisoners. *Crime, Law and Social Change* 57, 5, 493–519.

Dum, C. (2016). *Exiled in America.* Columbia University Press.

Durr, M. (2015). What is the difference between slave patrols and modern day policing? Institutional violence in a community of color. *Critical Sociology* 41, 6, 873–879.

Eren, O., and Mocan, N. (2021). Juvenile punishment, high school graduation, and adult crime: Evidence from idiosyncratic judge harshness. *Review of Economics and Statistics* 103, 1, 34–47.

Estelle, S.M., and Phillips, D.C. (2018). Smart sentencing guidelines: The effect of marginal policy changes on recidivism. *Journal of Public Economics* 164, 270–293.

Ethridge, G., Dunlap, P.N., Boston, Q., and Staten, B.H. (2014). Ex-offenders in rural settings seeking employment. *Journal of Applied Rehabilitation Counseling*, 45, 4, 56–63.

Evans Jr., R. (1968). The labor market and parole success. *Journal of Human Resources*, 3, 2, 201–212.

Farrall, S., (2021). Politics, research design, and the 'architecture' of criminal careers studies. *The British Journal of Criminology* 61, 6: 1575–1591.

Farrington, D.P. (2000). Explaining and preventing crime: The globalization of knowledge— The American Society of Criminology 1999 presidential address. *Criminology* 38, 1, 1–24.

Fazio, R.L., Pietz, C.A., and Denney, R.L. (2012). An estimate of the prevalence of autism-spectrum disorders in an incarcerated population. *Journal of Forensic Psychology* 4, 69–80.

Federal Interagency Reentry Council. (2016). A Record of Progress and a Roadmap for the Future. Available: https://nicic.gov/federal-interagency-reentry-council-record-progress-and-roadmap-future-0.

Felsenthal, J. (2018). *A Matter of Justice.* Vogue. Available: https://www.vogue.com/projects/ 13541665/criminal-justice-reform, accessed July 2021.

Flage, A. (2019). Discrimination against gays and lesbians in hiring decisions: A meta-analysis. *International Journal of Manpower* 41, 6, 671–691.

Flores, J. (2016). *Caught Up: Girls, Surveillance, and Wraparound Incarceration*. University of California Press.

Fontaine, J. (2013). The role of supportive housing in successful reentry outcomes for disabled prisoners. *Cityscape* 15, 3, 53–76.

Fontaine, J., and Biess, J. (2012). *Housing as a Platform for Formerly Incarcerated Persons*. Washington, DC: Urban Institute.

Fox, K.J. (2010). Second chances: A comparison of civic engagement in offender reentry programs. *Criminal Justice Review* 35, 3, 335–353.

Fullilove, R.E., Cortes, A., Gamarra, R., and Maxis, H. (2020). The Bard Prison Initiative: Education, incarceration, and public health. *American Journal of Public Health.* 110, S33–S34.

Gaes, G.G., and Camp, S.D. (2009). Unintended consequences: Experimental evidence for the criminogenic effect of prison security level placement on post-release recidivism. *Journal of Experimental Criminology* 5, 2, 139–162.

Garfinkel, H. (1956). Conditions of successful degradation ceremonies. *American Journal of Sociology* 61, 5, 420–424.

Garland, D. (Ed.). (2001). *Mass Imprisonment: Social Causes and Consequences*. Sage.

Garretson, H.J. (2016). Legislating forgiveness: A study of post-conviction certificates as policy to address the employment consequences of a conviction. *Boston University Public Interest Law Journal* 25, 1–43.

Gary, F.A. (2005). Stigma: Barrier to mental health care among ethnic minorities. *Issues in Mental Health and Nursing* 26, 979–999.

Gendreau, P., Little, T., and Goggin, C. (1996). A meta-analysis of the predictors of adult offender recidivism: What works! *Criminology* 34, 4, 575–607.

Giordano, P. (2021, July 28). *Research Perspectives: Desistance and Identity Change Remarks made before the Committee*. Committee on Evaluating Success Among People Released from Prison Meeting #2: Public Information Gathering Session. Washington, DC: National Academies of Sciences, Engineering, and Medicine.

Giordano, P.C., Cernkovich, S.A., and Rudolph, J.L. (2002). Gender, crime, and desistance: Toward a theory of cognitive transformation. *American Journal of Sociology* 107, 4, 990–1064.

Glaze, L., and Maruschak, L.E. (2008). *Parents in Prison and Their Minor Children*. NCJ 222984. Washington, DC: U.S. Department of Justice, Bureau of Justice Statistics.

Glueck, S., and Glueck, E. (1940). *Juvenile Delinquents Grown Up*. Commonwealth Fund.

Goddard, T., Myers, R.R., and Robison, K.J. (2015). Potential partnerships: Progressive criminology, grassroots organizations and social justice. *International Journal for Crime, Justice and Social Democracy* 4, 4, 76–90.

Goffman, E. (1963). *Stigma: Notes on the Management of Spoiled Identity*. New York: Simon and Schuster.

Goldstein, P.J. (1985). The drugs/violence nexus: A tripartite conceptual framework. *Journal of Drug Issues* 15, 493–506.

Golembeski, C., and Fullilove, R. (2005). Criminal (in)justice in the city and its associated health consequences. *American Journal of Public Health* 95, 1701–1706.

Gottfredson, M.R., and Hirschi, T. (1990). *A General Theory of Crime*. Stanford University Press.

Green, D.P., and Winik, D. (2010). Using random judge assignments to estimate the effects of incarceration and probation on recidivism among drug offenders. *Criminology* 48, 2, 357–387.

Greenberg, G.A., and Rosenheck, R.A. (2008). Jail incarceration, homelessness, and mental health: A national study. *Psychiatric Services* 59, 2, 170–177.

Griffin, M.L., and Armstrong, G.S. (2003). The effect of local life circumstances on female probationers' offending. *Justice Quarterly* 20, 2, 213–239.

Gurusami, S. (2019). Motherwork under the state: The maternal labor of formerly incarcerated Black women. *Social Problems* 66, 128–143.

Hadden, S. (2021). Police and slave patrols. Forthcoming in *The Ethics of Policing: New Perspectives on Law Enforcement*, edited by B. Jones and E. Mendieta. New York: NYU Press.

Hagan, J. (1993). The social embeddedness of crime and unemployment. *Criminology* 31, 4, 465–491.

Hagan, J. (1997). Crime and capitalization: Toward a developmental theory of street crime in America. *Advances in Criminological Theory* 7, 287–308.

Hall, T.L., Wooten, N.R., and Lundgren, L.M. (2016). Post-incarceration-policies and prisoner reentry: Implications for policies and programs aimed at reducing recidivism and poverty. *Journal of Poverty* 20, 1, 56–72.

Halsey, M., Armstrong, R., and Wright, S. (2017). 'F*ck It!': Matza and the mood of fatalism in the desistance process. *The British Journal of Criminology* 57, 5, 1041–1060. Available: https://doi.org/10.1093/bjc/azw041.

Hamilton-Smith, G.P., and Vogel, M. (2012). The violence of voicelessness: The impact of felony disenfranchisement on recidivism. *Berkeley La Raza Law Journal* 22, 407.

Hansen, C.D. (2018). *Risk and Resiliency Factors in Predicting Recidivism Among Native Americans on a Montana Reservation.* (Doctoral dissertation). The University of Montana.

Harding, D.J., Morenoff, J.D., Nguyen, A.P., and Bushway, S.D. (2017). Short- and long-term effects of imprisonment on future felony convictions and prison admissions. *Proceedings of the National Academies of Sciences* 114, 11103–11108.

Harding, D.J., Morenoff, J.D., and Wyse, J.J.B. (2019). *On the Outside: Prisoner Reentry and Reintegration.* Chicago: University of Chicago Press.

Harding, D.J., Wyse, J.J., Dobson, C., and Morenoff, J.D. (2014). Making ends meet after prison. *Journal of Policy Analysis and Management* 33, 2, 440–470.

Harlow, C.W. (1999). *Prior Abuse Reported by Inmates and Probationers.* NCJ 172879. Rockville, MD: U.S. Department of Justice.

Harlow, C.W. (2003). *Education and Correctional Populations.* Washington, DC: U.S. Department of Justice, Office of Justice Programs.

Harm, N.J., and Phillips, S.D. (2001). You can't go home again: Women and criminal recidivism. *Journal of Offender Rehabilitation* 32, 3, 3–21.

Harner, H.M., Budescu, M., Gillihan, S.J., Riley, S., and Foa, E.B. (2015). Post-traumatic stress disorder in incarcerated women: A call for evidence-based treatment. *Psychological Trauma: Theory, Research, Practice, and Policy* 7, 1, 58.

Harris, A. (2016). *A Pound of Flesh: Monetary Sanctions as Punishment for the Poor.* New York: Russell Sage Foundation.

Harris, M.H., Nakamura, K., and Bucklen, K.B. (2018). Do cell mates matter? A causal test of the schools of crime hypothesis with implications for differential association and deterrence theories. *Criminology* 56, 1, 87–122.

Harrison, P.M., and Beck, A.J. (2002). *Prisoners in 2001.* Washington, D.C. Bureau of Labor Statistics.

Hastings, A., and Kall, K. (2020). *Opening the Door to Healing: Reaching and Serving Crime Victims Who Have a History of Incarceration.* New York, NY: Vera Institute of Justice, National Resource Center for Reaching Victims.

Henson, A. (2020). Desistance, persistence, resilience and resistance: A qualitative exploration of how Black fathers with criminal records navigate employer discrimination. *Punishment & Society*, 24, 2, 262–283.

Herman, J.L. (2003). The mental health of crime victims: Impact of legal intervention. *Journal of Traumatic Stress* 159, 159.

Hester, R. (2019). Prior record and recidivism risk. *American Journal of Criminal Justice* 44, 3, 353–375.

Hipp, J.R., Petersilia, J., and Turner, S. (2010). Parolee recidivism in California: The effect of neighborhood context and social service agency characteristics. *Criminology* 48, 4, 947–979.

Hipp, J.R., and Yates, D.K. (2009). Do returning parolees affect neighborhood crime? A case study of Sacramento. *Criminology* 47, 3, 619–656.

Hirschi, T., and Gottfredson, M. (1983). Age and the explanation of crime. *American Journal of Sociology* 89, 3, 552–584.

Hoffman, P.B., and Beck, J.L. (1984). Burnout—Age at release from prison and recidivism. *Journal of Criminal Justice* 12, 6, 617–623.

Holtfreter, K., Reisig, M.D., and Morash, M. (2004). Poverty, state capital, and recidivism among women offenders. *Criminology and Public Policy* 3, 2, 185–208.

Hooks, Bell. (1995). *Killing Rage: Ending Racism*. New York: Henry Holt.

Hoover, H. (2021). *Civil Rights Restoration and Recidivism*. Available at: https://ssrn.com/abstract=3773572.

Horney, J., Osgood, D.W., and Marshall, I.H. (1995). Criminal careers in the short-term: Intra-individual variability in crime and its relation to local life circumstances. *American Sociological Review* 60, 5, 655–673.

Huebner, B.M., and Berg, M.T. (2011). Examining the sources of variation in risk for recidivism. *Justice Quarterly* 28, 1, 146–173.

Huebner, B.M., and Cobbina, J. (2007). The effect of drug use, drug treatment participation, and treatment completion on probationer recidivism. *Journal of Drug Issues* 37, 3, 641.

Huebner, B.M., DeJong, C., and Cobbina, J. (2010). Women coming home: Long-term patterns of recidivism. *Justice Quarterly* 27, 2, 225–254.

Huebner, B.M., Kras, K. R., and Pleggenkuhle, B., (2019). Structural discrimination and social stigma among individuals incarcerated for sexual offenses: Reentry across the rural–urban continuum. *Criminology* 57, 4, 715–738.

Huebner, B.M., and Pleggenkuhle, B. (2015). Residential location, household composition, and recidivism: An analysis by gender. *Justice Quarterly* 32, 5, 818–844.

Huebner, B.M., Varano, S.P., and Bynum, T.S. (2007). Gangs, guns, and drugs: Recidivism among serious, young offenders. *Criminology and Public Policy* 6, 2, 187–222.

Hyatt, S.N., Andersen, S.L., Chanenson, S., Horowitz, V.L., and Uggen, C. (2021). 'We can actually do this': Adapting Scandinavian correctional culture in Pennsylvania. *American Criminal Law Review* 58, 1715–1746.

Hyde, J., Bolton, R., Kim, B., Yakovchenso, V., Petrakis, B. A., Visher, C., and McInnes, K. (2021). "I've just never done that." The influence of transitional anxiety on post-incarceration reentry and reintegration experiences among veterans. *Health and Social Care in the Community*, 00, 1–10.

James, D.J., and Glaze, L.E. (2006). *Mental Health Problems of Prison and Jail Inmates*. American Psychological Association.

Jett, B.T. (2021). *Race, Crime, and Policing in the Jim Crow South: African Americans and Law Enforcement in Birmingham, Memphis, and New Orleans, 1920–1945*. LSU Press.

Johnson Listwan, S., Colvin, M., Hanley, D., and Flannery, D. (2010). Victimization, social support, and psychological well-being: A study of recently released prisoners. *Criminal Justice and Behavior* 37, 10, 1140–1159.

Jones, L., and Sayegh, G. (2021). *Grassroots Movements Are Needed to End Mass Incarceration*. Katal Center for Equity, Health, and Justice. Available: https://www.katalcenter.org/grassrootsnyc.

Junger-Tas, J., and Marshall I. (1999). *The Self-Report Methodology in Crime Research*. Washington, D.C. National Institute of Justice.

Katz, A.H. (1981). Self-help and mutual aid: An emerging social movement? *Annual Review of Sociology* 7, 129–155.

Kazemian, L. (2021). *Evaluating Success Among People Released from Prison: Lessons from Abroad.* Paper prepared for the Committee on Evaluating Success Among People Released from Prison. Washington DC: National Academies of Sciences, Engineering, and Medicine. https://nap.nationalacademies.org/resource/26459/Evaluating_Success_Among_People_Released_from%20Prison_Lessons%20from%20Abroad_Kazemian.pdf.

Kennedy, R. (1997). *Race, Crime, and the Law.* Vintage.

Kimpel, A.F. (2018). Coordinating community reintegration services for "deportable alien" defendants: A moral and financial imperative. *Florida Law Review* 70, 1019.

King, R. and Elderbroom, B. (2014). *Improving Recidivism as a Performance Measure.* Urban Institute.

Kirk, D.S. (2015). A natural experiment of the consequences of concentrating former prisoners in the same neighborhoods. *Proceedings of the National Academy of Sciences* 112, 22, 6943–6948.

Kirk, D.S. (2016). Prisoner reentry and the reproduction of legal cynicism. *Social Problems* 63, 2, 222–243.

Kirk, D.S., and Wakefield, S. (2018). Collateral consequences of punishment: A critical review and path forward. *Annual Review of Criminology* 1, 171–194.

Kornhauser, R.R. (1978). *Social Sources of Delinquency: An Appraisal of Analytic Models.* NCJ 55611. Washington DC: U.S. Department of Justice, Office of Justice Programs.

Kreager, D.A., Schaefer, D.R., Bouchard, M., Haynie, D.L., Wakefield, S., Young, J., and Zajac, G. (2016). Toward a criminology of inmate networks. *Justice Quarterly* 33, 6, 1000–1028.

Kreager, D.A., Young, J.T. N., Haynie, D.L., Bouchard, M., Schaefer, D.R., and Zajac, G. (2017). Where "old heads" prevail: Inmate hierarchy in a men's prison unit. *American Sociological Review* 82, 4, 685–718.

Kubrin, C., Squires, G., and Stewart, E. (2007). Neighborhoods, race, and recidivism: The Community reoffending nexus and its implications for African Americans. In *SAGE Race Relations Abstracts* 32, 7–37.

Kubrin, C.E., and Weitzer, R. (2003). Retaliatory homicide: Concentrated disadvantage and neighborhood culture. *Social Problems* 50, 2, 157–180.

Kurlychek, M.C., Brame, R., and Bushway, S.D. (2006). Scarlet letters and recidivism: Does an old criminal record predict future offending? *Criminology and Public Policy* 5, 3, 483–504.

Kurlychek, M.C., Brame, R., and Bushway, S.D. (2007). Enduring risk? Old criminal records and predictions of future criminal involvement. *Crime and Delinquency* 53, 1, 64–83.

Kuziemko, I. (2013). How should inmates be released from prison? An assessment of parole versus fixed-sentence regimes. *The Quarterly Journal of Economics* 128, 371–424.

La Vigne, N.G. (2004). *Chicago Prisoners' Experiences Returning Home.* Washington, DC: Urban Institute.

La Vigne, N., Visher, C.A., and Castro, J. (2004). *Chicago Prisoners' Experiences Returning Home.* Washington, DC: The Urban Institute.

Lageson, S.E. (2016). Digital punishment's tangled web. *Contexts* 15, 1, 22–27.

Lageson, S.E. (2020). *Digital Punishment: Privacy, Stigma, and the Harms of Data-Driven Criminal Justice.* Oxford University Press.

Larson, R.P., and Uggen, C. (2017). Felon disenfranchisement. In B. Kerley (Ed.) *The Encyclopedia of Corrections*, 1–5. New York: Wiley.

Lattimore, P.K., Dawes, D., and Barrick, K. (2018). *Desistance from Crime over the Life Course.* Washington, DC: National Institute of Justice.

Lattimore, P., and Visher, C. (2021). Considerations on the multi-site evaluation of the serious and violent offender reentry initiative. In P.K. Lattimore, B.M. Huebner, and F.S. Taxman (Eds.), *Handbook on Moving Corrections and Sentencing Forward: Building on the Record*, 312–335. New York, NY: Routledge.

Laub, J.H. and Sampson, R.J. (2001). Understanding desistance from crime. *Crime and Justice*, 28, 1–69.

Laub, J.H., and Sampson, R.J. (2006). *Shared Beginnings, Divergent Lives: Delinquent Boys to Age 70*. Harvard University Press.

Lauritsen, J.L. and Laub, J.H. (2007). Understanding the link between victimization and offending: new reflections on an old idea. *Crime Prevention Studies*, 22, 55–76.

Lawrence, K., and Keleher, T. (2004, November). *Structural Racism*. Paper prepared for the Race and Public Policy Conference, Berkeley. Available: http://www.intergroupresources. com/rc/Definitions%20of%20Racism.pdf.

LeBel, T.P. (2007). An examination of the impact of formerly incarcerated persons helping others. *Journal of Offender Rehabilitation* 46, 1–2, 1–24.

LeBel, T.P. (2017). Housing as the tip of the iceberg in successfully navigating prisoner reentry. *Criminology and Public Policy* 16, 889.

LeBel, T.P., Burnett, R., Maruna, S., and Bushway, S. (2008). The 'chicken and egg' of subjective and social factors in desistance from crime. *European Journal of Criminology* 5, 2, 131–159.

LeBel, T.P., Richie, M., and Maruna, S. (2015). Helping others as a response to reconcile a criminal past: The role of the wounded healer in prisoner reentry programs. *Criminal Justice and Behavior* 42, 1, 108–120.

Lee, J.J.H., Guilamo-Ramos, V., Muñoz-Laboy, M., Lotz, K., and Bornheimer, L. (2016). Mechanisms of familial influence on reentry among formerly incarcerated Latino men. *Social Work* 61, 3, 199–207.

Lemert, E.M. (1951). *Social Pathology: A Systematic Approach to the Theory of Sociopathic Behavior*. American Psychological Association.

Lemert, E.M. (1972). *Human Deviance, Social Problems, and Social Control* (2nd Ed.). Englewood Cliffs, NJ: Prentice-Hall.

Lerman, A.E., and Weaver, V.M. (2014). *Arresting Citizenship*. Chicago: University of Chicago Press.

Levenson, J.S., and Willis, G.M. (2018). Implementing trauma-informed care in correctional treatment and supervision. *Journal of Aggression, Maltreatment and Trauma* 28, 4, 481–501.

Leverentz A. (2011). Neighborhood context of attitudes toward crime and reentry. *Punishment & Society* 13, 1, 64–92.

Leverentz, A. (2020). Beyond neighborhoods: Activity spaces of returning prisoners. *Social Problems* 67, 1, 150–170.

Lewis, O. (1965). *La Vida: A Puerto Rican Family in the Culture of Poverty*. New York, NY: Random House.

Lewis, S. (2021, July 28). *Practitioner Perspectives on Reentry Programs remarks made before the Committee*. Committee on Evaluating Success Among People Released from Prison Meeting #2: Public Information Gathering Session. Washington, DC: National Academies of Sciences, Engineering, and Medicine.

Li, S.D., and MacKenzie, D.L. (2003). The gendered effects of adult social bonds on the criminal activities of probationers. *Criminal Justice Review* 28, 2, 278–298.

Li, S.D., Priú, H. and MacKenzie, D.L. (2000). Drug involvement, lifestyles, and criminal activities among probationers. *Journal of Drug Issues* 30, 593–619.

Light, M., He, J., and Robey, J.P. (2020). Comparing crime rates between undocumented immigrants, legal immigrants, and native-born U.S. citizens in Texas. *PNAS* 117, 51, 32340–32347. NCJ 301717.

Link, N.W., and Hamilton, L.K. (2017). The reciprocal lagged effects of substance use and recidivism in a prisoner reentry context. *Health and Justice* 5, 1, 1–14.

Link, N.W., Ward, J., and Stansfield, R. (2019). Consequences of mental and physical health for reentry and recidivism: Toward a health-based model of desistance. *Criminology* 57, 3, 544–573.

Listwan, S.J., Sullivan, C.J., Agnew, R., Cullen, F.T., and Colvin, M. (2013). The pains of imprisonment revisited: The impact of strain on inmate recidivism. *Justice Quarterly* 30, 1, 144–168.

Liu, L. (2020). Family, parochial, and public levels of social control and recidivism: An extension of the systemic model of social disorganization. *Crime and Delinquency* 66, 6–7, 864–886.

Liu, L., and Visher, C.A. (2019). The crossover of negative emotions between former prisoners and their family members during reunion: A test of general strain theory. *Journal of Offender Rehabilitation* 58, 567–591.

Liu, L., and Visher, C.A. (2021). Decomposition of the role of family in reentry: Family support, tension, gender, and reentry outcomes. *Crime and Delinquency* 67, 6–7, 970–996.

Loeffler, C.E., and Nagin, D.S. (2021). The impact of incarceration on recidivism. *Annual Review of Criminology* 5.

Loughran, T.A., Mulvey, E.P., Schubert, C.A., Fagan, J., Piquero, A.R., and Losoya, S.H. (2009). Estimating a dose-response relationship between length of stay and future recidivism in serious juvenile offenders. *Criminology* 47, 3, 699–740.

Love, M.C. (2022). *The Many Roads from Reentry to Reintegration: A National Survey of Laws Restoring Rights and Opportunities after Arrest or Conviction.* Collateral Consequences Resource Center (March 3, 2022).

Love, M.C., Roberts, J., and Klingele, C. (2013). *Collateral Consequences of Criminal Convictions: Law, Policy and Practice.* Eagan, MN: Thompson West.

Lutze, F.E., Rosky, J.W., and Hamilton, Z.K. (2014). Homelessness and reentry: A multisite outcome evaluation of Washington State's reentry housing program for high-risk offenders. *Criminal Justice and Behavior* 41, 4, 471–491.

Lynch, S.M., DeHart, D.D., Belknap, J., and Green, B.L. (2012a). *Women's Pathways to Jail: The Roles and Intersections of Serious Mental Illness and Trauma.* Washington, DC: US Department of Justice, Bureau of Justice Assistance.

Lynch, S.M., Fritch, A., and Heath, N.M. (2012b). Looking beneath the surface: The nature of incarcerated women's experiences of interpersonal violence, treatment needs, and mental health. *Feminist Criminology* 7, 4, 381–400.

MacKenzie, D.L. (2006). *What Works in Corrections: Reducing the Criminal Activities of Offenders and Delinquents.* Cambridge University Press.

MacKenzie, D.L., and Li, S.D. (2002). The impact of formal and informal social controls on the criminal activities of probationers. *Journal of Research in Crime and Delinquency* 39, 3, 243–276.

Mallory, C., Flores, A.R., Sears, B. (2021). *Workplace Discrimination and Harassment Against LGBT State and Local Government Employees.* UCLA School of Law, Williams Institute.

Marsden, P.V. (1987). Core discussion networks of Americans. *American Sociological Review* 52, 122–131.

Martin, M.S., Eljdupovic, G., McKenzie, K., and Colman, I. (2015). Risk of violence by inmates with childhood trauma and mental health needs. *Law and Human Behavior* 39, 6, 614.

Martin, L.L. (2011). Debt to society: Asset poverty and prisoner reentry. *The Review of Black Political Economy* 38, 2, 131–143.

Martinez, D.J., and Christian, J. (2009). The familial relationships of former prisoners: Examining the link between residence and informal support mechanisms. *Journal of Contemporary Ethnography* 38, 2, 201–224.

Maruna, S. (2001). *Making Good: How Ex-Convicts Reform and Rebuild Their Lives.* Washington, DC: American Psychological Association.

Maruna, S., and Toch, H. (2005). The impact of imprisonment on the desistance process. *Prisoner Reentry and Crime in America*, 139–178.

Maruschak, L.M., Bronson, J., and Alper, M. (2021a). *Alcohol and Drug Use and Treatment Reported by Prisoners. Statistical Tables*. NCJ 252641, Washington, DC: Bureau of Justice Statistics.

Maruschak, L.M., Bronson, J., and Alper, M. (2021b). *Disabilities Reported by Prisoners: Survey of Prison Inmates, 2016*. NCJ 252642. Washington, DC: Bureau of Justice Statistics.

Massey, D., and Denton, N.A. (1993). *American Apartheid: Segregation and the Making of the Underclass*. Harvard University Press.

Massoglia, M., and Pridemore, W.A. (2015). Incarceration and health. *Annual Review of Sociology* 41, 291–310. doi:10.1146/annurev-soc-073014-112326.

Massoglia, M., and Remster, B. (2019). Linkages between incarceration and health. *Public Health Reports* 134, 1, 8S-14S.

Massoglia, M., Firebaugh, G., and Warner, C. (2012). Racial variation in the effect of incarceration on neighborhood attainment. *American Sociological Review* 78, 1, 142–165.

Matsueda, R.L., and Heimer, K. (1997). A symbolic interactionist theory of role-transitions, role-commitments, and delinquency. *Developmental Theories of Crime and Delinquency*, 163–213.

McKay, T., Comfort, M., Lindquist, C., and Bir, A. (2016). If family matters: Supporting family relationships during incarceration and reentry. *Criminology and Public Policy* 15, 2, 529.

McNeeley, S. (2018). Do ecological effects on recidivism vary by gender, race, or housing type? *Crime and Delinquency* 64, 6, 782–806.

McPherson, M., Smith-Lovin, L., and Brashears, M.E. (2006). Social isolation in America: Changes in core discussion networks over two decades. *American Sociological Review* 71, 1, 353–375.

McShane, M.D., Williams III, F.P., and Dolny, H.M. (2003). The effect of gang membership on parole outcome. *Journal of Gang Research* 10, 25–38.

Meade, B., Steiner, B., Makarios, M., and Travis, L. (2013). Estimating a dose–response relationship between time served in prison and recidivism. *Journal of Research in Crime and Delinquency* 50, 4, 525–550.

Meade, B., Wasileski, G., and Hunter, A. (2021). The effects of victimization prior to prison on victimization, misconduct, and sanction severity during incarceration. *Crime & Delinquency* 67(12), 1856–1878.

Mears, D.P., Cochran, J.C., Bales, W.D., and Bhati, A.S. (2016). Recidivism and time served in prison. *The Journal of Criminal Law and Criminology* 106, 1, 81–122.

Mears, D.P., Wang, X., Hay, C., and Bales, W.D. (2008). Social ecology and recidivism: Implications for prisoner reentry. *Criminology* 46, 2, 301–340.

Mellow, J., Schlager, M.D., and Caplan, J.M. (2008). Using GIS to evaluate post-release prisoner services in Newark, New Jersey. *Journal of Criminal Justice* 36, 416–425.

Melton, A.P., Joshua, L., and Melton, D.J. (2010). *Strategies for Creating Offender Reentry Programs in Indian Country*. National Criminal Justice Reference Service.

Merton, R.K. (1938). Social structure and anomie. *American Sociological Review* 3, 5, 672–682.

Metraux, S., and Culhane, D.P. (2004). Homeless shelter use and reincarceration following prison release. *Criminology and Public Policy* 3, 2, 139–160.

Metraux, S., and Culhane, D. (2006). Recent incarceration history among sheltered homeless population. *Crime and Delinquency* 52, 3, 504–517.

Metraux, S., Hunt, D., and Yetvin, W. (2020). Criminal justice reentry and homelessness. *Center for Evidence-based Solutions to Homelessness*. Available: https://udspace.udel.edu/bitstream/handle/19716/25636/Reentry+and+Homelessness_Synthesis+of+the+Evidence_Final_2.6.2020.pdf?sequence=1.

Meyer, I.H., Flores, A.R., Stemple, L., Romero, A.P., Wilson, B.D.M., and Herman, J.L. (2017). Incarceration rates and traits of sexual minorities in the United States: National Inmate Survey, 2011–2012. *American Journal of Public Health* 107, 2, 267–273.

Michalsen, V. (2011). Mothering as a life course transition: Do women go straight for their children? *Journal of Offender Rehabilitation* 50, 6, 349–366.

Middlemass, K.M., and Smiley, C. (2019). Introduction: Critical reentry in the 21st century. In Middlemass, K.M., and Smiley, C. (Eds), *Prisoner Reentry in the 21st Century: Critical Perspectives of Returning Home*. London, UK: Routledge.

Miller, R.J. (2021). *Halfway Home: Race, Punishment, and the Afterlife of Mass Incarceration*. New York: Little, Brown and Company.

Miller, J., Caplan, J.M., and Ostermann, M. (2016). Home nodes, criminogenic places, and parolee failure: Testing an environmental model of offender risk. *Crime and Delinquency* 62, 2, 169–199.

Miller, R.J., and Stuart, F. (2017). Carceral citizenship: Race, rights and responsibility in the age of mass supervision. *Theoretical Criminology* 21, 4, 532–548.

Miller, R.J. (2014). Devolving the carceral state: Race, prisoner reentry, and the micro-politics of urban poverty management. *Punishment & Society* 16, 3, 305–335.

Mills, C.W. (1997) *The Racial Contract*. Ithaca, NY: Cornell University Press.

Mitchell, M.B., and Davis, J.B. (2019). Formerly incarcerated black mothers matter too: Resisting social constructions of motherhood. *The Prison Journal* 99, 4, 420–436.

Moore, G. (1990). Structural determinants of men's and women's personal networks. *American Sociological Review* 55, 726–735.

Moore, K.E., Hacker, R.L., Oberleitner, L., and McKee, S.A. (2020). Reentry interventions that address substance use: A systematic review. *Psychological Services* 17, 1, 93–101.

Morash, M. (2010), *Women on Probation and Parole: A Feminist Critique of Community Programs and Services*. Northeastern University Press.

Morash, M. (2021, July 28). *Research Perspectives: Desistance and Identity Change*. Committee on Evaluating Success Among People Released from Prison Meeting #2: Public Information Gathering Session. Washington, DC: National Academies of Sciences, Engineering, and Medicine.

Morash, M., Kashy, D.A., Smith, S.W., and Cobbina, J.E. (2015). The effects of probation or parole agent relationship style and women offenders' criminogenic needs on offenders' responses to supervision interactions. *Criminal Justice and Behavior* 42, 4, 412–434.

Morgenstern, J., and Blanchard, K.A. (2006). Welfare reform and substance abuse treatment for welfare recipients. *Alcohol Research and Health* 29, 1, 63–67.

Movement Advancement Project. (2016). *LGBT People with Criminal Records Face Challenges to Rebuilding Their Lives*. Available: https://www.lgbtmap.org/file/lgbt-criminal-justice-reentry.pdf.

Mowen, T.J., and Visher, C.A. (2015). Drug use and crime after incarceration: The role of family support and family conflict. *Justice Quarterly* 32, 2, 337–359.

Mowen, T.J., Wodahl, E., Brent, J.J., and Garland, B. (2018). The role of sanctions and incentives in promoting successful reentry: Evidence from the SVORI data. *Criminal Justice and Behavior* 45, 8, 1288–1307.

Mumola, C.J. (1999). *Substance Abuse and Treatment of State and Federal Prisoners, 1997*. NCJ 172871. Washington, DC: Bureau of Justice Statistics.

Nagin, D.S., Cullen, F.T., and Jonson, C.L. (2009). Imprisonment and reoffending. *Crime and Justice* 38, 1, 115–200.

Nagin, D.S., and Paternoster, R. (1991). On the relationship of past to future participation in delinquency. *Criminology* 29, 2, 163–189.

Nagin, D., and Paternoster, R. (2000). Population heterogeneity and state dependence: State of the evidence and directions for future research. *Journal of Quantitative Criminology* 16, 2, 117–144.

Naser, R.L., and La Vigne, N.G. (2006). Family support in the prisoner reentry process: Expectations and realities. *Journal of Offender Rehabilitation* 43, 1, 93–106.

Naser, R.L., and Visher, C.A. (2006). Family members' experiences with incarceration and reentry. *Western Criminology Review* 7, 2, 21–31.

National Academies of Sciences, Engineering, and Medicine. 2020. *Decarcerating Correctional Facilities during COVID-19: Advancing Health, Equity, and Safety*. Washington, DC: The National Academies Press. Available https://doi.org/10.17226/25945.

National Center for Transgender Equality. (2018). *LGBTQ People Behind Bars: A Guide to Understanding the Issues Facing Transgender Prisoners and their Legal Rights*. Available: https://transequality.org/sites/default/files/docs/resources/TransgenderPeopleBehindBars.pdf.

National Institute on Drug Abuse. (2020). *What Are the Unique Treatment Needs of Women in the Criminal Justice System?* Available: https://nida.nih.gov/publications/principles-drug-abuse-treatment-criminal-justice-populations-research-based-guide/what-are-unique-treatment-needs-women-in-criminal-justice-system.

National Research Council. (2014). *The Growth of Incarceration in the United States: Exploring Causes and Consequences*. Washington, DC: The National Academies Press. Available: https://doi.org/10.17226/18613.

Nelson, M., Deess, P., and Allen, C. (1999). The first month out: Post-incarceration experiences in New York City. *Federal Sentencing Reporter* 24, 1, 72–75.

Nur, A.V., and Nguyen, H. (2022). Prison work and vocational programs: A systematic review and analysis of moderators of program success, *Justice Quarterly*. Available: 10.1080/07418825.2022.2026451. Published online 18 Feb 2022.

Orth, U. (2002). Secondary Victimization of Crime Victims by Criminal Proceedings. *Social Justice Research* 15, 4, 313–325.

Owen, B., and Bloom, B. (1995). Profiling women prisoners: Findings from national surveys and California sample. *Prison Journal* 75, 2, 165–185.

Pager, D. (2003). The mark of a criminal record. *American Journal of Sociology* 108, 5, 937–975.

Paikowsky, D. (2019). Jails as polling places: Living up to the obligation to enfranchise the voters we jail. *Harvard Civil Rights-Civil Liberties Law Review* 54, 829.

Paternoster, R., and Bushway, S. (2009). Desistance and the "feared self": Toward an identity theory of criminal desistance. *Journal of Criminal Law and Criminology* 99, 4, 1103–1156.

Paternoster, R., and Iovanni, L. (1989). The labeling perspective and delinquency: An elaboration of the theory and an assessment of the evidence. *Justice Quarterly* 6, 3, 359–394.

Patterson, E.J. (2003). The dose-response of time served in prison on mortality: New York State, 1989–2003. *American Journal of Public Health* 103, 523–528.

Patterson, G.T. (2013). Prisoner reentry: A public health or public safety issue for social work practice? *Social Work in Public Health* 28, 2, 129–141.

Petersilia, J., and Turner, S. (1993). Intensive probation and parole. *Crime and Justice* 17, 281–335.

Petersilia, J. (1997). Justice for all? Offenders with mental retardation and the California corrections system. *The Prison Journal* 77, 4, 358–380.

Peterson, R.D., and Krivo, L.J. (2010). *Divergent Social Worlds: Neighborhood Crime and the Racial-Spatial Divide*. New York: Russell Sage Foundation.

Petrich, D.M., Pratt, T.C., Jonson, C.L., and Cullen, F.T. (2021). Custodial sanctions and reoffending: A meta-analytic review. *Crime and Justice* 50, 1.

Phelps, M.S. (2017). Mass probation: Toward a more robust theory of state variation in punishment. *Punishment and Society* 19, 1, 53–73.

Phelps, M.S., and E.L. Ruhland. (2021). Governing marginality: Coercion and care in probation. *Social Problems*. Available: https://doi.org/10.1093/socpro/spaa060.

Piquero, A.R., and Jennings, W.G. (2017). Research note: Justice system–imposed financial penalties increase the likelihood of recidivism in a sample of adolescent offenders. *Youth Violence and Juvenile Justice* 15, 3, 325–340.

Pompa, L. (2013). One brick at a time: The power and possibility of dialogue across the prison wall. *The Prison Journal* 93, 2, 127–34.

Pringer, S.M., and Wagner, N.J. (2020). Use of trauma-informed care with incarcerated offenders. *Journal of Addictions and Offender Counseling* 41, 1, 52–64.

Pugliesi, K., and Shook, S.L. (1998). Gender, ethnicity, and network charactersistics: Variation in social support resources. *Sex Roles* 38, 3/4, 215–238.

Pyrooz, D.C., Clark, K.J., Tostlebe, J.J., Decker, S.H., and Orrick, E. (2021). Gang affiliation and prisoner reentry: Discrete-time variation in recidivism by current, former, and non-gang status. *Journal of Research in Crime and Delinquency* 58, 2, 192–234.

Rafei, L. (2021). Meet the activists fighting to free people from LA jails. *ACLU News and Commentary.* Available: https://www.aclu.org/news/criminal-law-reform/meet-the-activists-fighting-to-free-people-from-la-jails/.

Ramos, J., and Wenger, M.R. (2019). Immigration and recidivism: What is the link? *Justice Quarterly* 37, 3, 436–460.

RAND Health Care. 36-Item Short Form Survey (SF-36). The RAND Corporation.

Reisig, M.D., Bales, W.D., Hay, C., and Wang, X. (2007). The effect of racial inequality on Black male recidivism. *Justice Quarterly* 24, 3, 408–434.

Reisig, M.D., Holtfreter, K., and Morash, M. (2002). Social capital among women offenders: Examining the distribution of social networks and resources. *Journal of Contemporary Criminal Justice* 18, 2, 167–187.

Rhodes, W., Gaes, G.G., Kling, R., and Cutler, C. (2018). Relationship between prison length of stay and recidivism: A study using regression discontinuity and instrumental variables with multiple break points. *Criminology and Public Policy* 17, 3, 731–769.

Rice, D. (2021, July 28). *Practitioner Perspectives: Education, Employment, Health, Housing and Beyond remarks made before the Committee.* Committee on Evaluating Success Among People Released from Prison Meeting #2: Public Information Gathering Session. Washington, DC: National Academies of Sciences, Engineering, and Medicine.

Richie, B.E. (2001). Challenges incarcerated women face as they return to their communities: Findings from life history interviews. *Crime and Delinquency* 47, 3, 368–389.

Riessman, F. (1965). The "helper" therapy principle. *Social Work* 10, 2, 27–32.

Roe-Sepowitz, D.E., Hickle, K.E., Loubert, M.P., and Egan, T. (2011). Adult prostitution recidivism: Risk factors and impact of a diversion program. *Journal of Offender Rehabilitation* 50, 272–285.

Rose, D.R., and Clear, T.R. (1998). Incarceration, social capital, and crime: Implications for social disorganization theory. *Criminology* 36, 3, 441–480.

Rose, D.R., Clear, T.R., and Ryder, J.A. (2001). Addressing the unintended consequences of incarceration through community-oriented services at the neighborhood level. *Corrections Management Quarterly* 5, 3, 62–71.

Rosenfeld, R., Messner, S.F., and Baumer, E.P. (2001). Social capital and homicide. *Social Forces* 80, 1, 283–310.

Rydberg, J., and Clark, K. (2016). Variation in the incarceration length-recidivism dose-response relationship. *Journal of Criminal Justice* 46, 118–128.

Sampson, R.J., and Laub, J.H. (1993). Structural variations in juvenile court processing: Inequality, the underclass, and social control. *Law and Society Review* (Jan.), 285–311.

Sampson, R.J., and Laub, J.H. (1996). Socioeconomic achievement in the life course of disadvantaged men: Military service as a turning point, circa 1940–1965. *American Sociological Review* 61, 347–367.

Sampson, R.J., and Laub, J.H. (1997). Unraveling the social context of physique and delinquency. In Raine, A., Brennan, P., and Farrington, D. (Eds), *Biosocial Bases of Violence,* 175–188. Boston, MA: Springer.

Sampson, R.J., and Laub, J.H. (2003). Desistance from crime over the life course. In Mortimer, J.T., and Shanahan, M.J. (Eds), *Handbook of the Life Course,* 295–309. Boston, MA: Springer.

Sampson, R.J., and Loeffler, C. (2010). Punishment's place: The local concentration of mass incarceration. *Daedalus* 139, 20–31.

Sampson, R.J., Raudenbush, S.W., and Earls, F. (1997). Neighborhoods and violent crime: A multilevel study of collective efficacy. *Science* 277, 5328, 918–924.

Santos, T. (2021). Justice in reentry for formerly incarcerated LGBTQ people and people living with HIV. *Center for American Progress.* Available: https://www.american-progress.org/issues/lgbtq-rights/news/2021/04/23/498211/justice-reentry-formerly-incarcerated-lgbtq-people-people-living-hiv/, accessed July 2021.

Sawyer, W. (2018). *The Gender Divide: Tracking Women's State Prison Growth.* Northampton, MA: Prison Policy Initiative.

Schaefer, D.R., Bouchard, M., Young, J.T., and Kreager, D.A. (2017). Friends in locked places: An investigation of prison inmate network structure. *Social Networks* 51, 88–103.

Schafhalter-Zoppoth, I., Walther, A., and Flattery, D. (2013). Exclusion of non-English speaking, recently released prisoners. *American Journal of Public Health* 103, 6, E6.

Schiraldi, V.N., and Arzu, J.L. (2018). *Less Is More in New York: An Examination of the Impact of State Parole Violations on Prison and Jail Populations.* Columbia University, Justice Lab. Available: https://academiccommons.columbia.edu/doi/10.7916/D8RZ0Q06.

Schnepel, K.T. (2018). Good jobs and recidivism. *The Economic Journal* 128, 447–469.

Schnittker, J., Massoglia, M., and Uggen, C. (2012). Out and down: Incarceration and psychiatric disorders. *Journal of Health and Social Behavior* 53, 4, 448–64.

Schur, E.M. (1971). *Labeling Deviant Behavior: Its Sociological Implications.* New York: Harper and Row.

Schwegman, D. (2018). Rental market discrimination against same-sex couples. Evidence from a pairwise-matched email correspondence test. *Housing Policy Debate* 29, 2, 250–272.

Sharkey, P., Torrats-Espinosa, G., and Takyar, D. (2017). Community and the crime decline: The causal effect of local nonprofits on violent crime. *American Sociological Review* 82, 6, 1214–1240.

Sharp, S.F., and Hope, T.L. (2001). The professional ex -revisited: cessation or continuation of a deviant career? *Journal of Contemporary Ethnography* 30, 6, 678–703.

Shaw, C.R., and McKay, H.D. (1942). *Juvenile Delinquency and Urban Areas.* University of Chicago Press.

Shaw, C.R., Zorbaugh, F.M., McKay, H.D., and Cottrell, L.S. (1929). *Delinquency Areas: A Study of the Geographic Distribution of School Truants, Juvenile Delinquents, and Adult Offenders in Chicago.* Chicago: University of Chicago Press.

Sherman, L.W. (1993). Defiance, deterrence, and irrelevance: A theory of the criminal sanction. *Journal of research in Crime and Delinquency* 30, 4, 445–473.

Sherman, L.W., Gottfredson, D.C., MacKenzie, D.L., Eck, J., Reuter, P., and Bushway, S. D. (1998). *Preventing Crime: What Works, What Doesn't, What's Promising: A Report to the United States Congress.* Washington, DC: National Institute of Justice.

Shineman, V. (2018). *Restoring Rights, Restoring Trust: Evidence that Reversing Felony Disenfranchisement Penalties Increases Both Trust and Cooperation with Government.* (October 25, 2018). SSRN Working Paper Available: https://ssrn.com/abstract=3272694 or http://dx.doi.org/10.2139/ssrn.3272694.

Shlanger, M. (2017). Prisoners with disabilities. In E. Luna (Ed.), *Reforming Criminal Justice: Punishment, Incarceration, and Release,* 4, 295–323. Phoenix, AZ: Academy for Justice.

Simes, J.T. (2018) Place after prison: Neighborhood attainment and attachment during reentry. *Journal of Urban Affairs,* 41, 4, 443–463. DOI: 10.1080/07352166.2018.1495041.

Skeem, J.L., Louden, J.E., Polaschek, D., and Camp, J. (2007). Assessing relationship quality in mandated community treatment: Blending care with control. *Psychological Assessment* 19, 4, 397.

Sloas, L., Murphy, A., and Taxman, F.S. (2019). Assessing the use and impact of points and rewards across four federal probation districts: A contingency management approach. *Victims and offenders*, 14, 7, 811–831.

Slocum, L.A., Rengifo, A.F., Choi, T., and Herrmann, C.R. (2013). The elusive relationship between community organizations and crime: An assessment across disadvantaged areas of the South Bronx. *Criminology* 51, 1, 167–216.

Smith, D.L. (2011). *Less than Human: Why We Demean, Enslave, and Exterminate Others*. New York: Macmillan.

Søgaard, T.F., Kolind, T., Thylstrup, B., and Deuchar, R. (2016). Desistance and the micro-narrative construction of reformed masculinities in a Danish rehabilitation centre. *Criminology and Criminal Justice* 16, 1, 99–118.

Sonnenberg, L. (2017). A former felon leads the way in criminal justice reform. *Forbes*. Available: https://www.forbes.com/sites/laurensonnenberg/2017/08/26/a-former-felon-leads-the-way-in-criminal-justice-reform/?sh=811157d7bb91, accessed August 2021.

Stafford, M.C., and Warr, M. (1993). A reconceptualization of general and specific deterrence. *Journal of Research in Crime and Delinquency* 30, 2, 123–135.

Steadman, H.J., Osher, F.C., Robbins, P.C., Case, B., and Samuels, S. (2009). Prevalence of serious mental illness among jail inmates. *Psychiatric Services* 60, 6, 761–765.

Stevenson, B. (2017). A Presumption of Guilt: A Legacy of America's History of Racial Injustice. In A. Davis (Ed.), *Policing the Black Man*, 3–30. New York: Pantheon Books.

Stewart, R.A., Watters, B., Horowitz, V., Larson, R., Sargent, B., and Uggen, C. (2021). Native Americans and monetary sanctions. Forthcoming in *RSF: The Russell Sage Foundation Journal of the Social Sciences*.

Substance Abuse and Mental Health Services Administration. SAMHSA's Concept of Trauma and Guidance for a Trauma-Informed Approach. HHS Publication No. (SMA) 14-4884. Rockville, MD: Substance Abuse and Mental Health Services Administration, 2014.

Sugie, N.F., and Lens, M.C. (2017). Daytime locations in spatial mismatch: Job accessibility and employment at reentry from prison. *Demography* 54, 2, 775–800.

Sutherland, E.H. (1947). *Principles of Criminology* (4th Ed.). Philadelphia: Lippincott.

Swavola, E., Riley, K., and Subramanan, R. (2016). *Overlooked: Women and Jails in an Era of Reform*. New York: Vera Institute of Justice.

Szifris, K., Fox, C., and Bradbury, A. (2018). A realist model of prison education, growth, and desistance: A new theory. *Journal of Prison Education and Reentry* 5, 1, 41–62.

Taxman, F.S. (2002). Supervision—exploring the dimensions of effectiveness. *Federal Probation* 66, 2, 14–27.

Taxman, F.S., and Ainsworth, S. (2009). Correctional milieu: The key to quality outcomes. *Victims and Offenders* 4, 4, 334–340.

Taxman, F.S., Smith, L., and Rudes, D.S. (2020). From Mean to Meaningful Probation: The Legacy of Intensive Supervision Programs. In Lattimore, P., Huebner, B., and Taxman, F.S. (Eds.), *Handbook on Moving Corrections and Sentencing Forward: Building on the Record*. Routledge Press.

Taxman, F.S., and Thanner, M.H. (2004). Probation from a therapeutic perspective: Results from the field. *Contemporary Issues in Law*, 7, 1, 39–63.

Taylor, C.J. (2016). The family's role in the reintegration of formerly incarcerated individuals: The direct effects of emotional support. *Prison Journal* 96, 3, 331–354.

Tiedt, A.D., and Sabol, W.J. (2015). Sentence length and recidivism among prisoners released across 30 states in 2005: Accounting for individual histories and state clustering effects. *Justice Research and Policy* 16, 1, 50–64.

Tillyer, M.S., and Vose, B. (2011). Social ecology, individual risk, and recidivism: A multilevel examination of main and moderating influences. *Journal of Criminal Justice* 39, 5, 452–459.

Tonry, M., and Wilson, J.Q. (Eds.). (1990). *Drugs and Crime. Crime and Justice: A Review of Research*, 13. Chicago: University of Chicago Press.

Travis, J. (2002). *Invisible Punishment: An Instrument of Social Exclusion*. Urban Institute.

Travis, J., and Visher, C. (Eds.). (2005). *Prisoner Reentry and Crime in America*. Cambridge University Press.

Uggen, C. (1999). Ex-offenders and the conformist alternative: A job quality model of work and crime. *Social Problems* 46, 1, 127–151.

Uggen, C. (2000). Work as a turning point in the life course of criminals: A duration model of age, employment, and recidivism. *American Sociological Review* 65, 4, 529–546. DOI:10.2307/2657381.

Uggen, C., and Inderbitzin, M. (2010). Public criminologies. *Criminology and Public Policy* 9, 4, 725–749.

Uggen, C., Larson, R., Shannon, S., and Pulido-Nava, A. (2020). *Locked Out 2020: Estimates of People Denied Voting Rights Due to a Felony Conviction*. The Sentencing Project. Available: https://www.sentencingproject.org/publications/locked-out-2020-estimates-of-people-denied-voting-rights-due-to-a-felony-conviction/.

Uggen, C., Manza, J., and Behrens, A. (2004). Less than the average citizen: stigma, role transition and the civic reintegration of convicted felons. In S. Maruna and R. Immarigeon (Eds.), *After Crime and Punishment: Pathways to Offender Reintegration*, 261–293. NCJ-205080.

Uggen, C., Manza, J., and Thompson, M. (2006). Citizenship, democracy, and the civic reintegration of criminal offenders. *The Annals of the American Academy of Political and Social Science* 605, 1, 281–310.

Uggen, C., and Piliavin, I. (1998). Asymmetrical causation and criminal desistance. *The Journal of Criminal Law and Criminology*, 88, 4, 1399–1422.

Uggen, C., and Stewart, R. (2014). Piling on: Collateral consequences and community supervision. *Minnesota Law Review* 99, 1871.

Uggen, C., Wakefield, S., and Western, B. (2005). Work and family perspectives on reentry, in J. Travis and C. Visher, eds. *Prisoner Reentry and Crime in America*, 209–243. Cambridge, UK: Cambridge University Press.

Upadhyayula, S., Ramaswamy, M., Chalise, P., Daniels, J., and Freudenberg, N. (2017). The association of ethnic pride with health and social outcomes among young Black and Latino men after release from jail. *Youth and Society* 49, 8, 1057–1076.

U.S. Department of Health and Human Services, Office of Disease Prevention and Health Promotion. *Healthy People 2030*. Available: https://health.gov/healthypeople/objectives-and-data/social-determinants-health.

U.S. Government Accountability Office. (2005). *Drug Offenders: Various Factors May Limit the Impacts of Federal Laws That Provide for Denial of Selected Benefits*. Available: https://www.gao.gov/products/gao-05-238.

Valverde, J. (2021, July 27). Remarks made before the Committee. Committee on Evaluating Success Among People Released from Prison, Meeting #2: Public Information Gathering Session. Washington, DC: National Academies of Sciences, Engineering, and Medicine.

Van Voorhis, P., Wright, E.M., Salisbury, E., and Bauman, A. (2010). Women's risk factors and their contributions to existing risk/needs assessment: The current role of a gender responsive supplement. *Criminal Justice and Behavior* 37, 3, 261–288.

Visher, C.A., and Courtney, S.M. (2006). *Cleveland Prisoners' Experiences Returning Home*. Washington, DC: Urban Institute.

Visher, C.A., Kachnowski, V., La Vigne, N.G., and Travis, J. (2004). *Baltimore Prisoners' Experiences Returning Home*. Washington, DC: Urban Institute. Available: https://www.urban.org/research/publication/baltimore-prisoners-experiences-returning-home.

Visher, C.A., and La Vigne, N. (2021). Returning home: A pathbreaking study of prisoner reentry and its challenges. In *Handbook on Corrections and Sentencing, Volume 5: Moving Corrections and Sentencing Forward: Building on the Record*. New York: Routledge. 2021.

Visher, C.A., and Mallik-Kane, K. (2007). Reentry experiences of men with health problems, 434–460 in *Public Health Behind Bars*, R. Greifinger, ed. Springer, New York, NY.

Visher, C.A., and Travis, J. (2003). Transitions from prison to community: Understanding individual pathways. *Annual Review of Sociology* 29, 89–113.

Visher, C.A., Winterfield, L., and Coggeshall, M.B. (2005). Ex-offender employment programs and recidivism: A meta-analysis. *Journal of Experimental Criminology* 1, 3, 295–315. Available: https://doi.org/10.1007/s11292-005-8127-x.

Vitale, A.S. (2017). *The End of Policing*. Verso Books.

Vuolo, M., Schneider, L.E., and Laplant, E.G. (2022). Surveillance and the experience of the COVID-19 pandemic for formerly incarcerated individuals. *Punishment & Society* (February 2022). Available:10.1177/14624745221080696.

Wacquant, L. (2010). Class, race and hyperincarceration in revanchist America. *Daedalus* 139, 3, 74–90.

Wakefield, S., and Uggen, C. (2010). Incarceration and stratification. *Annual Review of Sociology*, 36, 387–406.

Walker, S.C., and Bishop, A.S. (2016). Length of stay, therapeutic change, and recidivism for incarcerated juvenile offenders. *Journal of Offender Rehabilitation* 55, 6, 355–376.

Wallace, D. (2015). Do neighborhood organizational resources impact recidivism? *Sociological Inquiry* 85, 2, 285–308.

Wallace, D., and Papachristos, A.V. (2014). Recidivism and the availability of health care organizations. *Justice Quarterly* 31, 3, 588–608.

Wallace, D., and Wang, X. (2020). Does in-prison physical and mental health impact recidivism? *SSM-population Health* 11, 100569.

Waller, E. (2000). Disjunction and integration in prison education. In D. Wilson and A. Ruess, *Prisoner(er) Education: Stories of Change and Transformation*, 106–173. Winchester: Waterside Press. 106–137.

Wang, E.A., Pletcher, M., and Lin, F. (2009). Incarceration, incident hypertension, and access to health care: Findings from the coronary artery risk development in young adults (CARDIA) study. *Archives of Internal Medicine* 169, 7, 687–693. doi:10.1001/archinternmed.2009.

Warr, M. (1998). Life-course transitions and desistance from crime. *Criminology* 36, 2, 183–216.

Wattanaporn, K.A., and Holtfreter, K. (2014). The impact of feminist pathways research on gender-responsive policy and practice. *Feminist Criminology* 9, 3, 191–207.

Weaver, B. (2019). Understanding desistance: A critical review of theories of desistance. *Psychology, Crime & Law* 25, 6, 641–658.

Weaver, V.M., and Lerman, A.E. (2010). Political consequences of the carceral state. *American Political Science Review* 104, 4, 817–833.

Wehrman, M.M. (2010). Race, concentrated disadvantage, and recidivism: A test of interaction effects. *Journal of Criminal Justice* 38, 4, 538–544.

Western, B. (2006). *Punishment and Inequality in America*. Russell Sage Foundation.

Western, B. (2018). *Homeward: Life in the Year After Prison*. Russell Sage Foundation.

Western, B., Braga, A.A., Davis, J., and Sirois, C. (2015). Stress and hardship after prison. *American Journal of Sociology* 120, 5, 1512–1547.

Western, B., and Simes, J.T. (2019). Drug use in the year after prison. *Social Science & Medicine* 235, 112357.

Western, B., and Smith, N. (2018). Formerly incarcerated parents and their children. *Demography* 55, 3, 823–847.

Wilkerson, I. (2020). *Caste: The Origins of Our Discontents*. Random House.

Wilkins, E.J., Whiting, J.B., Watson, M.F., Russon, J.M., and Moncrief, A.M. (2013). Residual effects of slavery: What clinicians need to know. *Contemporary Family Therapy* 35, 14–28.

Williams, K. (2015). *Our Enemies in Blue: Police and Power in America*. Oakland: AK.

Williams, J.M., Wilson, S.K., and Bergeson, C. (2019). It's hard out here if you're a Black felon: Critical examination of Black male reentry. *The Prison Journal* 99, 4, 437–458.

Wilson, W. (1987). *The Truly Disadvantaged*. Chicago: University of Chicago Press.

Wilson, W.J. (1996). *When Work Disappears: The World of the New Urban Poor*. New York, NY: Knopf.

Wilson, B.D., Choi, S.K., Harper, G.W., Lightfoot, M., Russell, S., and Meyer, I.H. (2020). *Homelessness among LGBT Adults in the US*. UCLA School of Law, Williams Institute. https://williamsinstitute.law.ucla.edu/publications/lgbt-homelessness-us/.

Wilson, D.J. (2000). *Drug Use, Testing, and Treatment in Jails*. NCJ 179999. Washington, DC: Bureau of Justice Statistics.

Wilson, B.D.M, Bouton, L., and Mallory, C. (2022). *Racial Differences Among LGBT Adults in the US: LGBT Well-Being at the Intersection of Race*. UCLA School of Law: Williams Institute.

Winkler, A. (1993). Expressive voting. *New York University Law Review* 68, 330–388.

Wo, J.C., Hipp, J.R., and Boessen, A. (2016). Voluntary organizations and neighborhood crime: A dynamic perspective. *Criminology* 54, 2, 212–241.

Wo, J.C., and Park, J. (2019). Places not cases? Rethinking probation: The effects of nonprofit organizations on rearrest rates of probationers. *Crime and Delinquency* 65, 5, 657–680.

Wodahl, E.J. (2006). The Challenges of Prisoner Reentry from a Rural Perspective. *Western Criminology Review* 7, 2.

Wodahl, E.J., Garland, B., Culhane, S.E., and McCarty, W.P. (2011). Utilizing behavioral interventions to improve supervision outcomes in community-based corrections. *Criminal Justice and Behavior* 38, 4, 386–405.

Wodahl, E.J., and Freng, A. (2017). The challenges of prisoner reentry faced by Native American returning offenders. *Journal of Ethnicity in Criminal Justice* 15, 2, 160–184.

Wolff, K.T., Baglivio, M.T., Intravia, J., and Piquero, A.R. (2015). The protective impact of immigrant concentration on juvenile recidivism: A statewide analysis of youth offenders. *Journal of Criminal Justice* 43, 6, 522–531.

Wolff, N., Shi, J., and Siegel, J. (2009). Patterns of victimization among male and female inmates: Evidence of an enduring legacy. *Violence and Victims*, 24, 4, 469–484.

Wong, K., and Horan, R. (2019). Early testing and formative evaluation of the enablers of change. *European Journal of Probation* 11, 1, 30–48.

Woodward, C.V. (1955). *The Strange Career of Jim Crow*. New York: Oxford University Press.

Wright, K.A. (2020). Time well spent: Misery, meaning, and the opportunity of incarceration. *The Howard Journal of Crime and Justice* 59, 1, 44–64.

Wright, K.A., and Rodriguez, N. (2014). A closer look at the paradox: Examining immigration and youth reoffending in Arizona. *Justice Quarterly* 31, 5, 882–904.

Wright, K.A., Morse, S.J, and Sutton, M.M. (2021). The limits of recidivism reduction: Advancing a more comprehensive understanding of correctional success. In J. Gould and P. Metzger (Eds.), *Big Ideas in Criminal Justice Reform*. New York, NY: New York University Press.

Yang, C.S. (2017). Local labor markets and criminal recidivism. *Journal of Public Economics* 147, 16–29.

Yoon, I.A., Slade, K., and Fazel, S. (2017). Outcomes of psychological therapies for prisoners with mental health problems: A systematic review and meta-analysis. *Journal of Consulting and Clinical Psychology* 8, 783–802.

Young, S., González, R.A., Mullens, H., Mutch, L., Malet-Lambert, I., and Gudjonsson, G.H. (2018). Neurodevelopmental disorders in prison inmates: Comorbidity and combined associations with psychiatric symptoms and behavioural disturbance. *Psychiatry Research* 261, 109–115.

Zajac, G., Hutchison, R., and Meyer, C.A. (2013). *An Examination of Rural Prisoner Reentry Challenges*. Justice Center for Research. Pennsylvania State University.

Zamble, E., and Quinsey, V.L. (1997). *The Process of Criminal Recidivism*. Cambridge, UK.

Zemore, S.E., Kaskutas, L.A., and Ammon, L.N. (2004). In 12-step groups, helping helps the helper. *Addiction* 99, 8, 1015–1023.

Ziegelheim, D. (2018). Grassroots organizations are leading the way on justice reform. *Pacific Standard*, Available: https://psmag.com/social-justice/the-grassroots-organizations-leading-criminal-justice-reform, accessed September 2021.

Zweig, J.M., Yahner, J., Visher, C.A., and Lattimore, P.K. (2015). Using general strain theory to explore the effects of prison victimization experiences on later offending and substance use. *The Prison Journal* 95, 1, 84–113.

4

Measuring Success Beyond Recidivism

Behavioral change is a multifaceted process shaped by structural, institutional, and environmental contexts. Hence, it is unreasonable to expect that a single behavioral indicator can truly identify whether an individual has "succeeded" or "failed" in making a transition from prison to the community. Moreover, the transition to a prosocial lifestyle will likely be different for different individuals. Individuals are likely to vary as to which behaviors are more or less important for their overall reintegration. This perspective was one of the most consistent themes of the committee's listening session with those with lived experiences in making a transition from prison to the community.

Previous research and practice have not sufficiently recognized the importance of individual differences in understanding pathways to successful reintegration, and there is a dearth of literature reflecting the voices of criminal legal system (CLS) involved individuals in understanding markers of success. Measures of success for this population would be better-informed and more effective if official sources of recidivism were supplemented by the point of view of the individuals themselves and the way they view success. Such a conceptual shift in measuring success would then include domains that are referred to in other literatures as the social determinants of health, such as an individual's economic stability, health status, housing conditions and living environment, educational needs, and the broader social and community context of which they are a part (See Box 4-1).

139

BOX 4-1
Listening Session: Partnering with Individuals with
Lived Experience in Reentry Research and Programming

During a public information-gathering session held by the Committee on Evaluating Success Among People Released from Prison, practitioners and those with lived experience emphasized that those who have been formerly incarcerated have often been omitted from the process of research question development, study execution, and data analysis and dissemination. This is true of studies of recidivism. Centering research on those with lived experience adds crucial insight into what works and what does not, creates opportunities for meaningful work for those with direct experience, and may build trust in communities where generations of neglect and harmful actions have built a foundation of earned distrust (Israel et al., 1998).

Kara Nelson, Director of Public Relations and Development at True North Recovery: "We have to be at the table. We aren't just redemption stories, we're leaders who have something to say and something to offer and we will be the ones with the solutions to make that change."

Sam Lewis, Executive Director of Anti-Recidivism Coalition: "I say this with all due respect. There needs to be a lot more people who were formerly incarcerated—I don't describe myself as directly impacted, I was formerly incarcerated—in the world of academia."

Susan Burton, Founder of A New Way of Life Reentry Center: "The program and the participants need to define what success means, and [we] need to collect [qualitative] data around that."

Venus Woods, Director of HIV Prevention and Education with the Alaskan AIDS Assistance Program: "I also agree that successful reentry programming has to be set by the person that was incarcerated. I think that there's no one-size-fits-all-solution to reentry programming. . . . People that have been in prison need to be the ones making decisions for their programming."

SOURCE: See Committee on Evaluating Success Among People Released from Prison Meeting #2: Public Information Gathering Session (July 27–28, 2021). Session 1: https://www.nationalacademies.org/event/07-27-2021/evaluating-success-among-people-released-from-prison-meeting-2-public-information-gathering-session-1. Session 2: https://www.nationalacademies.org/event/07-28-2021/evaluating-success-among-people-released-from-prison-meeting-2-public-information-gathering-session-2.

Research on reentry experiences indicates that most individuals transitioning from incarceration need time to adapt to an identity as a prosocial community member who is living and positively interacting in their community. Desistance from criminal activity is increasingly understood as a process and it is possible, even likely, that individuals who are successful in one area at the same time face challenges in another area. For example, individuals may be engaged in a job training program but also experience a relapse to substance use. Or a person may have reunited with their children and family and engaged with health care providers yet be unable to find a job. Signaling theory can be used to help identify individuals who are in the process of desisting from criminal behavior (Bushway and Apel, 2012). As discussed in Chapter 3, greater attention to incremental indicators of individual success (as opposed to failure) may help to identify markers of desistance (Andersen et al., 2020). These indicators encompass more than criminal legal system involvement, but also progress in other domains such as health, housing, employment, education, social relationships, and civic and community life.

Further, the path to reintegration for individuals is also shaped by broader structural and contextual conditions. Post-release success is also affected by the supports or obstacles that individuals face within prison and in the community. As oral reports gathered by the Committee suggest and as discussed in Chapter 3, being in prison can be a turning point and facilitate desistance, but this depends on the prison environment and supports within prison (Wright, 2020). Individuals assigned to maximum security or restricted movement are ineligible for programming, and interpersonal contact, including with visitors, is reduced (Crittenden and Koons-Witt, 2017; Gaes and Camp, 2009; Mears and Bales, 2009). Once released, individuals face monetary sanctions, the conditions of supervision, and the collateral consequences of incarceration. Often these post-release circumstances impede successful post-release trajectories and also have disproportionate effects on Black and Latinx individuals (see National Research Council, 2014).

Previous research and comments during the committee's listening session indicate that the importance of community and structural factors that shape successful reintegration has not been recognized sufficiently by researchers and evaluators (see Box 4-2 below). Success following incarceration cannot be understood without attention to the social and environmental context to which people return. For example, if people are returning to communities where the unemployment rate is high at baseline (Western, 2006), how likely is it that they will find a job? If the nearest opioid treatment program is more than 60 minutes away, how will they manage their addiction (Joudrey, Edelman, and Wang, 2019)? Without understanding how community contextual factors shape an individual's return from prison, policy makers, service providers, and communities miss opportunities to increase the likelihood of success following release from prison.

This chapter begins with a review of the state of the science around evidence-based correctional and reentry-focused programs on post-release outcomes, with attention to the most pressing needs facing the field. The next

BOX 4-2
Listening Session: Social Context, Structural
Conditions, and Post-Release Success

During a public information-gathering session held by the Committee on Evaluating Success Among People Released from Prison, practitioners and those with lived experience spoke to the impact of social ties and structural conditions on reentry success.

George Braucht, co-founder of the Certified Addiction Recovery Empowerment Specialist Academy: "It's about pushing through the idea that the problem is solely within the individual. Behavior is always a function of the interaction between people and their environment. It's building places, community, and having people have a sense of really being valued and belong within community . . ." (Braucht, 2021).

John Valverde, President and CEO of Youthbuild USA: "Structural injustice exits and has done multi-generational harm to people living in poverty and on the margins, especially people of color. And that criminal justice involvement is intricately connected to this. The barriers to success can feel insurmountable to some people and those barriers are real" (Valverde, 2021).

Sam Lewis, Executive Director of the Anti Recidivism Coalition: "When a person comes home from incarceration, you're trying to fit back into society and you need to feel like you're welcome. And often because of all of the stereotypes that go along with it, and the red scarlet letter, and the boxes you have to check, make you feel like you're not part of society. But if you have a community of people who have gone through the same thing you've gone through and overcome those things, then you know you can do it too. And not only that but should you stumble and fall you have a community that is going to reach down and lift you up and walk with you and tell you we can overcome these barriers together and we've got your back. That makes you feel comfortable and as you progress with your transition from incarceration you become comfortable knowing that you not only belong to this community but you belong to a broader community" (Lewis, 2021).

section addresses broader approaches to evaluation, offering suggestions that can be applied to the measurement of success across different life domains. We build on Chapter 3's discussion of how larger structural and community contexts shape post-release success and offer specific measures that account for structural and community contexts. A brief discussion of the value of self-report data follows. We then consider alternatives to official measures of recidivism as indicators of post-release success, including proposed measures of criminal desistance.

Finally, the chapter turns to research on the measurement of overall well-being as a more holistic, multidimensional, and person-centered measure of post-release progress. This includes a review of research on indicators in specific domains that could be used as complementary or alternative measures of progress. Domains discussed include physical and mental health status, housing status, employment, educational attainment, civic and community engagement, and social relationships with family, peers, and other social supports. The chapter concludes with a discussion of research needs to improve the measurement of post-release outcomes for criminal legal system-involved individuals, with attention to needs for shared data collection standards and data sharing across policy domains.

THE STATE OF THE SCIENCE: EVIDENCE-BASED REHABILITATION AND REENTRY

Within corrections, a significant research focus in the 2000s has been what Francis Cullen has called "reaffirming rehabilitation" through science (Cullen and Gilbert, 2012; Cullen and Gendreau, 2000; 2001). Research emphasizing what works in rehabilitation programming, including meta-analyses of previous and more contemporary correctional programs, has aimed to develop knowledge to help policy makers and practitioners choose evidence-based reentry programs (Sherman et al., 2006; Weisburd, Farrington, and Gill, 2017; Wilson, Gallagher, and MacKenzie, 2000).[1] Evaluations in this vein using randomized controlled trial methodology have found that substance abuse treatment, cognitive behavioral therapy, and some educational programs are effective approaches to reducing recidivism as measured by official records of rearrest, reconviction, and reincarceration (Doleac, 2018; Lacoe and Betesh, 2019; MacKenzie, 2006; Moore et al., 2019; Visher et al., 2017). Despite at least a decade of evaluation on employment-focused interventions such as transitional jobs, job readiness, or job training connected to immediate employment, such programming only minimally affects longer-term employment and has little effect on official measures of recidivism (Lacoe and Betesh, 2019; Muhlhausen, 2015), although it is likely that conceptual and measurement issues hinder stronger conclusions.

Reentry programming faces a number of pressing challenges. One key area of correctional programming is discharge planning or specific programming to help individuals transition from prison to the community (La Vigne et al., 2008). However, despite decades of discussion that "reentry begins at prison entry" (Wilkinson, Rhine, and Henderson-Hurly, 2005),

---

[1] See https://crimesolutions.ojp.gov/.

reentry planning and programming in prison is often not initiated until a few months before release. Such in-prison reentry programming is rarely adequate for the needs of people returning from incarceration (Duwe, 2018; Wilkinson, Rhine, Henderson-Hurly, 2005) and seldom acknowledges the structural barriers and community contexts to which people return.

In addition, despite the diverse needs facing individuals after release from prison (highlighted in Chapter 3), correctional programming is often narrowly focused. For example, reentry programs commonly focus solely on job training or substance use, or are only situated in the criminal legal system without considering how other social support or "safety net" systems act as important agents of success following prison release (Hawks et al., 2021). Connections are lacking between correctional systems and the community service agencies that provide substantial assistance to criminal legal system-involved individuals (Byrne, 2019; Muhlhausen, 2015; Shavit et al., 2017; Visher, 2007).

Correctional programming has also been insufficiently attentive to the heterogeneity of criminal legal system-involved individuals, particularly women, racial and ethnic minorities, and other distinct subgroups. The depth of challenges these populations face, described in Chapter 3, sometimes including persisting poverty and disadvantage dating back to childhood (Western, 2018), makes it particularly important to develop individualized approaches to reentry and community reintegration. Also, scholars have recommended that effective in-prison programming and evaluation requires attention to program dosage, timing, and sequencing (Duwe, 2018; Visher, 2007; Wilkinson, Rhine, and Henderson-Hurly, 2005). As discussed in Chapter 3, the use of peer mentors and other supportive relationships can also improve the delivery of reentry and correctional programming.

Reentry and transition from incarceration back to the community is best conceived as a process, one that can begin in prison but continues with services and other support in the community, especially in the first six months after release (Latessa, Johnson, and Koetzle, 2020). Better analytic methods are needed for modeling these processes longitudinally, including measures of incremental progress. People exiting prison face a host of challenges, and many reentry programs attempt to develop multicomponent or wrap-around service models to address their numerous needs. However, these approaches are difficult to evaluate and may require longer follow-up periods (Doleac, 2019; Lattimore, 2020; Lindquist, Willison, and Lattimore, 2021).

Other reentry and rehabilitation approaches, such as reentry courts, swift-certain-fair supervision (Cullen, Pratt, and Turanovic, 2017; Lattimore et al., 2016), and comprehensive approaches, such as programs funded by the Second Chance Act, have shown limited impacts on post-release outcomes, including substance-use relapse, rearrest, or reincarceration (Bitney et al., 2017; D'Amico and Kim, 2016; Lindquist, Willison, and Lattimore, 2021). A common result in reentry program evaluations is that individuals do receive more services, but reentry outcomes do not improve. However, historically, the evaluation literature on correctional programming has been tied to the inadequate measures of repeated contact with the criminal legal system that were discussed in Chapter 2. Rare are the studies that have linked program evaluations for justice-involved individuals to broader measures of desistance and reintegration (Wright et al., 2021; Hawks et al., 2021).

Even rarer are studies that acknowledge the community and structural contexts to which people come home (Puglisi, 2021). The science of measuring success following release has, by and large, not taken into account the realities of the communities to which people return. Yet people's pathway to success following release, even if understood as heterogeneous and evolving over the life course, cannot be accurately measured without accounting for community and structural factors, including racism. (For an example of work accounting for racism and health inequities from a life course perspective, see Gee, Walsemann, and Brondolo, 2012.) Neighborhoods vary significantly in terms of availability of employment, health care, and housing opportunities, which makes these places even more difficult for minority populations (National Research Council, 2014; Western, 2006). The community context includes both the general environment to which people return and also the resources an individual has been offered (or has access to). Measuring this context which can be difficult, given that public services lack coordination, their record keeping systems lack compatibility, and their accessibility is often restricted for people with felony records, either directly through laws or policies or indirectly through discriminatory practices. This makes it difficult or impossible to measure the challenges or successes of individuals returning from incarceration as they navigate the health care system, secure housing and employment, and obtain access to welfare benefits (Chen and Meyer, 2020; Wang et al., 2019).

Thus, despite substantial progress in the past two decades on understanding the challenges facing people released from prison and their pathways to desistance and reintegration, U.S. research on the topic seems to have reached a critical moment (Jonson and Cullen, 2015). Current methods of evaluation do not serve the most pressing needs of policy makers and reentry practitioners. The barriers to reintegration are clear—a 2000s study of the longitudinal studies of individuals' transitions from prison to the community conducted by the Urban Institute and RTI International in the early 2000s find similar obstacles facing returning citizens and high rates of continued involvement with the criminal legal system (Harding, Morenoff, and Wyse, 2019; Western et al., 2015; Western, 2018).

What appears to be lacking is measurement grounded in a theory of change and specification of causal mechanisms that have been rigorously tested (Lindquist, Willison, and Lattimore, 2021, p. 353). Logic models that predict that reentry programming will influence intermediate outcomes, such as employment, stable housing, and substance use, which will then facilitate desistance and reintegration have not been validated (Lattimore, 2020; Mulhausen, 2015). Thus, better measures of reentry outcomes could address a critical need in rehabilitative and reentry programming (Butts and Schiraldi, 2018). Further development and testing of the possible theoretical frameworks in Chapter 3 of this report are needed to make progress on this front (see Box 4-3).

NEW APPROACHES TO MEASUREMENT: CONTEXTUAL CONDITIONS AND DATA COLLECTION

This section considers broader shifts in approach to evaluating success. Specifically, it considers the role of contextual conditions in shaping post-release outcomes and the value of self-report and qualitative data in informing the evaluation of success. These shifts in approach could be productively applied to efforts to measure success in the domains discussed in the following sections.

As detailed in Chapter 3, community and macro-level contexts play an important role in shaping post-release outcomes. Communities vary widely in the strength of their social networks and in the resources that are available to individuals returning from incarceration. Reintegration is supported by a return to communities that are characterized by ample access to basic resources and services and strong supportive community networks, and it is undermined by a return to neighborhoods characterized by inequality and socioeconomic disadvantage (Kubrin and Weitzer, 2003; Simes, 2018; Visher and Travis, 2005). There are also important differences in how community and macro-level impacts shape the success of Black and Latino/a individuals, who are more likely to return to neighborhoods that lack cohesion and material resources (Kubrin, Squires, and Stewart, 2007; National Research Council, 2014). Finally, as explained in Chapter 3, particular groups also experience special reentry needs. For example, formerly incarcerated women are more likely than men to have been primary caregivers for their children before incarceration, and they generally place a higher priority on reunification with children following their release (Giordano, Cernkovich, and Rudolph, 2002; Glaze and Maruschak, 2016; Richie, 2001).

Similarly, given racial and ethnic health inequalities and the disproportionate incarceration of Black, Latino/a, and Indigenous communities, success for people, particularly people belonging to these communities, will

---

BOX 4-3
Listening Session:
Defining Reentry Success, and the Need for Resources

Formerly incarcerated individuals, policy practitioners, and scholarly experts who participated in the committee's information-gathering sessions discussed their definitions of success in reentry and how context and access to resources shape successful reintegration.

John Valverde, President and CEO of Youthbuild USA: "For me, success is not about being out of prison and struggling to survive—or out of prison but homeless, unemployed, living in constant fear of judgment and rejection from the world—or addicted to substances and without a network of support of caring positive people." (Valverde, 2021)

John Valverde, President and CEO of Youthbuild USA: "As I said earlier [success] really isn't about just surviving. It's about the sense of belonging and feeling you can contribute to society that you're accepted. Even as a CEO of a global organization, when I moved from NY to Boston I was denied my first apartment because I had to check the box. Even though I was on TV and there were press releases and they knew who I was they said we cannot set a precedent and allow a formerly incarcerated person to live in this community. It's real even for people who have overcome so much. Imagine for those who don't have the opportunities that some of us have had."

Kara Nelson, Director of Public Relations and Development at True North Recovery: "To me, success is better quality of life. Can just be basic needs, getting access to food then looking at housing, peer support, education, employment comes later after basic needs get met." (Nelson, 2021)

Walter Strauss, (retired) New York City Housing Court Judge: "I think the way we have a system now is that someone is incarcerated and then they're suddenly released and then if it's an agency or individuals or a group [reentry program] it's all—'okay here's this individual and now you make them whole again.' It's like starting from scratch. . . . [returning citizens] need more intensive counseling, more assistance in finding housing, in finding jobs, in dealing with discrimination." (Strauss, 2021)

SOURCE: See Committee on Evaluating Success Among People Released from Prison Meeting #2: Public Information Gathering Session (July 27, 28, 2021). Session 1: https://www. nationalacademies.org/event/07-27-2021/evaluating-success-among-people-released-from-prison-meeting-2-public-information-gathering-session-1.

be shaped by systemic inequalities in exposure to barriers and access to resources (Bailey, Feldman, and Bassett, 2021; Churchwell et al., 2020). Evidence has shown that racial disparities not only impact economic and social opportunities, but also produce trauma, harms to psychosocial health, and poor coping behaviors while also weakening access to health care and to political inclusion (Bailey et al., 2017). A Black individual returning to a community with discriminatory policies that further stigmatize and marginalize individuals with incarceration histories is much more likely to struggle to achieve a successful return from incarceration than the same individual would be if returning to a community without such policies. Indeed, some analysts have argued that the entire system developed to help individuals succeed is heavily influenced by structural conditions that impede success (Ortiz and Jackey, 2019).

Evaluating how well institutions and organizations act as facilitators of success following release is essential, especially evaluating how the systems that provide health care, food, transportation, education, and employment support the needs of recently released individuals. Linking data from correctional systems to other administrative data from within state and local government could provide further understanding of how different sectors support the success of individuals following release (Willoughby et al., 2021). Studies have linked data from correctional systems and health systems or payors and used measures such as "preventable hospitalizations" as an indicator of the quality and accessibility of primary care for individuals leaving incarceration (Wang, Wang, and Krumholz, 2013). Low rates of preventable hospitalizations among people just released from correctional facilities could indicate success, from the perspective of the health care system, in caring for this population. Other studies have linked data from correctional systems to opioid overdose databases and cancer tumor registries, which indicates how data linkages can provide windows into how health systems can better serve people who are being released from prison (Krawczyk et al., 2020; Puglisi et al., 2021). To be sure, these administrative linkages would need to be carefully designed and monitored with input from individuals with a history of incarceration to avoid additional surveillance leading to repeat encounters with the criminal legal system. Modern day examples of cross-system surveillance are numerous (see Brayne, 2014; Harada et al., 2021). For example, they include individuals being arrested at methadone treatment centers as well as the case of Operation Talon, where people obtaining food stamps were first screened for pending arrests (Gustafson, 2009).

In summary, communities may lack the resources to help individuals succeed after prison, and these contextual circumstances are rarely accounted for in current observational and intervention studies of people released from prison. Individual success (and failure) for individuals returning from prison results from a combination of individual behaviors and decisions, their social context, and the systemic supports or barriers they face. Thus, measures of success are incomplete if they fail to capture a holistic understanding of an individual's surroundings, particularly whether the neighborhood they live in has the resources and supports to facilitate success, if the place they return to has policies and practices that actively prohibit their progress and eventual desistance after incarceration, and lastly if the organizations and institutions which provide these resources and supports, such as health care systems or safety net structures, are attentive to or dismissive of their needs. Metrics of progress following release that do not account for whether an individual's surroundings will facilitate or deter their successful reintegration are inadequate.

Methods for Measuring Community and Structural Conditions

The most effective measures of success following release from prison include measures of the structural and social context of the communities to which people return, both for understanding what facilitates success and for identifying interventions that promote individual and community well-being. To start, recording the residential address (as is available in administrative data) or zip code of returning individuals within intervention studies and program evaluations will enable a broader understanding of how a person's community and structural factors affect the potentiality of success following release (Chambers et al., 2018; Vilda et al., 2021).

Having participant-level residential address data enables linkages to existing small-area measures of the structural and social context of communities, such as the Area Deprivation Index (ADI). The ADI allows census tracts to be compared by socioeconomic disadvantages based on income, education, employment, and housing (Kind and Buckingham, 2018; Link and Phelan, 1995; Ludwig et al., 2011). A growing literature in the health services field shows that a community's ADI is associated with health utilization (Kind and Buckingham, 2018) and is a stronger (or as strong as) predictor of health outcomes as individual-level characteristics (Powell et al., 2020). For example, in a national sample of Medicare patients with severe health conditions (congestive heart failure, pneumonia, or myocardial infraction), ADI is associated with more rehospitalizations in 30 days in the most disadvantaged places (Kind et al., 2014), even after adjusting for individual-level factors. This finding has been corroborated with other research showing that those living in the most disadvantaged places based on ADI are 70 percent more likely to be readmitted to the hospital compared to those in the least disadvantaged places (Hu, Kind, and Nerenz, 2018). Similar analyses for studying outcomes among persons released from prison could reveal important geographic patterns of post-release success and failure. (Further discussion of this issue appears in the section on "Research Needs" below.)

In addition to offering a richer, more accurate measurement of success, measures that account for local disadvantage and structural context could also result in more effective prison- and community-based interventions (Kubrin and Stewart, 2006). In one of the committee's information-gathering sessions, Nneka Jones-Tapia, managing director of Justice Initiatives at Chicago Beyond and former warden of the Cook County jail, discussed the need for measures of community capacity, noting the need for resources and programs to support individuals returning from incarceration (Jones-Tapia, 2021). University of North Carolina public health professor and former public health practitioner Dana Rice emphasized the need to supplement measurements of individual success with indicators of social determinants of health such as community cohesion, health care access, quality education, economic stability, and features of the built environment. It is especially worth noting that given persistent racial and ethnic inequalities in health, education, and employment, and especially the disproportionate incarceration of Black, Brown, and Indigenous populations, success for people belonging to these communities returning home from incarceration will vary by how intensely these inequalities are embedded within each of these systems and the community at large (Rice, 2021).

Finally, measuring and evaluating an individual's success within the context of their community supports and (especially) structural barriers for historically marginalized populations released from corrections requires that researchers recognize how race and ethnicity are being measured and operationalized in studies. In quantitative studies, self-identified race is used as a confounder, implying that a person's race is associated with the probability of success, as opposed to self-identified race being seen as an indirect proxy of embedded inequalities and a root cause for health inequities or inequities in success following release. This, in the words of Boyd and colleagues (2020) "renders racism less visible and thus less accessible as a preventable etiology of inequity." To avoid the quantitative erasure of this crucial aspect of mass incarceration, the explicit operationalization of race and ethnicity in studies is needed; it is needed, that is, both to be concrete about racism's outsized role in success following release and also to illuminate opportunities for intervention (Krieger, 2000).

New Approaches to Data Collection: Self-Report Data

Improving the evaluation of success for individuals released from prison will benefit from changes in approach, in addition to new metrics. One prominent area for such improvement is in data collection itself. In many instances, subjective measures of success from individual self-reports may be more informative than objective measures gathered from officially recorded data. In order to both center experiences of formerly incarcerated people in the measurement of success and also use more holistic measures of individual success, we draw on both administrative data and self-reported indicators of each domain of success, including individual well-being, health, education, employment, civic engagement, and social relationships. As mentioned previously, this represents a conceptual shift in research, moving away from using only administrative or expert-ascertained data and instead anchoring the design and implementation of programs, services, and policies in measures of success that are better suited to capture individual perceptions of well-being, health, and quality of life in other domains.

ALTERNATIVE INDICATORS OF SUCCESS

A shift in approach is needed to move researchers, practitioners, and policy makers beyond the conceptually limited definitions of success that focus solely on criminal legal system involvement (recidivism) or even on criminal behavior (desistance). As previously discussed, the vast majority of the research on individual transitions from criminal activity to a prosocial identity, including transitions from prison to the community, focuses on measures of failure, principally official measures of recontact with the criminal legal system. Studies of desistance from crime illuminate other outcomes that correlate with desistance processes including cognitive changes, conventional ties (e.g., family, employment, prosocial peers), and sobriety (Bachman et al., 2013; Butts and Schiraldi, 2018; Lattimore, Dawes, and Barrick, 2018; Paternoster et al., 2016; Sampson and Laub, 1993; 2003). For people leaving prison to achieve personal well-being, avoid contact with the criminal legal system, and become productive citizens, studies may also need to capture engagement with multiple other domains, including health care, housing, education, employment, and social and community integration. However, rigorous research on the measures of individual progress within these domains is rather limited (Butts and Schiraldi, 2018). The need for multidimensional, holistic measures of success following release from prison leads us to a measure of overall well-being as an important indicator of individual success. In this section, we discuss existing measures of well-being, proposed measures of criminal desistance, and how measures of success in other domains could be constructed. In addition, the text refers to Table 4-1, which presents suggestions for alternate measures of individual outcomes that could be used in various circumstances, including probation officers' progress reports, research on individual post-release trajectories, and evaluation studies on the effectiveness of reentry programs.

TABLE 4-1 Subjective and Objective Measures of Post-Release Success

Individual Level Measures

Domain	Subjective Measures	Objective Measures	Notes
Overall Well-being	Cantril Self-Anchoring Striving Scale 100 Million Healthier Lives* Well-Being in the Nation*	N/A	*Includes the individual domains of physical health, mental health, spiritual support, financial support, and social support
Health			
Overall Health	MOS-1 In general, would you say your health is (Excellent, Very Good, Good, Fair, Poor)	N/A	
Mental Health Disorder	Depression, PHQ-9 or PHQ-2; Post-Traumatic Stress Disorder, Primary Care Post Traumatic Stress Disorder Screen	Can be ascertained with International Classification of Diseases (ICD-10) codes and pharmacy records in electronic health records or administrative claims	
Substance Use Disorder	Addiction Severity Index Subjective self-report item: Compared to 1 year ago (or other time frame), do you engage in more, less, or about the same amount of alcohol and substance use?	Can be ascertained with ICD10 codes and pharmacy records in electronic health records or administrative claims	Avoid using urine drug screen as singular measure of relapse
Engagement in Health Care	Is there a place that {you/someone} usually {go/goes} when {you are/he/she is} sick or {you/s/he} need{s} advice about {your/his/her} health? {What kind of place is it—a clinic, doctor's office, emergency room, or some other place?} {What kind of place {do you/do they} go to most often—a clinic, doctor's office, emergency room, or some other place?}	Administrative claims data, All-payor databases. ICD10 codes also enable measurement of emergency department visits or hospitalizations that are preventable with engagement in primary care	Measures drawn from the National Health Interview Survey, National Health and Nutrition Examination Survey, and CDC Hospital Utilization and Access to Care Questionnaire

{During the past 12 months, how/How} many times {have you/have they} seen a doctor or other health care professional about {your/his/her} health at a doctor's office, a clinic or some other place? Do not include times {you were/s/he was} hospitalized overnight, visits to hospital emergency rooms, home visits or telephone calls.

{During the past 12 months, were you/they a patient in a hospital overnight? Do not include an overnight stay in the emergency room.

How many different times did {you/they} stay in any hospital overnight or longer {during the past 12 months}? (Do not count total number of nights, just total number of hospital admissions for stays which lasted 1 or more nights.)

During the past 12 months, that is since {CURRENT MONTH} of {LAST YEAR}, {have you/they} seen or talked to a mental health professional such as a psychologist, psychiatrist, psychiatric nurse or clinical social worker about {your/his/her} health?

continued

TABLE 4-1 Continued

Individual Level Measures

Domain	Subjective Measures	Objective Measures	Notes
Housing and Homelessness	Item: Do you feel safe in your current housing? Item: Are you satisfied with your living arrangement? Item: Are you living in a private residence? Item: Are you living in a household with employed adults? Item: Do you expect to move within the next month? Item: How long do you expect to live where you are now?	From supervision records: Number of residential moves in specific time period Number of moves to institutional housing in specific time period Housing location (zip code)	Proposed items are suggestions and would need to be validated.
Employment and Job Retention	Item: Are you employed? Item: Is this a job you wish to keep? Item: Is your salary on this job enough to make ends meet? Item: How satisfied are you with your wage? Item: Are you learning new skills on this job? Item: How easy is it for you to get to and from work? Item: How long do you think you will stay at this job? Item: Do you go to work after drinking alcohol or using drugs? Item: Do you get along with your boss and co-workers?	Type of employment (FT, PT, occasional) Seasonality of employment Number of hours worked per week Work schedule (regular 9-5 job, irregular schedule) Hourly wage or annual salary Nature of pay (paycheck versus cash) Type of work (North American Industry Classification System codes and Standard Industrial Classification codes.) Class of worker (private company, government, self-employment, family business)	Proposed items are suggestions and would need to be validated.

	Item: Have you experienced any unfair treatment because of your criminal record?	List of benefits attached to job, if any	
	Item: Are there career opportunities with this job?	Length of time at current job	
	Item: Do you have any flexibility in your work schedule?	Distance between residence and workplace	
		Job satisfaction measures	
		Method of obtaining the job (application process, length of time searched, how found out about the job)	
		If not employed, job search activity	
Educational Attainment	Item: Do you desire additional education?	If no HS diploma, enrollment in GED/TASC prep course	Proposed items are suggestions and would need to be validated.
	Item: Have you asked for assistance in locating additional education options?	Completion of GED/TASC Completion of practice exams if no HS diploma	
	Item: Has someone helped you complete the necessary paperwork to engage in additional education? (i.e., FAFSA and application)	Enrollment in certification course	
		Completion of certification course	
	Item: Have you received assistance in securing funds needed to engage in additional education?	Enrollment in course(s) for college credit	
		Number of courses completed	
	Item: Is educational tutoring and/or mentoring available to you?	Attainment of degree (AA, BA, MA, PhD)	
		Number of certifications or degrees earned	

continued

TABLE 4-1 Continued

Individual Level Measures

Domain	Subjective Measures	Objective Measures	Notes
Social Relationships	Item: Do you feel close to your family? Item: Do you have friends you can go to if you need help? Item: Would a friend or family member loan you money if you needed it? Item: Do you have support from a faith community? Item: If you have children, how often do you play a caregiving or parental role? Item: What frequency of contact do you have with your children? Degree of connection to others for social support Receiving peer support Involvement in peer support groups	Medical Outcomes Study social support survey Positive Social Engagement—5 Key Model Positive Relationships—5 Key Model Engagement with children (scale) Responsible fathering (scale) Parent contact with children (scale)	Proposed items are suggestions and would need to be validated.
Civic Engagement	INDIVIDUAL-LEVEL ITEMS Item: Individual-level political efficacy (e.g., belief that "people like me have no say" about the government; "you get nowhere talking to public officials") Item: Individual-level importance of engagement in the community	INDIVIDUAL-LEVEL ITEMS Item: Political participation (turnout), gathered through self-reports and/or administrative records Item: Volunteering; type and time commitment to volunteer service Item: Attending rallies, demonstrations, and other political events	Proposed items are suggestions and would need to be validated.

	Item: Political engagement (self-reports of talking with partners, friends, and relatives about politics)		
	SYSTEM-LEVEL ITEMS		
	Legal restrictions on right to vote or other collateral sanctions limiting civic participation at the federal, state, and municipal level		
	Political participation (turnout) rates		
Neighborhood Context	Item: Do you feel safe in your neighborhood? Item: Is public transportation available in your neighborhood?	Residential Zip code	Zip code data enables measurement of neighborhood context: area deprivation index, census tract measures, housing segregation. Individual items would need to be validated.

continued

TABLE 4-1 Continued

Individual Level Measures

Domain	Subjective Measures	Objective Measures	Notes
Desistance	Subjective self-report item: Compared to 5 years ago, do you now do more, less, or about the same amount of these activities?	Self-reported item: Deceleration (of number activities reported in time interval)	Proposed items are suggestions and would need to be validated.
	Reference group self-report item: Compared to other people (your age; in your neighborhood; who have been to prison) do you think you do more, less, or about the same amount of these activities?	Self-reported item: De-escalation in the severity level of offense categories (e.g., movement away from violent activities)	
		Self-reported item: Cessation of criminal activity within broad offense categories over a follow-up period	
		Administrative data item: Deceleration in rate of convictions in time interval	
		Administrative data item: De-escalation in the severity level of convictions	
		Administrative data item:	
		Cessation or absence of criminal convictions over a follow-up period	

SOURCE: Table derived from analysis and discussion of the committee as a whole. See "Notes" column for references to specific existing instruments and direct sources.

Overall Well-Being

Well-being concerns whether people perceive that their lives are going well. Living conditions such as stable housing, meaningful employment, and safe neighborhoods are fundamental to well-being. How people think and feel about their lives is equally important, including the quality of their relationships, their emotions and resilience, their realization of their potential, and their overall satisfaction with life. As such, well-being holds promise as a positively framed metric that reflects an individual's current state of being with a focus on health and life satisfaction (Stiefel et al., 2016). Such a measure aligns squarely with the World Health Organization's definition of health and moves beyond solely examining the absence of physical or mental illness to evaluating a range of life experiences (World Health Organization, 1948). To be sure, release from prison is challenged by infirmity and worsening of health conditions, hospitalizations, and even higher rates of death. Past studies have catalogued a worsening of HIV disease, hypertension, and hospitalizations and even deaths from preventable conditions (Massoglia and Pridemore, 2015; Wildeman and Wang, 2017). However, even health outcomes researchers are moving away from direct measures of specific physical (i.e., diabetes) and mental (i.e., depression) health conditions to include more holistic measures of health and well-being.

Previous research has validated several self-reported questionnaires aimed at assessing individual well-being. One promising measure of overall well-being is the Cantril Self-Anchoring Striving Scale (Sundaresh et al., 2021), which has been used extensively in research on well-being in the United States and internationally. Respondents rank their current life satisfaction and future life optimism on scales from 0 to 10. To help conceptualize and visualize the scale, an image of a ladder is used. Current life satisfaction responses of greater than or equal to 7 and future life optimism responses of greater than or equal to 8 are classified as a *thriving* life evaluation. Responses of current life satisfaction and future life optimism less than or equal to 4 are classified as a *suffering* life evaluation. All combinations of responses between *suffering* and *thriving* are classified as a *surviving* life evaluation. Estimates of life expectancy are based on the Life Evaluation Index, which is calculated for any population group as (% Thriving-% Suffering)*100. An increase of one standard deviation (SD) in the Life Evaluation Index (mean 48, SD 5.4) is associated with an estimated 1.54-year longer life expectancy at the population level (Arora et al., 2016).

Recent studies using this measure of well-being have shown that well-being in each measured domain was lower for individuals with exposure to police stops, arrests, and incarceration, compared to those not exposed (Sundaresh et al., 2020). Further, longer durations of incarceration and multiple incarcerations were each associated with progressively lower well-being, and those exposed to police stops with searches (i.e., stop-and-frisk) reported levels of well-being as low as those who experienced multiple incarcerations. As the authors suggest, this illustrates "the extent to which even lower-level contact with the criminal legal system is negatively associated with quality of life" (Sundaresh et al., 2020, p. 5120). Another study found that a family member's incarceration was associated with lower well-being in every domain of well-being and an estimated 3.6-year shorter life expectancy compared with those without an incarcerated family member (Sundaresh et al., 2021). Among individuals with any family incarceration, Black respondents had a lower life expectancy (an estimated 0.46 fewer years) than White respondents.

In addition to the Cantril Self-Anchoring Striving Scale, there are other instruments that are validated and used with Cantril's ladder that can measure individual and community-level well-being.[2] These include the 100 Million Healthier Lives measure (led by the Institute of Healthcare Improvement, which includes the domains of physical health, mental health, spiritual support, financial support, and social support) and the Well-being in the Nation measures[3] (Stiefel et al., 2016). These two measures are being used both at the individual level and at the community level. Selecting a well-being measure like these three which are being used among non-incarcerated individuals and entire communities enables comparisons with a never-incarcerated group. This achieves two aims: (1) to have benchmarks to compare how incarceration may impact well-being, and (2) to humanize those who are currently or formerly incarcerated. These surveys enable measurement of individual factors that contribute to success following release, including physical and mental health, but also the social environments that directly influence individual well-being.

Already underway is a multisite randomized controlled trial of a six-week mental health intervention, the 5-Key Model for Reentry, where the primary outcome is individual-level psychological well-being. This intervention targets five key domains proposed to influence well-being: healthy thinking patterns, positive coping strategies, positive interpersonal relationships, positive social activities, and occupational balance (Veeh, Renn, and Pettus-Davis, 2018). According to the oral presentation made by Carrie Pettus-Davis to the committee, the model was developed in part with formerly incarcerated individuals and researchers to focus on an individual's strengths, in contrast to a deficit-based model. It is highly adaptive to accommodate individual needs; for example, substance-use treatment

---

[2] See https://www.rand.org/capabilities/solutions/measuring-wellbeing-to-help-communities-thrive.html.

[3] See https://web.archive.org/web/20210126145106/https://wellbeingtrust.org/areas-of-focus/community-transformation/well-being-in-the-nation-win-network/.

is implemented into the intervention for individuals with substance-use disorders. Further, there are validated assessments of each core domain, which allows for an individual's progress to be tracked over time and allows for specific services and treatment plans to be adjusted as needed. For example, throughout the duration of the intervention, a fidelity monitoring tool is implemented to ensure consistency across different practitioners implementing the intervention while also allowing for the flexibility needed for individual participants.

This intervention is being tested using a randomized controlled trial design with more than 2,000 incarcerated individuals across 100 U.S. prisons and jails. Preliminary data suggest that not only does the intervention group have improved well-being in each of the domains, but also lower rates of being reincarcerated compared to a control group. Further, the five well-being domains are associated with increases in overall well-being, which is in return associated with decreased likelihood of reincarceration. Early data also suggest that participants of color and those who have been incarcerated several times are more likely to engage with the 5-Key Model intervention than their White peers or those who have been incarcerated only once (Pettus-Davis and Veeh, 2021). This model serves as an important proof of concept that such interventions, targeting various components of well-being, may have large impacts on recontact with the criminal legal system and that measures of well-being can be effectively used to measure success following prison release, including avoiding return to prison. Examples of the measurement of individual well-being are presented in Table 4-1.

Criminal Desistance

As a supplement to official measures of recidivism, formal measures of criminal desistance would provide useful information about an individual's post-release progress related to any continuation of criminal activity. As discussed in Chapter 3, the measurement of desistance tracks positive outcomes that indicate reduced involvement in offending over time, ultimately including the complete cessation of criminal behavior. A 2021 National Institute of Justice report, *Desistance-Focused Criminal Justice Practice*, identifies three basic approaches to understanding and measuring desistance: (1) deceleration, (2) de-escalation, and (3) "reaching a ceiling" or cessation (Bucklen, 2021, p. 1). As Bucklen describes these terms, deceleration refers to a slowdown in the frequency of criminal offending and may be measured by comparing the frequency of criminal activity in fixed periods of time. De-escalation indicates a reduction in the severity of criminal activity and may be measured by changes in gravity scores for offenses. Cessation or reaching a ceiling refers to the absence of offending for some follow-up period, which might be considered the inverse of recidivism. Although measuring such changes is difficult and fraught with potential biases stemming from use of official or self-reported data, the modalities are helpful in distinguishing important qualitative differences in trajectories of criminal behavior over time. De-escalation and desistance from more serious violent offenses such as robbery and aggravated assault may represent reentry success, even when there is little to no deceleration in the rate of low-level law violations.

Although the National Institute of Justice report recommends use of arrest data in operationalizing these concepts, the committee cautions that arrest may not be an accurate indicator of individual offending because of the potential biases in arrest data that were discussed in Chapter 2. Nevertheless, the concepts of deceleration, de-escalation, and cessation may also be measured using administrative data on criminal convictions, self-report survey data based on checklists and frequency counts of criminal activities within a time interval, and self-report data on both subjective desistance (e.g., "Compared to 5 years ago, do you now do more, less, or the same amount of these activities?") and reference group desistance (Uggen and Massoglia, 2007; Massoglia and Uggen, 2010). Some basic sample measures in each of these categories are included in Table 4-1.

Historically, standard measures of both recidivism and desistance have typically been based on official statistics, which can provide some indication of the occurrence and relative frequency and severity of criminal events but also reflect criminal legal system activity. As described in Chapter 2, such official data are subject to known biases. Although self-reported information on the type, frequency, and severity of post-release criminal activity is more expensive to gather, it offers an important alternative to data derived from police, courts, and correctional agencies and officials (Farrington, 2007). Despite these advantages, self-report data also raise concerns about potential errors and biases, including those related to sampling, response rates, measurement, and differential validity across groups (see, e.g., Gomes et al., 2019; Junger-Tas and Marshall, 1999). A smaller number of studies have examined "subjective desistance," based on measures of whether people believe they are engaging in more, less, or about the same amount of criminal activity relative to an earlier baseline period or a peer reference group (Massoglia and Uggen, 2007; 2010). Survey items and qualitative research based on such self-appraisals can provide a sensitive measure of whether people believe they are desisting from crime even when such changes are not reflected in official statistics.

International measurement efforts also offer some promise for the measurement of desistance. Recent research from the United Kingdom uses a "proxy measure of desistance" by measuring outcomes such as client engagement with services, changes in individual needs resulting from provided services, and "changes in well-being, agency, and relationships" (Wong and Horan, 2019, p. 7). Another group in the United Kingdom has focused on the measurement of "intermediate outcomes," which are defined as "measurable changes in individuals that are directly or indirectly associated with reductions in reoffending" (Maguire et al., 2019, p. 5). These outcomes are referred to as intermediate because they indicate positive changes that may reflect progress toward ceasing criminal behavior and eventually lead to the complete abandonment of criminal behavior, although individuals may not have completely ceased offending at the time of measurement (Burrowes et al., 2013). Maguire and colleagues (2019) developed a 29-item instrument, the Intermediate Outcomes Measurement Instrument (IOMI), to assess the impact of mentoring and arts interventions, but the instrument is likely applicable to a wider range of interventions. This tool aims to support service providers in evaluating their work with individuals under supervision.

The IOMI includes eight key dimensions (Maguire et al., 2019, p. 19): resilience, agency and self-efficacy, hope, well-being, motivation to change, impulsivity/problem-solving, interpersonal trust, and practical problems.

- *Resilience* refers to the ability to bounce back after exposure to adversity; this is similar to the adversarial growth narrative noted in the discourse of prisoners in France (Kazemian, 2020).
- *Agency/self-efficacy* measures an individual's ability to take control of one's own life, to make decisions, and to take action.
- *Hope* refers to a "calculation about perceived scope for positive future change" (Maguire et al., 2019, p. 19).
- *Well-being* assesses overall mental, emotional, and psychological health.
- *Motivation to change* reflects an internal desire to change, an increased engagement in interventions, and a reduced motivation to engage in offending.
- *Impulsivity/problem-solving* measures the ability to reflect, plan, and exercise self-control.
- *Interpersonal trust* is linked to the concept of social capital and indicates "positive attitudes toward and connectedness with others" (p. 19).
- *Practical problems* documents perceived problems in key areas such as housing, education, employment, substance use, financial situation, and family relationships.

While the IOMI is still in preliminary stages of development and requires more validity and reliability testing, it offers valuable guidance for efforts to measure key positive outcomes that are known to be linked to the process of desistance from crime.

Overall Health

In 1989, the RAND Corporation published the results of The Medical Outcomes Study, a multiyear, multisite study aimed at explaining variations in patient outcomes and developing new tools for monitoring patient health outcomes (Tarlov et al., 1989). Building on this work, RAND developed the 36-Item Short Form Health Survey (SF-36), a set of "generic, coherent, and easily administered quality-of-life measures," that rely on participant self-reporting (RAND Health Care). These measures have been widely used by health care organizations, in national population-based health studies, and in studies of incarcerated people. In particular, the singular question of the Medical Outcomes Study, which asks individuals to rate their perceived health into one of five categories ("excellent," "very good," "good," "fair," "poor"), has been studied extensively in various contexts and populations, and shown to be independently associated with morbidity, functional status, and mortality, even after controlling for key demographics such as socioeconomic status (Idler and Kasl, 1995; for more examples of self-reporting on overall health see Kaplan and Camacho, 1983; Manor, Matthews, and Power, 2001; Siegel, Bradley, and Kasl, 2003).

Self-reported metrics for specific physical health conditions (e.g., hypertension, diabetes, etc.) are best avoided given the potential of recall bias. For example, self-reported data across 12 European countries among working-age populations underestimated the prevalence of obesity by four percent among the total population; for men, self-reported data underestimated hypertension by 10 percent. Further, recall bias related to health varies by key demographic characteristics, such as sex, race and ethnicity, and education, which can thwart accurate measurements of health inequalities (Brusco and Watts, 2015; Dowd and Todd, 2011; Kislaya et al., 2019; Tolonen et al., 2014). Greater accuracy, instead, would be obtained using data from health systems with electronic health records (i.e., blood pressure measurement or prescription of antihypertension medication), more accurate than self-reported data on specific health conditions.

However, recognizing the challenges associated with accessing health records and that people released from prison often have limited health care access, several national health surveys include self-reported measures of specific physical health and mental health conditions that can be used in research, thereby providing a benchmark of study participants' responses with national rates (see Table 4-1). The National Survey on Drug Use and Health (NSDUH), a nationally representative, annual survey of approximately 70,000 individuals, includes self-reported questions about physical health, substance use, and mental health conditions, as well as a measure of criminal legal system contact (whether a person has been arrested or been on parole or probation in the last year). By using the same questions to measure health outcomes that NSDUH uses, researchers can then benchmark participants against a nationally representative population of people on community supervision. Survey questions from the Bureau of Justice Statistics' Survey of Prison Inmates and Survey of Inmates in Local Jails can also be used in this same way.

Mental Health and Substance Use Disorder

Given the high prevalence of mental health conditions and substance use disorder among criminal legal system-involved individuals, using specific mental health and substance use indicators that are short and widely used in non-incarcerated populations can complement measures of well-being and can be used in evaluating the success of specific interventions. For instance, the Patient Health Questionnaire-9 (PHQ-9) evaluates the severity of depression and has been used in studies of criminal legal system-involved individuals (Kroenke, Spitzer, and Williams, 2001). To measure post traumatic disorder and the severity of symptoms, the PTSD-Primary Care, a four-item screening tool, can be used to identify who is experiencing current symptoms as well as the worsening of symptomatology over time.

One challenge in defining success for people with substance use disorders returning from prison is identifying appropriate criteria for relapse. Any measure of relapse, if used, needs to be defined by clinical practice and based on the recognition that episodic use (lapse) is inherent to the illness and not pathologic or necessarily health-harming. While a positive drug screen is often used in studies as a measure of failure following prison release (and cause for reincarceration), addiction medicine experts, including the American Society of Addiction Medicine, do not define a single positive urine drug screen as pathologic or a treatment failure, but an expected consequence of a chronic health condition (Jarvis et al., 2017). Even in clinical practice, where urine drug screening is used to help guide treatment plans for either harm reduction or recovery, its use is of questionable value (Jarvis et al., 2017). Studies of licensed physicians with years of clinical training have found confusion about proper implementation and that misinterpretations of urine drug screening results are common (Ceasar et al., 2016; Chua et al., 2020). For these reasons, urine drug screening, which is currently used to surveil and sanction addiction relapse for those on probation and parole, is not an appropriate measure of success (or failure) by researchers or practitioners. Instead, reliance on self-reported measures of substance use that define success as *a progression of health-promoting behaviors over time* may be more reliable indicators of improvement and offer better insights for those making decisions about probation and parole supervision. For instance, a person who is using less and thus able to maintain better communication with their family or a person who has not overdosed in a year may be defined as "successful," when viewed in the context of that individual's past (see Table 4-1).

Engagement in Health Care

Success following release from incarceration can also be described by how and when individuals engage the health care system, especially for those with physical and mental health conditions. Consistent engagement of the health care system, whether for a chronic disease or in general, is potentially a metric of success following release. Examples of such measures are presented in Table 4-1. And for specific conditions, there are frameworks, or cascades of care, designed to measure successful engagement in the health care system, including an opioid treatment cascade, HIV treatment cascade, and now even a Hepatitis C treatment cascade (Kay, Batey, and Mugavero, 2016; Williams et al., 2018; Yehia et al., 2014). Identifying the challenges encountered by patients at each stage of the cascade can target individual-level opportunities for support. In addition, when these measures are used in the health care system, they can also identify hospital-based and local policy interventions to improve individual treatment outcomes, track health-related progress, and reduce related diseases and deaths.

Housing and Homelessness

People with criminal records face significant barriers to housing. As discussed in Chapter 3, formerly incarcerated individuals experience high rates of housing instability and homelessness. Housing instability makes it difficult for those with incarceration histories to successfully reenter the community and gain stability, establish social networks, and avoid reengagement with the criminal legal system. Individuals without housing who are placed in group shelters can enter a cycle of incarceration, release to shelter, homelessness, and reincarceration. In large urban areas, the "prison to shelter" pipeline fuels chronic homelessness (Sirois, 2019). Thus, stable housing is a necessary component of post-release success, yet an individual's housing situation can be influenced by a wide variety of personal circumstances. Gaining stable housing is also dependent on structural issues that need to be taken into account when assessing housing stability, including discrimination by owners of rental housing, the lack of affordable housing in urban areas, and risks associated with living in high crime and poverty areas (Metraux, Hunt, and Yetvin, 2020).

Recent research on housing challenges among people released from prison point to a variety of possible housing-related metrics and measures of housing stability, which could be additional indicators of success. However, few of these studies have included measures of housing status as outcomes. One exception is a multi-site evaluation of housing programs for high-risk individuals, which found that the timing of achieving residential stability in the first weeks and months following release was important in achieving longer-term housing stability and preventing convictions and readmission to prison for new crimes (Lutze, Rosky, and Hamilton, 2014). This finding about the importance of housing stability shortly after release (i.e., in the first month) was also supported in an evaluation of the Fortune Society's reentry program (McDonald, Dyous, and Carlson, 2008).

In other housing demonstration programs, the receipt of temporary housing subsidies, housing vouchers, general rental assistance, or housing-related case management led to more successful outcomes for individuals leaving prison (Metraux, Hunt, and Yetvin, 2020). An untested but promising approach to improving housing stability for returning citizens is to provide support for their families in the form of rental assistance or other resources as part of a holistic reentry plan prior to discharge from prison. Living in a well-resourced household (i.e., stable employment of household members) can improve positive outcomes following release (Hamilton, Kigerl, and Hays, 2015; Harding et al., 2014; Sirois, 2019). One study in Ohio examined whether individuals lived with a parent, spouse, boyfriend/girlfriend, or other relative and found that individuals who lived with a spouse or parent had more positive outcomes (measured by felony arrest) than those in other living arrangements (Steiner, Makarios, and Travis, 2015). Thus, addressing housing issues faced by returning citizens can be a pathway to successful reentry (see Fontaine and Biess, 2012).

Given how limited the research on reentry and housing has been, future research in this area would benefit from attention to an individual's housing situation shortly after release, type of housing arrangement, whether housing is temporary (e.g., shelters, halfway house) or not, number of residential moves within a time period, receipt of housing subsidies or rental assistance, and the duration of any assistance. Subjective self-reported measures of housing status could be a plausible source of information (see Table 4-1). An individual's choice to reside in a supportive housing arrangement that combines rental assistance with onsite services, mental health or drug treatment, and case management could also be an indicator of progress towards desistance and community integration (see, Metraux, Hunt, and Yetvin, 2020). Data on housing can also include indicators of housing quality, affordability, and segregation by using links to residential zip codes. Such information is sometimes available in official sources, such as community supervision records. More research is needed to establish relationships between housing status and post-release success.

Employment and Job Retention

Employment is a core domain for overall reintegration and well-being, and recent efforts to assist men and women released from prison have heavily emphasized creating employment opportunities. Many such efforts aim to promote employment in the hope that it will also promote desistance, though relatively little is known about the extent to which, or the mechanism by which, post-release employment promotes desistance. In considering how employment is related to desistance following release from prison, Skardhamar and Savolainen (2014) found that most people with criminal histories had disengaged from crime before the transition to work, and that securing employment was not associated with further reductions in criminal behavior. Thus, the relationship between employment and desistance is complicated, as it may not be work alone but the social bonds formed at work that promote desistance (Sampson and Laub, 1990, p. 611). Moreover, employment programs that help individuals secure a job may not be helpful if individuals are not psychologically ready to give up criminal behavior (Lattimore and Visher, 2021; Muhlhausen, 2015). In short, finding a job may be a necessary but not sufficient condition for desistance.

For people recently released from prison or those who have recent criminal legal system involvement, finding a job is challenging, despite increased policy attention to reducing the likelihood of discrimination among these job seekers and new federal protections (U.S. Equal Employment Opportunity Commission, 2012). It is important to note that a person's "employability" potential may be preexisting to the period of incarceration. A sizeable minority of individuals leaving prison were unemployed prior to incarceration (Visher and La Vigne, 2020; Western, 2018). Because these individuals were often not sought after in the labor market before their imprisonment, it remains challenging to determine whether incarceration or pre-prison risk factors most influence post-release employment outcomes (Apel and Sweeten, 2010; Holzer, Raphael, and Stoll, 2003). In addition, among those who held jobs prior to confinement, the required skills may erode during a period of incarceration, and relationships with former employers are likely to be severed (Western, 2002).

Identifying the role employment plays in successful transitions begins with uncovering a broader range of employment-related measures as indicators of success following release from prison. The measurement of employment status among criminal legal system-involved individuals may account for the lack of positive findings about employment and success. Simply measuring employment status as present or absent is often not associated with reentry outcomes. In a longitudinal study of men released from prison in the Netherlands, Ramakers and colleagues (2017) found that it is not just employment but the quality of employment, especially perceived work conditions, that explains recidivism (measured by crimes officially registered) after release from prison. In particular, they found that both the subjective assessment of job quality and the distinction between primary and secondary sector jobs play a crucial role in explaining recidivism. Included in the secondary sector occupations are those filling manufacturing jobs, laborers, and unskilled service workers. Secondary sector occupations and employment are characterized by low wages, poor work conditions, and, most importantly, job instability, whereas the primary sector refers to employment with high wages, employment stability and security, and strong social relationships with others in the work force (Doeringer and Piore, 1971). Moreover, Tripodi, Kim, and Bender (2010) found that obtaining employment is associated with increased time to reincarceration, thus indicating that employment may be part of a process of behavioral change that unfolds over time (Apel et al., 2006; Crutchfield and Pitchford, 1997; Uggen, 1999).

Employment for many criminal legal system-involved individuals is likely to be intermittent, at least initially. Many have never held a job for any length of time (Bushway and Apel, 2012; Western, 2018). Thus, measures of employment stability, such as length of time employed during a specific time frame, as well as length of time employed in a specific workplace, would be indicators of a successful transition. Among the unanswered questions is whether holding jobs with greater career potential or higher wages or better benefits leads to a greater likelihood of success. In fact, it is unknown whether actively looking for work is an indicator of progress toward successful reintegration, although such activity could provide a signal that individuals are intent on a transition to a prosocial identity (Bushway and Apel, 2012).

Alternative measures of employment need to be explored as possible indicators of progress toward successful reintegration and overall well-being. Promising metrics could include wage rates, job retention, number of hours worked per week, and measures of job quality, including type of job, career opportunities, and whether the job includes benefits (see Table 4-1). Official data sources for measures of employment status could include state unemployment records, records held by state employment counselors, and self-reported employment experiences, including job applications submitted and job interviews. Other subjective measures of employment and current work experience may provide greater insight into an individual's progress in connecting successfully to the labor market after incarceration (see Table 4-1). Where appropriate, individual employment indicators could be compared to various national data sources on labor force participation, but care needs to be taken in making sure comparisons are made with populations with similar employment and education backgrounds.

Educational Attainment

The incarcerated population has been referred to as the "most educationally disadvantaged population in the United States" (Klein et al., 2004). People in prison have much lower educational attainment than those in the general population (Harlow, 2003). Roughly 19 percent of adults outside of prison have not attained a high school diploma or equivalent, compared to 36 percent of individuals in state prisons who have not completed high school (Davis et al., 2013). Thus, it seems reasonable that improvements in educational attainment (acquiring GED, taking college courses, completing college degrees) could be an important marker of success among individuals released from prison. Because people who end up in prison often have low educational attainment, many of them access educational opportunities during their incarceration. However, there has been an appreciable decline in prison-based programs (National Research Council, 2008), which has resulted in a dearth of recent knowledge about how education affects desistance and reentry transitions for people leaving prison and returning to the community.

Despite reduced programming through the 1990s and 2000s, prison has become a place where many people increase their literacy levels, earn GEDs and, when possible, college degrees (Crayton and Neusteter, 2008; Harlow, 2003). Many studies have found that the more education people acquire while in prison, the less likely they are to recidivate (Chappell, 2003; Cleere, 2013; Crayton and Neusteter, 2008; Harlow, 2003; Nuttall, Hollmen, and Staley, 2003), with often significant reductions for those who earn a GED (Macdonald and Bala, 1986; Nutall, Hollmen, Staley, 2003) or participate in post-secondary education toward achieving a college diploma (Anderson and Moore, 1995; Chappell, 2003; Denney and Tynes, 2021; Nuttall, Hollmen, Staley, 2003; Vacca, 2004). In a three-year study of GED completion for people released from prisons in New Jersey, about six in ten non-GED participants were rearrested once released, compared with about half of GED participants (Zgoba, Haugebrook, and Jenkins, 2008). The most recent systematic review of correctional education programs found promising evidence of the effectiveness of adult basic and post-secondary educational programs (Weisburd, Farrington, and Gill, 2017). Finally, the website CrimeSolutions,[4] which is funded and hosted by the U.S. Department of Justice, Office of Justice Programs, reports effectiveness ratings of crime prevention and rehabilitation programs. It rates adult basic education

---

[4]See www.crimesolutions.ojp.gov.

classes for incarcerated individuals as "promising" in reducing recidivism, and also "promising" in improving employment and job placement outcomes, although it calls for more rigorous studies of the relationship between education and individual outcomes.

Research on education and desistance is complicated by the fact that substantial selection effects are often not directly observed. That is, it may be that the individuals most likely to succeed are those who enroll and complete education courses in prison. In oral reports gathered during the committee's listening session, participants noted that educational opportunities influenced their transitions from prison and were important factors in their success. Similar to the role of employment in the desistance process, education may not be a self-defined 'turning point' but may instead be a critical component in the process of desistance from crime for some criminal legal system-involved individuals. Moreover, single (and binary) measures of educational attainment may obscure the full impact of educational engagement on post-release outcomes (see Box 4-4).

It is also difficult to untangle *how* prison education promotes desistance. Little is known about how people exiting prison use the education they have gained in prison to navigate the difficult terrain post-release, particularly how they deal with structural impediments. Education may propel individuals into a new trajectory, but documenting this process is difficult and more research in this area is needed. Runell (2015) conducted in-depth interviews with 34 criminal legal system-involved individuals who enrolled in a state university and found that post-secondary education increased the participants' social and academic networks. While participants expressed a desire to remain crime-free, some of them noted that they had

---

BOX 4-4
Listening Session: Education and Post-Release Success

One central theme of the committee's listening session with formerly incarcerated individuals was the importance of education in contributing to success after release. Walter Strauss, who became a New York Housing Court judge following his release from incarceration, credited his focus on getting an education with his success (Strauss, 2021). John Valverde, CEO of YouthBuild USA, agreed that education is "key to everything," (Valverde, 2021) and Jai Diamond of the New York City Criminal Justice Agency cited "education, a strong voice, and a strong mind" as her core needs to validate herself and "set the tone for the success I've found today" (Diamond 2021). Kenneth Cooper of the Game Changers Reentry Program identified the day he began seeking education in prison as the day he became free, explaining, "I was in prison, confined, locked up, but I wasn't locked out" (Cooper, 2021).

not completely ruled out committing another crime. Most importantly, despite increases in education, their desistance pathways were affected by structural elements of neighborhood disadvantage (Runell, 2015).

As with other measures of success, improvement in educational attainment is best viewed as a process that individuals experience over some period of time. Measures of educational attainment can include improvement in literacy skills, participation in courses, whether during prison or in the community, enrollment in community college, progress towards a degree, and other educational milestones (see Table 4-1). Moreover, as with measures of employment, housing and health, indicators of educational attainment could be compared to various national data sources on education status, but care needs to be taken to ensure that comparisons are made among populations with similar backgrounds.

Social Relationships: Children, Families, Peer Support

Strong social relationships are an important component of a successful transition from prison to the community or after other criminal legal system involvement. For example, family support for criminal legal system-involved individuals, though it is largely invisible, can be critical to an individual's success. Individuals who receive financial or emotional support from their families experience reentry differently from people whose families are unable to help or are not active in their lives (Berg and Huebner, 2011; Harding et al., 2014; Pettus-Davis and Kennedy, 2020; Western, 2018). In addition, as mentioned in Chapter 3, support from persons who have had prior contact with the criminal legal system can provide much-needed assistance and understanding during the transition from prison to the community. Such peer support is rarely included in studies examining the experiences of justice-involved individuals. For individuals with children, commitment to being in their children's lives may also be a critical marker of a successful transition from prison (see Eddy and Poehlmann-Tynan, 2019). In studies of fathers returning from incarceration, an important element of their transition from prison to community was being physically and emotionally available to their children, making up for lost time, and wanting to repair broken bonds (e.g., Charles et al., 2021).

The measurement of social relationships as indicators of post-release success for individuals involved in the criminal legal system is clearly a new area for understanding desistance processes. A recent evaluation of a New York City program that aimed to improve relationships between formerly incarcerated fathers and their children noted that their research was hampered by how to quantify family reconnection (Tomberg et al., 2021). Research on family relationships, connections with children, and support received from peers and other formal or informal arrangements (i.e., faith communities, community groups) has included various measures of involvement and commitment as intermediate constructs in studying reintegration pathways and desistance. These measures and other subjective indicators of social relationships would also be useful as markers of progress and success (see Table 4-1).

Qualitative studies have made important contributions to our understanding of the role of relationships in criminal behavior and desistance, but more attention is needed to understand the ways in which families and other social relationships and related social capital help individuals succeed, including within the domains of healthcare, education, and employment. Going forward, studies need to include interviews not only with the returning individuals but also with those who are in their families, communities, and other social networks. Measures of successful relationships could be gathered through these interviews and self-reports of social relationships, such as strength of ties with family members, reduction in connections with people who are actively committing crime or using illegal drugs, and time spent in positive social interaction including with other community members with social capital (see Table 4-1). As with other indicators of success, building positive social relationships is likely to be a process that unfolds over many months as legal system–involved individuals create new social networks and re-establish relationships with family members.

Civic Engagement

Criminologists typically use the term "citizens" in opposition to people convicted of crime. Uggen and Manza (2005, 67) suggest that this usage places "criminals on one side of the ledger and law-abiding community residents on the other." Yet people with criminal records are commonly citizens themselves, occupying roles as taxpayers, homeowners, volunteers, and voters. In contrast to the large literatures on work and family reintegration, the subject of reintegration into community life and civic participation has received comparatively little attention. If desistance is only possible when people "develop a coherent pro-social identity for themselves," as Shadd Maruna (2001, p. 7) contends, then community involvement and democratic participation need to be among the markers of post-release success. Additionally, developing a self-concept as a pro-social conforming citizen may be a key mechanism linking adult work and family roles with desistance from crime (Massoglia and Uggen, 2010).

As discussed in Chapter 3, research is lacking on whether civic engagement affects the trajectory of people who have been discharged from prison, yet it is clear that behaviors such as voting are associated with subsequent desistance from crime (Uggen and Manza, 2004). Nevertheless, a significant number of people who are entangled in the criminal legal system are formally prohibited from being civically engaged (Uggen et al., 2020; Lageson, 2020), which suggests that measures of engagement need to include both individual-level indicators (e.g., whether an individual votes) and system-level indicators (e.g., whether individuals have the right to vote in a particular jurisdiction).

In view of these ideas, it seems plausible to suggest that voting, volunteering, and other forms of civic and political participation may be considered markers of success after release from prison. Some sample measures of these concepts are included in Table 4-1. To measure such engagement at the individual level, well-established indicators of political engagement include political participation or voter turnout, attendance at political events such as rallies and demonstrations, and conversations with friends and neighbors about political issues and events. Refined self-report indicators and scales are available in the American National Election Studies, and basic voter registration and participation information is publicly available in administrative data. The type and timing of volunteer service has also been measured through self-report items in studies such as Add-Health (Ranapurwala, Casteel, and Peek-Asa, 2016) and the Youth Development Study (Uggen and Janikula, 1999). More subjective measures include political efficacy and trust (Niemi, Craig, and Mattei, 1991) and the perceived importance of engagement in the community (Uggen, Manza, and Behrens, 2004). Apart from these individual-level items, system-level measures of civic engagement include turnout rates and legal restrictions on the right to vote, volunteer, or otherwise participate in civic life.

RESEARCH NEEDS

Measuring improvement for those leaving prison and other justice-involved individuals is a new area of study for corrections researchers. Methods to measure incremental success need to be developed, including considerations about appropriate time dimensions, sources of data, and community context. Importantly, most studies have not examined thoroughly how the specific time course following release affects success, especially whether the first few hours, days, and weeks following release are essential to success and how individuals thrive over the life course. The measurement of success regarding health conditions following release may need to be undertaken in a less regimented way than is typical of other research studies and evaluation efforts (such as with surveys scheduled one month, three months, etc., following release). Instead, measurement should employ methods adapted to the fact that post-release success is often dictated by the events immediately following release (Binswanger et al., 2007; 2012). More studies are using new methodologies and smart phones to capture events immediately following release, including ecological momentary assessment (EMA), which captures individuals' behaviors in real time. EMA has been used in the criminal legal system with high rates (>95%) of participation, and it has been used in substance use research with 75–90 percent compliance when incentives were used. Thus, while longitudinal data collection is much preferred over cross-sectional data collection, it may still be inadequate to observe important points for success following release without more flexible methodologies.

Further, employing a life-course perspective in defining success following release from prison enables a more complete understanding concerning which individual- and community-level factors, especially structural factors, support thriving and what their intergenerational impacts are on families and communities. Two salient examples from other fields are the High Scope Interventions, an early childhood education intervention, and the Nurse-Family Partnership, intensive support for women and children perinatally. These two intervention studies targeting individuals at high risk for incarceration or who have been incarcerated found that participants in the treatment group, along with their children, were less likely to be incarcerated (Eckenrode et al., 2010; Kitzman et al., 2019; Olds et al., 1997; Olds et al., 1998; Schweinhart and Weikart, 1997; Weikart, 1998). Success that is achieved and maintained over the course of one's life, even if it is decades after their last release, may be as valuable as success obtained within the first 20 months. A holistic conceptualization of success after incarceration includes one that measures and evaluates the success of other individuals not directly incarcerated but substantially impacted by the incarceration of their family and community members.

Research is also needed to consider how to establish improvement, which is likely to vary depending on the outcome measure. There are national baselines for some outcomes, such as mental health and substance use, but baseline data would need to be culturally specific. Moreover, there are significant social structure and context considerations for adopting benchmarks for education and employment among criminal legal system-involved individuals. As discussed in Chapter 3, there is strong evidence of racial, ethnic, gender, socioeconomic, and geographic inequities facing criminal legal system-involved individuals which need to be taken into account. For example, an appropriate benchmark for employment of individuals released from prison might be the age-specific labor force participation rate for individuals with a high school degree living in urban areas. Care should be taken in establishing appropriate benchmarks so that they reflect reasonable improvements over the period before incarceration but also reflect structural considerations based on population and geographic characteristics.

Supplemental measures of post-release success also lend themselves quite well to benefit/cost analysis. Improvements in health, education, housing, and employment for people returning from prison would impact the life course of hundreds of thousands of people a year. Measuring the direct and indirect financial benefits to local communities of those improvements would provide evidence of the significance of supplementing official measures of recidivism with other measures of success. This would be a new area of research that could enhance our understanding of success as it is experienced by individuals during the months and years following release from prison.

This chapter has repeatedly mentioned the lack of sufficient administrative and statistical data to measure various forms of success experienced by people returning from prison. The lack of such quantitative data on measures of success limits our understanding of success and failure, as researchers usually fall back on inadequate measures of official recidivism based on recontact with the criminal legal system. The use of qualitative interview data can capture more detailed and nuanced information about success, particularly with respect to identity change, self-perception, and progress toward social reintegration. Indeed, these data are valuable because they elevate the perspectives of people who are experiencing these difficult transitions. We can gather qualitative data about "the strengths, skills, responsibilities, talents of people and how are they experiencing return [to the community] in terms of belonging and being valued members of the community" along with the "density and quality of people's social networks and degree to which they reintegrate people back into society" (Braucht, 2021).

Interviews can capture not just the presence or absence of a program but whether it matches participants' needs (Good Collins, 2021). Qualitative data can help us examine outcomes like stable relationships. Such data can also help investigators and policy makers understand not just who did not have further contact with the legal system, but why, and it can help capture the various stories of successful people (Lewis, 2021). Qualitative and ethnographic researchers who participated in the committee's information-gathering sessions—Jerry Flores (University of Toronto), Andrea Leverentz (University of Massachusetts, Boston), and Reuben Miller (University of Chicago)[5]—shared examples of situations where individuals they interviewed or observed made decisions that led them to be considered recidivists. The examples, including missing drug tests or appointments with a parole officer or accepting a plea deal that seemed avoidable, reflected these people's complicated relationships with agents of the criminal legal system rather than new criminal activity. The use of self-report interview

---

[5]See Committee on Evaluating Success Among People Released from Prison Meeting #2, Session 1: https://www.nationalacademies.org/event/07-27-2021/evaluating-success-among-people-released-from-prison-meeting-2-public-information-gathering-session-1.

or survey data to measure post-release improvements, progress, and success has notable strengths but, as discussed in Chapter 2, these data may also have weaknesses. Thus, research is needed to develop reliable and valid indicators of the possible metrics of success discussed in this chapter.

At the system level, an overhaul of data systems is needed so that indicators of success and reintegration are more readily available. Work from Hennepin County, Minnesota, illuminates how creating data linkages between correctional systems, health systems, and other state-run social services can be immediately useful to both practitioners and policy makers (Bodurtha et al., 2017). After merging data from four public sectors (health care, human services, housing, and the criminal legal system) for 98,282 Medicaid expansion enrollees in Hennepin County, researchers found that urban Medicaid expansion enrollees in the county had rates of emergency room use and hospitalization three times higher than the national average and had significant contact with housing shelters or supportive housing (13% of enrollees), the criminal legal system (34%), and the social service sector, including monetary and food support and case management (68%). In follow-up work, researchers have provided a more concise and nuanced examination of cross-sector patterns of use and used latent class analysis to identify patterns of cross-sector involvement, inclusive of the criminal legal system. These analyses illustrate the possibility of cross-sector data linkages to identify how the needs of criminal legal system–involved individuals are or are not being met by other sectors of local government and the social safety net system, recognizing that success after prison release depends on the availability of resources and services from various sectors (Andersen, 2020).

Further, documenting unmet needs creates systems of accountability within the local government that can be rapidly addressed. This cross-sector approach may offer an effective and efficient mechanism to improve success following release by highlighting system deficiencies and strengths within communities. Although some organizations now utilize integrated cross-sector data for evaluation, these data have not been extensively leveraged to explore the comprehensive network of public sector interactions for the justice-involved population.

An example of this approach might employ hierarchical models, a statistical model in which individuals are sorted under a hierarchy of successively higher-level units, in this case the community in which they are released. These models challenge traditional analyses that assume individual choice and behaviors are the sole causes of success following prison release. Hierarchical models require larger multisite studies and would incorporate a diverse set of communities to which people return, so that the clustering within communities can be taken into account in statistical analyses. Conducting larger-scale studies would provide richer and more accurate data on the efficacy of interventions, recognizing that people return home to communities that are diverse in resources and assets. Such studies would illuminate the complex and interconnected nature of various components of policy and social life that affect success following release, in all domains. As Jessica Simes (2021, p. 155) states, studying community context "necessitates a direct engagement between quantitative and qualitative scholars and takes seriously the nested scales of both place (neighborhoods, cities, regions) and punishment (police precincts, court districts, prison jurisdictions)." Where multisite studies are not possible, investigators need to recognize this as a limitation and, at the very least, first consider how the community in which the study is being conducted may be the primary determinant of whether the intervention is or is not successful or whether the location of the study itself is compromising the possibility of scientific discovery.

The ability to measure success following release from prison, and especially the ability to measure the community contexts to which people return, is hindered by data silos and restrictive data-sharing practices across criminal legal institutions. Few police departments routinely share information disaggregated by census tracts or by even smaller areas, like the block or longitude/latitude coordinates of stops and arrests, though many departments use such data in the practice of predictive policing. Even more challenging is accessing geographically disaggregated data from courts, prisons, jails, and probation and parole agencies. Disciplinary differences have created academic research silos, such that criminologists, for instance, often do not collect the most relevant and up-to-date health data, while health and public health colleagues would benefit from the expertise and data of sociologists, geographers, and environmental scientists in their attempts to study community-level phenomena. Synthesizing research efforts and data collections and sharing strategies for data gathering, analyses, and dissemination, while maintaining the highest ethical standards regarding public data sharing, are critical to moving this new science forward.

CONCLUSION

The foregoing review and discussion of alternative measures for assessing individual success and well-being after release from prison demonstrates that successful reintegration involves much more than what is conveyed through common measures of recidivism. Official recidivism measures such as rearrest, reconviction, and reincarceration are highly imperfect measures of criminal behavior and completely ignore improvements in multiple life domains that are central to successful reintegration and progress in an individual's life after imprisonment. Using person-centered, supplementary measures of success enables us to better understand what factors are important for success from the individual's perspective and avoid misinterpreting behavior in a way that could lead to misinformed and even harmful policy. A noted example is reincarceration for a technical violation of parole, such as a missed appointment, which then creates a major setback for the individual who otherwise may be making progress towards reintegration. Thus, the measurement of post-release success needs to be multidimensional, using both subjective and administrative data sources.

Whereas Chapter 3 of this report documented the existence of community-level and policy barriers to post-release success, this chapter proposed potential methods to account for those structural barriers in measuring success. As discussed here, the measurement of improvement, progress, and success for justice-involved individuals could benefit from a framework similar to that exemplified by the social determinants of health literature, which recognizes that multiple, overlapping factors influence individual outcomes, such as an individual's housing and neighborhood environment, employment and education status, civic engagement, and social relationships. We have also underlined the importance of sharing data across different life domains and of attending to the unique experiences of historically marginalized groups in evaluating success. Finally, this chapter has emphasized that individual outcomes are located within a community and societal context that includes substantial structural inequities which may affect individual transitions from prison to the community. The development and testing of new outcome and progress measures would benefit from measurement of these system inequalities.

Notable roadblocks remain that could undermine these promising methods for improving the measure of post-release success. Most prominently, they include the inability to link data across agencies and policy domains, lack of standard demographic, social, economic, and legal data to be collected by agencies, and the difficulty of sharing data across jurisdictions.

The potential impact of such improvements in measurement is significant. Research on the effectiveness of correctional programming and reentry programs has been hampered by several methodological issues, including an almost singular focus on narrow measures of official recidivism as the outcome measure. Measuring desistance and reintegration through the narrow lens of recontact with the criminal legal system is likely to undervalue the impacts of reentry programs and miss indicators of incremental progress, including changes in housing stability, job retention, or educational advancement, as indicated by participants in the committee's listening session. Research establishing relationships between non-criminal justice outcomes and reductions in criminal behavior could give policy makers the confidence to focus on those outcomes as a way to influence criminal behavior.

REFERENCES

Agan, A., and Starr, S. (2018). Ban the box, criminal records, and racial discrimination: A field experiment. *The Quarterly Journal of Economics* 133, 1, 191–235.

Anderson, S.V., and Moore, E.A. (1995). *Evaluation of the impact of correctional education programs on recidivism.* Columbus, OH: Ohio Department of Rehabilitation and Correction, Bureau of Planning and Evaluation.

Andersen, T.S., Scott, D.A.I., Boehme, H.M., King, S., and Mikell, T. (2020). What matters to formerly incarcerated men? Looking beyond recidivism as a measure of successful reintegration. *The Prison Journal* 100, 4, 488–509.

Andrews, D.A., Zinger, I., Hoge, R.D., Bonta, J., Gendreau, P., and Cullen, F.T. (1990). Does correctional treatment work? A clinically relevant and psychologically informed meta-analysis. *Criminology* 28, 3, 369–404.

Apel, R., Paternoster, R., Bushway, S.D., and Brame, R. (2006). A job isn't just a job: The differential impact of formal versus informal work on adolescent problem behavior. *Crime and Delinquency* 52, 2, 333–369.

Apel, R., and Sweeten, G. (2010). The impact of incarceration on employment during the transition to adulthood. *Social Problems* 57, 3, 448–479.

Arora, A., Spatz, E., Herrin, J., Riley, C., Roy, B., Kell, K., Coberley, C., Rula, E., and Krumholz, H.M. (2016). Population well-being measures help explain geographic disparities in life expectancy at the county level. *Health Affairs* 35, 11, 2075–2082.

Bachman, R., Kerrison, E., O'Connell, D., and Paternoster, R. (2013). *Roads diverge: Long-term patterns of relapse, recidivism and desistance for a cohort of drug-involved offenders.* Washington, DC: National Institute of Justice, United States Department of Justice.

Bachman, R., Kerrison, E.M., Paternoster, R., Smith, L., and O'Connell, D. (2016). The complex relationship between motherhood and desistance. *Women and Criminal Justice* 26, 212–231.

Bailey, Z.D., Feldman, J.M., and Bassett, M.T. (2021). How structural racism works—racist policies as a root cause of US racial health inequities. *New England Journal of Medicine* 384, 8, 768–773.

Bailey, Z.D., Krieger, N., Agénor, M., Graves, J., Linos, N., and Bassett, M.T. (2017). Structural racism and health inequities in the USA: Evidence and interventions. *The Lancet* 389, 10077, 1453–1463.

Barrick, K., Lattimore, P.K., and Visher, C.A. (2014). Reentering women: The impact of social ties on long-term recidivism. *The Prison Journal* 94, 279–304.

Bazemore, G., and Stinchcomb, J. (2004). A civic engagement model of reentry: Involving community through service and restorative justice. *Federal Probation* 68, 14.

Berg, M.T., and Huebner, B.M. (2011). Reentry and the ties that bind: An examination of social ties, employment, and recidivism. *Justice Quarterly* 28, 2, 382–410.

Binswanger, I.A., Nowels, C., Corsi, K.F., Glanz, J., Long, J., Booth, R.E., and Steiner, J.F. (2012). Return to drug use and overdose after release from prison: A qualitative study of risk and protective factors. *Addiction Science and Clinical Practice* 7, 1, 1–9.

Binswanger, I.A., Stern, M.F., Deyo, R.A., Heagerty, P.J., Cheadle, A., Elmore, J.G., and Koepsell, T.D. (2007). Release from prison—A high risk of death for former inmates. *New England Journal of Medicine* 356, 2, 157–165.

Bitney, K., Drake, E., Grice, J., Hirsch, M., and Lee, S. (2017). *The Effectiveness of Reentry Programs for Incarcerated Persons: Findings for the Washington Statewide Reentry Council (17-05-1901).* Olympia: Washington State Institute for Public Policy.

Blokland, A.A., and Nieuwbeerta, P. (2005). The effects of life circumstances on longitudinal trajectories of offending. *Criminology* 43, 4, 1203–1240.

Bodurtha, P., Van Siclen, R., Erickson, E., Legler, M., Thornquist, L., Vickery, K.D., Winkelman, T., Hougham, C., and Owen, R. (2017). *Cross-sector Service Use and Costs Among Medicaid Expansion Enrollees in Minnesota's Hennepin County*. Center for Health Care Strategies.

Bohmert, M. (2016). The role of transportation disadvantage for women on community supervision. *Criminal Justice and Behavior* 43, 1522–1540.

Boyd, R.W., Lindo, E.G., Weeks, L.D., and McLemore, M.R. (2020). On racism: A new standard for publishing on racial health inequities. *Health Affairs Blog* 10, 10.1377.

Braucht, G. (2021, July 28). Remarks made before the Committee. Committee on Evaluating Success Among People Released from Prison Meeting #2: Public Information Gathering Session. Washington, DC: National Academies of Sciences, Engineering, and Medicine.

Brayne, S. (2014). Surveillance and system avoidance: Criminal justice contact and institutional attachment. *American Sociological Review* 79, 3, 367–391.

Brusco, N.K., and Watts, J.J. (2015). Empirical evidence of recall bias for primary health care visits. *BMC Health Services Research* 15, 1, 1–8.

Bucklen, K.B. (2021, October 25). *Desistance-Focused Criminal Justice Practice*. Washington DC: National Institute of Justice. Available: https://nij.ojp.gov/topics/articles/desistance-focused-criminal-justice-practice.

Burrowes, N., Disley, E., Liddle, M., Maguire, M., Rubin, J., Taylor, J., and Wright, S. (2013). *Intermediate Outcomes of Arts Projects: A Rapid Evidence Assessment*. National Offender Management Services.

Burton, S. (2021, July 28). Remarks made before the Committee. Committee on Evaluating Success Among People Released from Prison Meeting #2: Public Information Gathering Session. Washington, DC: National Academies of Sciences, Engineering, and Medicine.

Bushway, S.D., and Apel, R. (2012). A signaling perspective on employment-based reentry programming: Training completion as a desistance signal. *Criminology and Public Policy* 11, 1, 21–50.

Butts, J.A., and Schiraldi, V. (2018). *Recidivism Reconsidered: Preserving the Community Justice Mission of Community Corrections*. Executive Session on Community Corrections. Harvard University, Kennedy School of Government.

Byrne, J.M. (2019). *The Effectiveness of Prison Programming: A Review of the Research Literature Examining the Impact of Federal, State, and Local Inmate Programming on Post-Release Recidivism*. First Step Act Independent Review Committee. Available: https://www.uscourts.gov/federal-probation-journal/2020/06/effectiveness-prison-programming-review-research-literature.

Ceasar, R., Chang, J., Zamora, K., Hurstak, E., Kushel, M., Miaskowski, C., and Knight, K. (2016). Primary care providers' experiences with urine toxicology tests to manage prescription opioid misuse and substance use among chronic noncancer pain patients in safety net health care settings. *Substance Abuse* 37, 1, 154–160.

Chambers, B.D., Erausquin, J.T., Tanner, A.E., Nichols, T.R., and Brown-Jeffy, S. (2018). Testing the association between traditional and novel indicators of county-level structural racism and birth outcomes among Black and White women. *Journal of Racial and Ethnic Health Disparities* 5, 5, 966–977.

Chappell, C.A. (2003). *Post-secondary Correctional Education and Recidivism: A Meta-Analysis of Research Conducted 1990–1999*. University of Cincinnati.

Charles, P., Frankham, E., Visher, C.A., and Kay, A.L. (2021). Father involvement in the first year after prison: Considerations for social work intervention research. *Research on Social Work Practice* 31, 8, 797–813.

Chen, E.Y., and Meyer, S. (2020). Beyond recidivism: Towards accurate, meaningful, and comprehensive data collection on the progress of individuals reentering society. In A. Leverentz, E.Y. Chen, and J. Christian (Eds.), *Beyond Recidivism: New Approaches to Research on Prisoner Reentry and Reintegration*, 13–38. New York University Press.

Chua, I., Petrides, A.K., Schiff, G.D., Ransohoff, J.R., Kantartjis, M., Streid, J., Demetriou, C.A., and Melanson, S.E. (2020). Provider misinterpretation, documentation, and follow-up of definitive urine drug testing results. *Journal of General Internal Medicine* 35, 1, 283–290.

Churchwell, K., Elkind, M.S., Benjamin, R.M., Carson, A.P., Chang, E.K., Lawrence, W., Mills, A., Odom, T.M., Rodriguez, C.J., Rodriguez, F., and Sanchez, E. (2020). Call to action: Structural racism as a fundamental driver of health disparities: A presidential advisory from the American Heart Association. *Circulation* 142, 24, e454–e468.

Cleere, G. (2013). *Prison Education, Social Capital and Desistance: An Exploration of Prisoners' Experiences in Ireland* (Doctoral dissertation). Waterford Institute of Technology.

Clone, S., and DeHart, D. (2014). Social support networks of incarcerated women: Types of support, sources of support, and implications for reentry. *Journal of Offender Rehabilitation* 53, 503–521.

Cobbina, J.E., Huebner, B.M., and Berg, M.T. (2012). Men, women, and post-release offending: An examination of the nature of the link between relational ties and recidivism. *Crime and Delinquency* 58, 331–361.

Cobbina, J.E., Morash, M., Kashy, D.A., and Smith, S.W. (2014). Race, neighborhood danger, and coping strategies among female probationers and parolees. *Race and Justice* 4, 3–28.

Cooper, K. (2021, July 27). Remarks made before the Committee. Committee on Evaluating Success Among People Released from Prison Meeting #2: Public Information Gathering Session. Washington, DC: National Academies of Sciences, Engineering, and Medicine.

Crayton, A., and Neusteter, S.R. (2008). *The Current State of Correctional Education: Paper to be presented at the Reentry Roundtable on Education.* John Jay College of Criminal Justice, Prisoner Reentry Institute.

Crittenden, C.A. and Koons-Witt, B.A. (2017). Gender and programming: A comparison of program availability and participation in US prisons. *International Journal of Offender Therapy and Comparative Criminology* 61, 6, 611–644.

Crutchfield, R.D., and Pitchford, S.R. (1997). Work and crime: The effects of labor stratification. *Social Forces* 76, 1, 93–118.

Cullen, F.T., and Gendreau, P. (2000). Assessing correctional rehabilitation: Policy, practice, and prospects. *Criminal Justice* 3, 1, 299–370.

Cullen, F.T., and Gendreau, P. (2001). From nothing works to what works: Changing professional ideology in the 21st century. *The Prison Journal* 81, 3, 313–338.

Cullen, F., and Gilbert, K. (2012). *Reaffirming Rehabilitation*. Routledge.

Cullen, F.T., Pratt, T., and Turanovic, J. (2017). The failure of swift, certain, and fair supervision: Choosing a more hopeful future. *Perspectives* 41, 66–78.

D'Amico, R., and Kim, H. (2016). *An Evaluation of Seven Second Chance Act Adult Demonstration Programs: Impact Findings at 18 months.* Social Policy Research Associates.

Davis, L.M., Bozick, R., Steele, J.L., Saunders, J., and Miles, J.N. (2013). *Evaluating the Effectiveness of Correctional Education: A Meta-Analysis of Programs That Provide Education to Incarcerated Adults.* RAND Corporation.

Denney, M.G.T., and Tynes, R. (2021). The effects of college in prison and policy implications. *Justice Quarterly* 38, 7, 1542–1566.

Diamond, J. (2021, July 27). Remarks made before the Committee. Committee on Evaluating Success Among People Released from Prison Meeting #2: Public Information Gathering Session. Washington, DC: National Academies of Sciences, Engineering, and Medicine.

Doeringer, P.B., and Piore, M.J. (1971). *Internal Labor Markets and Manpower Analysis*. Lexington, MA: DC Heath.

Doleac, J.L. (2018). Strategies to productively reincorporate the formerly incarcerated into communities: A review of the literature. *SSRN*. Available: http://dx.doi.org/10.2139/ssrn.3198112.

Doleac, J.L. (2019). Wrap-around services don't improve prisoner reentry outcomes. *Journal of Policy Analysis and Management* 38, 2, 508–514.

Dowd, J.B., and Todd, M. (2011). Does self-reported health bias the measurement of health inequalities in US adults? Evidence using anchoring vignettes from the Health and Retirement Study. *Journals of Gerontology Series B: Psychological Sciences and Social Sciences* 66, 4, 478–489.

Duwe, G. (2018). The effects of the timing and dosage of correctional programming on recidivism. *Journal of Offender Rehabilitation* 57, 3–4, 256–271.

Eckenrode, J., Campa, M., Luckey, D.W., Henderson, C.R., Cole, R., Kitzman, H., Anson, E., Sidora-Arcoleo, K., Powers, J., and Olds, D. (2010). Long-term effects of prenatal and infancy nurse home visitation on the life course of youths: 19-year follow-up of a randomized trial. *Archives of Pediatrics and Adolescent Medicine* 164, 1, 9–15.

Eddy, J.M., and Poehlmann-Tynan, J. (Eds.) (2019). In *Handbook on Children with Incarcerated Parents: Research, Policy, and Practice* (2nd Ed.). Springer Nature.

Farrington, D.P., 2007. Advancing knowledge about desistance. *Journal of Contemporary Criminal Justice* 23, 1, 125–134.

Fontaine, J., and Biess, J. (2012). *Housing as a Platform for Formerly Incarcerated Persons*. Washington, DC: Urban Institute.

Fox, K.J. (2010). Second chances: A comparison of civic engagement in offender reentry programs. *Criminal Justice Review* 35, 3, 335–353.

Gaes, G.G., and Camp, S.D. (2009). Unintended consequences: Experimental evidence for the criminogenic effect of prison security level placement on post-release recidivism. *Journal of Experimental Criminology* 5, 2, 139–162.

Gee, G.C., Walsemann, K.M., and Brondolo, E. (2012). A life course perspective on how racism may be related to health inequities. *American Journal of Public Health* 102, 5, 967–974.

Giordano, P.C., Cernkovich, S.A., and Rudolph, J.L. (2002). Gender, crime, and desistance: Toward a theory of cognitive transformation. *American Journal of Sociology* 107, 990–1106.

Glaze, L. and Maruschak, L. (2016) *Parents in Prison and Their Minor Children*. NCJ 222984. Washington, DC: U.S. Department of Justice, Bureau of Justice Statistics.

Gomes, H.S., Farrington, D.P., Maia, A., and Krohn, M.D. (2019). Measurement bias in self-reports of offending: A systematic review of experiments. *Journal of Experimental Criminology*. 15, 313–339. Available: https://doi.org/10.1007/s11292-019-09379-w.

Good Collins, D. (2021, July 28). Remarks made before Committee. Committee on Evaluating Success Among People Released from Prison Meeting #2: Public Information Gathering Session. Washington, DC: National Academies of Sciences, Engineering, and Medicine.

Gustafson, K. (2009). The criminalization of poverty. *The Journal of Criminal Law and Criminology* 99, 3, 643–716.

Hall, T.L., Wooten, N.R., and Lundgren, L.M. (2016). Postincarceration policies and prisoner reentry: Implications for policies and programs aimed at reducing recidivism and poverty. *Journal of Poverty* 20, 1, 56–72.

Hamilton, Z., Kigerl, A., and Hays, Z. (2015). Removing release impediments and reducing correctional costs: Evaluation of Washington State's housing voucher program. *Justice Quarterly* 32, 2, 255–287.

Hamilton-Smith, G.P., and Vogel, M. (2012). The violence of voicelessness: The impact of felony disenfranchisement on recidivism. *Berkeley La Raza Law Journal* 22, 407.

Harada, M.Y., Lara-Millán, A., and Chalwell, L.E. (2021). Policed patients: How the presence of law enforcement in the emergency department impacts medical care. *Annals of Emergency Medicine* 78, 6, 738–748

Harding, D.J., Morenoff, J.D., and Wyse, J.J. (2019). *On the Outside*. Chicago: University of Chicago Press.

Harding, D.J., Wyse, J.J., Dobson, C., and Morenoff, J.D. (2014). Making ends meet after prison. *Journal of Policy Analysis and Management* 33, 2, 440–470.

Harlow, C.W. (2003). *Education and Correctional Populations*. Bureau of Justice Statistics Special Report. Washington, DC: U.S. Department of Justice.

Hawks, L., Lopoo, E., Puglisi, L., Wang, E. (2021). *Towards a New Framework for Achieving Decarceration: A Review of the Research on Social Investments*. The Square One Project, Executive Session on the Future of Justice Policy. Available: https://squareonejustice.org/paper/anewframeworkforachievingdecarceration/.

Holzer, H.J., Raphael, S., and Stoll, M.A. (2003). Employment barriers facing ex-offenders. Washington, DC: *Urban Institute Reentry Roundtable*, 1–23.

Hu, J., Kind, A.J., and Nerenz, D. (2018). Area deprivation index predicts readmission risk at an urban teaching hospital. *American Journal of Medical Quality* 33, 5, 493–501.

Idler, E.L. and Kasl, S.V. (1995). Self-ratings of health: Do they also predict change in functional ability? *The Journals of Gerontology Series B: Psychological Sciences and Social Sciences* 50, 6, S344–S353.

Israel, B.A., Schulz, A.J., Parker, E.A. and Becker, A.B. (1998). Review of community-based research: Assessing partnership approaches to improve public health. *Annual Review of Public Health* 19, 1, 173–202.

Jarvis, M., Williams, J., Hurford, M., Lindsay, D., Lincoln, P., Giles, L., Luongo, P., and Safarian, T. (2017). Appropriate use of drug testing in clinical addiction medicine. *Journal of Addiction Medicine* 11, 3, 163–173.

Jones-Tapia, N. (2021, July 28). Remarks made before the Committee. Committee on Evaluating Success Among People Released from Prison Meeting #2: Public Information Gathering Session. Washington, DC: National Academies of Sciences, Engineering, and Medicine.

Jonson, C.L., and Cullen, F.T. (2015). Prisoner reentry programs. *Crime and Justice* 44, 1, 517–575.

Joudrey, P.J., Edelman, E.J., and Wang, E.A. (2019). Drive times to opioid treatment programs in urban and rural counties in 5 US states. *JAMA* 322, 13, 1310–1312.

Junger-Tas, J., and Marshall, I.H. (1999). *The Self-Report Methodology in Crime Research*. U.S. Department of Justice, Office of Justice Programs, Bureau of Justice Statistics, NCJ 178734.

Kaplan, G.A., and Camacho, T. (1983). Perceived health and mortality: A nine-year follow-up of the human population laboratory cohort. *American Journal of Epidemiology* 117, 3, 292–304.

Kay, E.S., Batey, D.S., and Mugavero, M.J. (2016). The HIV treatment cascade and care continuum: Updates, goals, and recommendations for the future. *AIDS Research and Therapy* 13, 1, 1–7.

Kazemian, L. (2020). *Positive Growth and Redemption in Prison: Finding Light Behind Bars and Beyond*. Abingdon, Oxon: Routledge.

Kazemian, L. (2021). *Evaluating Success Among People Released from Prison: Lessons from Abroad*. Paper presented to the Committee on Evaluating Success Among People Release from Prison. Washington DC: National Academies of Sciences, Engineering, and Medicine.

Kind, A.J.H., and Buckingham, W. (2018). Making neighborhood disadvantage metrics accessible: The neighborhood atlas. *New England Journal of Medicine* 378, 2456–2458. Available: https://doi.org/10.1056/NEJMp1802313.

Kind, A.J., Jencks, S., Brock, J., Yu, M., Bartels, C., Ehlenbach, W., Greenberg, C., and Smith, M. (2014). Neighborhood socioeconomic disadvantage and 30-day rehospitalization: A retrospective cohort study. *Annals of Internal Medicine* 161, 11, 765–774.

Kislaya, I., Tolonen, H., Rodrigues, A.P., Barreto, M., Gil, A.P., Gaio, V., Namorado, S., Santos, A.J., Dias, C.M., and Nunes, B. (2019). Differential self-report error by socioeconomic status in hypertension and hypercholesterolemia: INSEF 2015 study. *European Journal of Public Health* 29, 2, 273–278.

Kitzman, H., Olds, D.L., Knudtson, M.D., Cole, R., Anson, E., Smith, J.A., Fishbein, D., DiClemente, R., Wingood, G., Caliendo, A.M., and Hopfer, C. (2019). Prenatal and infancy nurse home visiting and 18-year outcomes of a randomized trial. *Pediatrics* 144, 6.

Klein, S., Tolbert, M., Bugarin, R., Cataldi, E.F., and Tauschek, G. (2004). *Correctional Education: Assessing the Status of Prison Programs and Information Needs*. Office of Safe and Drug-Free Schools, U.S. Department of Education.

Krawczyk, N., Schneider, K.E., Eisenberg, M.D., Richards, T.M., Ferris, L., Mojtabai, R., Stuart, E.A., Lyons, B.C., Jackson, K., Weiner, J.P., and Saloner, B. (2020). Opioid overdose death following criminal justice involvement: Linking statewide corrections and hospital databases to detect individuals at highest risk. *Drug and Alcohol Dependence* 213, 107997.

Krieger, N. (2000). Refiguring "race": Epidemiology, racialized biology, and biological expressions of race relations. *International Journal of Health Services* 30, 1, 211–216.

Kroenke, K., Spitzer, R.L., and Williams, J.B. (2001). The PHQ-9: Validity of a brief depression severity measure. *Journal of General Internal Medicine* 16, 9, 606–613.

Kubrin, C., Squires, G.D., and Stewart, E. (2007). Neighborhoods, race, and recidivism: the community reoffending nexus and its implications for African Americans. *Sage Race Relations Abstracts* 32, 7–37. Available: https://ssrn.com/abstract=2028179.

Kubrin, C.E., and Stewart, E.A. (2006). Predicting who reoffends: The neglected role of neighborhood context in recidivism studies. *Criminology* 44, 1, 165–197.

Kubrin, C.E., and Weitzer, R. (2003) New directions in social disorganization theory. *Journal of Research in Crime and Delinquency* 40, 374–402.

Lacoe, J., and Betesh, H. (2018). *Supporting Reentry Employment and Success: A Summary of the Evidence for Adults and Young Adults*. Mathematica Policy Research. Available: https://ideas.repec.org/p/mpr/mprres/26ce465de8784278a4bf28545a1a870a.html.

Lageson, S.E. (2020). *Digital punishment: Privacy, Stigma, and the Harms of Data-Driven Criminal Justice*. Oxford University Press.

Latessa, E.J., Johnson, S.L., and Koetzle, D. (2020). *What Works (and Doesn't) in Reducing Recidivism*. Routledge.

Lattimore, P. (2020). Considering program evaluation: Thoughts from SVORI (and other) evaluations. *Rethinking Reentry*. Washington, DC: American Enterprise Institute.

Lattimore, P.K., Dawes, D., and Barrick, K. (2018). *Desistance from Crime over the Life Course*. Washington, DC: National Institute of Justice.

Lattimore, P.K., MacKenzie, D.L., Zajac, G., Dawes, D., Arsenault, E., and Tueller, S. (2016). Outcome findings from the HOPE demonstration field experiment: Is swift, certain, and fair an effective supervision strategy? *Criminology and Public Policy* 15, 4, 1103–1141.

Lattimore, P., and Visher, C. (2021). Considerations on the multi-site evaluation of the serious and violent offender reentry initiative. In P.K. Lattimore, B.M. Huebner, and F.S. Taxman (Eds.), *Handbook on Moving Corrections and Sentencing Forward: Building on the Record*, 312–335. New York, NY: Routledge.

La Vigne, N., Davies, E., Palmer, T., and Halberstadt, R. (2008). Release planning for successful reentry. *A Guide for Corrections, Service Providers, and Community Groups*. Washington, DC: Urban Institute, Justice Policy Center. Available: https://core.ac.uk/download/pdf/71348466.pdf.

LeBel, T.P., Burnett, R., Maruna, S., and Bushway, S. (2008). The 'chicken and egg' of subjective and social factors in desistance from crime. *European Journal of Criminology* 5, 2, 131–159.

Lewis, S. (2021, July 28). Remarks made before the Committee. Committee on Evaluating Success Among People Released from Prison Meeting #2: Public Information Gathering Session. Washington, DC: National Academies of Sciences, Engineering, and Medicine.

Lindquist, C.H., Willison, J.B., and Lattimore, P.K. (2021). Key findings and implications of the cross-site evaluation of the bureau of justice assistance FY 2011 Second Chance Act adult offender reentry demonstration projects. In P.K. Lattimore, B.M. Huebner, and F.S. Taxman (Eds.), *Handbook on Moving Corrections and Sentencing Forward: Building on the Record*, 336–358. New York, NY: Routledge.

Link, B.G., and Phelan, J. (1995). Social conditions as fundamental causes of disease. *Journal of Health and Social Behavior, Extra Issue: Forty Years of Medical Sociology: The State of the Art and Directions for the Future*, 80–94.

Liu, L. (2020a). Family, parochial, and public levels of social control and recidivism: An extension of the systemic model of social disorganization. *Crime and Delinquency* 66, 6–7, 864–886.

Liu, L. (2020b). Parole, neighborhood and reentry outcomes: A contextualized analysis. *International Journal of Offender Therapy and Comparative Criminology* 65, 6–7, 741–762.

Ludwig, J., Sanbonmatsu, L., Gennetian, L., Adam, E., Duncan, G.J., Katz, L.F., Kessler, R.C., Kling, J.R., Lindau, S.T., Whitaker, R.C., and McDade, T.W. (2011). Neighborhoods, obesity, and diabetes—A randomized social experiment. *New England Journal of Medicine* 365, 16, 1509–1519.

Lutze, F.E., Rosky, J.W., and Hamilton, Z.K. (2014). Homelessness and reentry: A multi-site outcome evaluation of Washington State's reentry housing program for high-risk offenders. *Criminal Justice and Behavior* 41, 4, 471–491.

Macdonald, D.G., and Bala, G. (1986). *Follow-up Study of a Sample of Offenders Who Earned High School Equivalency Diplomas While Incarcerated*. State of New York, Department of Correctional Services, Division of Program Planning, Research and Evaluation.

MacKenzie, D.L. (2006). *What Works in Corrections: Reducing the Criminal Activities of Offenders and Delinquents*. Cambridge University Press.

Maguire, M., Disley, E., Liddle, M., Meek, R., and Burrowes, N. (2019) *Developing a Toolkit to Measure Intermediate Outcomes to Reduce Reoffending from Arts and Mentoring Interventions*. London: Ministry of Justice.

Manor, O., Matthews, S., and Power, C. (2001). Self-rated health and limiting longstanding illness: Inter-relationships with morbidity in early adulthood. *International Journal of Epidemiology* 30, 3, 600–607.

Manza, J., and Uggen, C. (2006). *Locked Out: Felon Disenfranchisement and American Democracy*. Oxford, UK: Oxford University Press.

Maruna, S. (2001). *Making Good: How Ex-Convicts Reform and Rebuild Their Lives*. Washington, DC: American Psychological Association.

Massoglia, M., and Pridemore, W.A. (2015). Incarceration and health. *Annual Review of Sociology* 41, 291–310.

Massoglia, M., and Uggen, C. (2007). Subjective desistance and the transition to adulthood. *Journal of Contemporary Criminal Justice* 23, 1, 90–103.

Massoglia, M., and Uggen, C. (2010). Settling down and aging out: Toward an interactionist theory of desistance and the transition to adulthood. *American Journal of Sociology* 116, 543–82.

McDonald, D., Dyous, C., and Carlson, K.E. (2008). *The Effectiveness of Prisoner Reentry Services as Crime Control: The Fortune Society*. Abt Associates, Incorporated.

Mears, D.P., and Bales, W.D. (2009). Supermax incarceration and recidivism. *Criminology* 47, 4, 1131–1166.

Metraux, S., Hunt, D., and Yetvin, W. (2020). *Criminal Justice Reentry and Homelessness.* Cambridge, MA: Abt Associates.

Miller, R.J. (2021). *Halfway Home: Race, Punishment, and the Afterlife of Mass Incarceration.* New York: Little, Brown and Company.

Moore, K.E., Roberts, W., Reid, H.H., Smith, K.M., Oberleitner, L.M., and McKee, S.A. (2019). Effectiveness of medication assisted treatment for opioid use in prison and jail settings: A meta-analysis and systematic review. *Journal of Substance Abuse Treatment* 99, 32–43.

Muhlhausen, D. (2015). *Studies Cast Doubt on Effectiveness of Prisoner Reentry Programs.* The Heritage Foundation, Crime and Justice.

National Academies of Sciences, Engineering, and Medicine. (2017). *Improving Collection of Indicators of Criminal Justice System Involvement in Population Health Data Programs: Proceedings of a Workshop.* Washington, DC: The National Academies Press. Available: https://doi.org/10.17226/24633.

National Research Council. (2008). *Parole, Desistance from Crime, and Community Integration.* Washington, DC: The National Academies Press. Available: https://doi.org/10.17226/11988

National Research Council. (2014). *The Growth of Incarceration in the United States: Exploring Causes and Consequences.* Washington, DC: The National Academies Press. Available: https://doi.org/10.17226/18613.

Nelson, K. (2021, July 27). Remarks made before the Committee. Committee on Evaluating Success Among People Released from Prison, Meeting #2: Public Information Gathering Session. Washington, DC: National Academies of Sciences, Engineering, and Medicine.

Niemi, R.G., Craig, S.C., and Mattei, F. (1991). Measuring internal political efficacy in the 1988 National Election Study. *American Political Science Review* 85, 4, 1407–1413. Available: http://doi.org/10.2307/1963953.

Nuttall, J., Hollmen, L., and Staley, E.M. (2003). The effect of earning a GED on recidivism rates. *Journal of Correctional Education* 54, 3, 90–94.

Olds, D.L., Eckenrode, J., Henderson, C.R., Kitzman, H., Powers, J., Cole, R., Sidora, K., Morris, P., Pettitt, L.M., and Luckey, D. (1997). Long-term effects of home visitation on maternal life course and child abuse and neglect: Fifteen-year follow-up of a randomized trial. *Journal of the American Medical Association* 278, 8, 637–643.

Olds, D., Henderson, Jr., C.R., Cole, R., Eckenrode, J., Kitzman, H., Luckey, D., Pettitt, L., Sidora, K., Morris, P., and Powers, J. (1998). Long-term effects of nurse home visitation on children's criminal and antisocial behavior: 15-year follow-up of a randomized controlled trial. *Journal of the American Medical Association* 280, 14, 1238–1244.

Ortiz, J.M., and Jackey, H. (2019). The system is not broken, it is intentional: The prison reentry industry as deliberate structural violence. *The Prison Journal* 99, 4, 484–503.

Paikowsky, D. (2019). Jails as polling places: Living up to the obligation to enfranchise the voters we jail. *Harvard Civil Rights-Civil Liberties Law Review* 54, 2, 829–873.

Paternoster, R., Bachman, R., Bushway, S., Kerrison, E., and O'Connell, D. (2015). Human agency and explanations of criminal desistance: Arguments for a rational choice theory. *Journal of Developmental and Life-Course Criminology* 1, 3, 209–235.

Paternoster, R., Bachman, R., Kerrison, E., O'Connell, D., and Smith, L. (2016). Desistance from crime and identity: An empirical test with survival time. *Criminal Justice and Behavior* 43, 9, 1204–1224.

Paternoster, R., and Bushway, S. (2009). Desistance and the "feared self": Toward an identity theory of criminal desistance. *The Journal of Criminal Law and Criminology* 99, 4, 1103–1156.

Pettus-Davis, C., and Kennedy, S. (2020). Early lessons from the multistate study of the 5-key model for reentry. *Perspectives: The Journal of the American Probation and Parole Association* 44, 19–31.

Pettus-Davis, C., and Veeh, C. (2021). *Associations Between Well-Being and Reincarceration: Early Data on the 5-Key Model*. Florida State University, Institute for Justice Research and Development. Available: https://ijrd.csw.fsu.edu/sites/g/files/upcbnu1766/files/Publications/Associations_between_Well-Being_and_Incarceration.pdf.

Powell, W.R., Buckingham, W.R., Larson, J.L., Vilen, L., Yu, M., Salamat, M.S., Bendlin, B.B., Rissman, R.A., and Kind, A.J. (2020). Association of neighborhood-level disadvantage with Alzheimer disease neuropathology. *JAMA Network Open* 3, 6, e207559–e207559.

Puglisi, L. (2021, July 28). Remarks made before the Committee. Committee on Evaluating Success Among People Released from Prison Meeting #2: Public Information Gathering Session. Washington, DC: National Academies of Sciences, Engineering, and Medicine.

Puglisi, L., Halberstam, A.A., Aminawung, J., Gallagher, C., Gonsalves, L., Schulman-Green, D., Lin, H.J., Metha, R., Mun, S., Oladeru, O.T., and Gross, C. (2021). Incarceration and Cancer-Related Outcomes (ICRO) study protocol: Using a mixed-methods approach to investigate the role of incarceration on cancer incidence, mortality and quality of care. *British Medical Journal Open* 11, 5, e048863.

Ranapurwala, S.I., Casteel, C., and Peek-Asa, C. (2016). Volunteering in adolescence and young adulthood crime involvement: A longitudinal analysis from the add health study. *Injury Epidemiology* 3, 26. Available: https://doi.org/10.1186/s40621-016-0091-6.

RAND, 36-Item Short Forum Survey (SF-36). Available: https://www.rand.org/health-care/surveys_tools/mos/36-item-short-form.html.

Ramakers, A., Nieuwbeerta, P., Van Wilsem, J., and Dirkzwager, A. (2017). Not just any job will do: A study on employment characteristics and recidivism risks after release. *International Journal of Offender Therapy and Comparative Criminology* 61, 16, 1795–1818.

Rice, D. (2021, July 28). Remarks made before the Committee. Committee on Evaluating Success Among People Released from Prison Meeting #2: Public Information Gathering Session. Washington, DC: National Academies of Sciences, Engineering, and Medicine.

Richie, B. (2001). Challenges incarcerated women face as they return to their communities: Findings from life history interviews. *Crime and Delinquency* 47, 368–389.

Runell, L.L. (2015). Life-course engagement in crime, post-secondary education and desistance for formerly incarcerated college students (Doctoral dissertation). Newark, NJ: Rutgers University Graduate School.

Sampson, R.J., and Laub, J.H. (1990). Crime and deviance over the life course: The salience of adult social bonds. *American Sociological Review* 55, 609–627.

Sampson, R.J., and Laub, J.H. (1993). *Crime in the Making: Pathways and Turning Points through Life*. Harvard University Press.

Sampson, R.J., and Laub, J.H. (2003). Desistance from crime over the life course. In *Handbook of the Life Course*, 295–309. Mortimer, J.T. and Shanahan, M.J. eds. Springer, Boston, MA.

Schweinhart, L.J., and Weikart, D.P. (1997). The High/Scope preschool curriculum comparison study through age 23. *Early Childhood Research Quarterly* 12, 2, 117–143.

Shavit, S., Aminawung, J.A., Birnbaum, N., Greenberg, S., Berthold, T., Fishman, A., Busch, S.H., and Wang, E.A. (2017). Transitions clinic network: Challenges and lessons in primary care for people released from prison. *Health Affairs* 36, 6, 1006–1015.

Sherman, L.W., Farrington, D.P., Welsh, B.C., and MacKenzie, D.L. (Eds.). (2006). *Evidence-based Crime Prevention* (2nd Ed.). New York: Routledge.

Sherman, L.W., Gottfredson, DC, MacKenzie, D.L., Eck, J., Reuter, P., and Bushway, S. (1997). *Preventing Crime: What Works, What Doesn't, What's Promising: A Report to the United States Congress*. Washington, DC: National Institute of Justice.

Siegel, M., Bradley, E.H., and Kasl, S.V. (2003). Self-rated life expectancy as a predictor of mortality: Evidence from the HRS and AHEAD surveys. *Gerontology* 49, 4, 265–271.

Simes, J.T. (2018). Place after prison: Neighborhood attainment and attachment during reentry. *Journal of Urban Affairs* 41, 4, 443–463. DOI: 10.1080/07352166.2018.1495041.

Sirois, C. (2019). Household support and social integration in the year after prison. *Sociological Forum* 34, 4, 838–860.

Skardhamar, T., and Savolainen, J. (2014). Changes in criminal offending around the time of job entry: A study of employment and desistance. *Criminology* 52, 2, 263–291.

Skeem, J.L., Louden, J.E., Manchak, S., Vidal, S., and Haddad, E. (2009). Social networks and social control of probationers with co-occurring mental and substance abuse problems. *Law and Human Behavior* 33, 122–135.

Steiner, B., Makarios, M.D., and Travis III, L.F. (2015). Examining the effects of residential situations and residential mobility on offender recidivism. *Crime and Delinquency* 61, 3, 375–401.

Stiefel, M.C., Riley, C.L., Roy, B., Ramaswamy, R., and Stout, S. (2016). *100 Million Healthier Lives Measurement System: Progress to Date*. 100 Million Healthier Lives Metrics Development Team Report. Cambridge, MA: Institute for Healthcare Improvement.

Strauss, W. (2021, July 27). Remarks made to the Committee. Committee on Evaluating Success Among People Released from Prison Meeting #2: Public Information Gathering Session. Washington, DC: National Academies of Sciences, Engineering, and Medicine.

Sundaresh, R., Yi, Y., Harvey, T.D., Roy, B., Riley, C., Lee, H., Wildeman, C., and Wang, E.A. (2021). Exposure to family member incarceration and adult well-being in the United States. *Journal of the American Medical Association (network open)* 4, 5, e2111821–e2111821.

Sundaresh, R., Yi, Y., Roy, B., Riley, C., Wildeman, C., and Wang, E.A. (2020). Exposure to the US criminal legal system and well-being: A 2018 cross-sectional study. *American Journal of Public Health* 110, S1, S116–S122.

Tarlov, A.R., Ware, J.E., Greenfield, S., Nelson, E.C., Perrin, E., and Zubkoff, M. (1989). The Medical Outcomes Study: An application of methods for monitoring the results of medical care. *Journal of the American Medical Association* 262, 7, 925–930.

Tolonen, H., Koponen, P., Mindell, J.S., Männistö, S., Giampaoli, S., Dias, C.M., Tuovinen, T., Gößwald, A., and Kuulasmaa, K. (2014). Under-estimation of obesity, hypertension and high cholesterol by self-reported data: Comparison of self-reported information and objective measures from health examination surveys. *The European Journal of Public Health* 24, 6, 941–948.

Tomberg, K.A., Moreno, G., Cobar, P., and Alexander, N. (2021). *Returning Home: A Descriptive Evaluation of Prepare in New York City*. New York, NY: Research and Evaluation Center, John Jay College of Criminal Justice, City University of New York. Available: https://johnjayrec.nyc/2021/10/11/osborne_prepare/.

Tripodi, S.J., Kim, J.S., and Bender, K. (2010). Is employment associated with reduced recidivism? The complex relationship between employment and crime. *International Journal of Offender Therapy and Comparative Criminology* 54, 5, 706–720.

Uggen, C. (1999). Ex-offenders and the conformist alternative: A job quality model of work and crime. *Social Problems* 46, 1, 127–151.

Uggen, C., and Inderbitzin, M. (2010). Public criminologies. *Criminology and Public Policy* 9, 4, 725–749.

Uggen, C., and Janikula, J. (1999). Volunteerism and arrest in the transition to adulthood. *Social Forces* 78, 331–62.

Uggen, C., Larson, R., Shannon, S., and Pulido-Nava, A. (2020). *Locked Out 2020: Estimates of People Denied Voting Rights Due to a Felony Conviction*. The Sentencing Project. Available: https://www.sentencingproject.org/publications/locked-out-2020-estimates-of-people-denied-voting-rights-due-to-a-felony-conviction/.

Uggen, C., and Manza, J. (2004). Voting and subsequent crime and arrest: Evidence from a community sample. *Columbia Human Rights Law Review* 36, 193–215.

Uggen, C., and Manza, J. (2005). Disenfranchisement and the civic reintegration of convicted felons. In C. Mele and T.A. Miller (Eds.), *Civil Penalties, Social Consequences*, 67–8. Routledge.

Uggen, C., Manza, J., and Behrens, A. (2004). Less than the average citizen: Stigma, role transition, and the civic reintegration of convicted felons. In S. Maruna and R. Immarigeon (Eds.), *After Crime and Punishment: Pathways to Offender Reintegration*, 258–290. Cullompton, Devon, UK: Willan Publishing.

Uggen, C., Manza, J., and Thompson, M. (2006). Citizenship, democracy, and the civic reintegration of criminal offenders. *The Annals of the American Academy of Political and Social Science* 605, 1, 281–310.

Uggen, C. and Massoglia, M. (2007). Subjective desistance and the transition to adulthood. *Journal of Contemporary Criminal Justice* 23, 90.

U.S. Equal Employment Opportunity Commission. (2012). *Enforcement Guidance on the Consideration of Arrest and Conviction Records in Employment Decisions under Title VII of the Civil Rights Act.* Available: https://www.eeoc.gov/laws/guidance/enforcement-guidance-consideration-arrest-and-conviction-records-employment-decisions.

Vacca, J.S. (2004). Educated prisoners are less likely to return to prison. *Journal of Correctional Education* 55, 4, 297–305.

Valverde, J. (2021, July 27). Remarks made before the Committee. Committee on Evaluating Success Among People Released from Prison Meeting #2: Public Information Gathering Session. Washington, DC: National Academies of Sciences, Engineering, and Medicine.

Veeh, C.A., Renn, T., and Pettus-Davis, C. (2018). Promoting reentry well-being: A novel assessment tool for individualized service assignment in prisoner reentry programs. *Social Work* 63, 1, 91–96.

Vilda, D., Hardeman, R., Dyer, L., Theall, K.P., and Wallace, M. (2021). Structural racism, racial inequities and urban–rural differences in infant mortality in the U.S. *Journal of Epidemiology and Community Health* 75, 8, 1–6.

Visher, C.A. (2007). Returning home: Emerging findings and policy lessons about prisoner reentry. *Federal Sentencing Reporter* 20, 1, 93–102.

Visher, C.A., and La Vigne, N. (2020). Returning home: A pathbreaking study of prisoner reentry and its challenges. In P.K. Lattimore, B.M. Huebner, and F. Taxman (Eds.), *Handbook on Moving Corrections and Sentencing Forward*, 278–311. Routledge.

Visher, C.A. and Travis, J. (2003). Transitions from prison to community: Understanding individual pathways. *Annual Review of Sociology*, 29, 81–113.

Wang, E.A., Long, J.B., McGinnis, K.A., Wang, K.H., Wildeman, C.J., Kim, C., Bucklen, K.B., Fiellin, D.A., Bates, J., Brandt, C., and Justice, A.C. (2019). Measuring exposure to incarceration using the electronic health record. *Medical Care* 57, S157–S163.

Wang, E.A., Macmadu, A., and Rich, J.D. (2019). Examining the impact of criminal justice involvement on health through federally funded, national population-based surveys in the United States. *Public Health Reports* 134, 1, 22S–33S.

Wang, E.A., Wang, Y., and Krumholz, H.M. (2013). A high risk of hospitalization following release from correctional facilities in Medicare beneficiaries: A retrospective matched cohort study, 2002 to 2010. *JAMA Internal Medicine* 173, 17, 1621–1628.

Weaver, V.M. and Lerman, A.E. (2010). Political consequences of the carceral state. *American Political Science Review* 104, 4, 817–833. Available: http://doi.org/10.1017/S0003055410000456.

Weikart, D.P. (1998). Changing early childhood development through educational intervention. *Preventive Medicine* 27, 2, 233–237.

Weisburd, D., Farrington, D.P., and Gill, C. (2017). What works in crime prevention and rehabilitation: An assessment of systematic reviews. *Criminology and Public Policy* 16, 2, 415–449.

Western, B. (2002). The impact of incarceration on wage mobility and inequality. *American Sociological Review* 67,4, 526–546.

Western, B. (2006). *Punishment and Inequality in America.* New York, NY: Russell Sage Foundation.

Western, B. (2018). *Homeward: Life in the Year After Prison.* Russell Sage Foundation.

Western, B., Braga, A.A., Davis, J., and Sirois, C. (2015). Stress and hardship after prison. *American Journal of Sociology* 120, 5, 1512–1547.

Wildeman, C., and Wang, E.A. (2017). Mass incarceration, public health, and widening inequality in the USA. *The Lancet* 389, 10077, 1464–1474.

Wilkinson, R., Rhine, E., and Henderson-Hurly, M. (2005). Reentry in Ohio corrections: A catalyst for change. *Journal of Correctional Education* 56, 2, 158–172.

Williams, A.R., Nunes, E.V., Bisaga, A., Pincus, H.A., Johnson, K.A., Campbell, A.N., Remien, R.H., Crystal, S., Friedmann, P.D., Levin, F.R., and Olfson, M. (2018). Developing an opioid use disorder treatment cascade: A review of quality measures. *Journal of Substance Abuse Treatment* 91, 57–68.

Willoughby, M., Keen, C., Young, J.T., Spittal, M.J., Borschmann, R., Janca, E., and Kinner, S.A. (2021). Violence-related morbidity among people released from prison in Australia: A data linkage study. *Drug and Alcohol Review* 41, 2, 457–466.

Wilson, D.B., Gallagher, C.A., and MacKenzie, D.L. (2000). A meta-analysis of corrections-based education, vocation, and work programs for adult offenders. *Journal of Research in Crime and Delinquency* 37, 4, 347–368.

Winkler, A. (1993). Expressive voting. *New York University Law Review* 68, 330.

Wong, K., and Horan, R. (2019). Early testing and formative evaluation of enablers of change assessment and sentence planning tools for adults with convictions. *European Journal of Probation* 11, 1, 30–48.

Woods, V. (2021, July 28). *Practitioner Perspectives on Reentry Programs remarks made before the Committee.* Committee on Evaluating Success Among People Released from Prison Meeting #2: Public Information Gathering Session. Washington, DC: National Academies of Sciences, Engineering, and Medicine.

World Health Organization. (1948). Preamble to the Constitution of the World Health Organization. *Official Records of the World Health Organization, 1948.*

Wright, K.A. (2020). Time well spent: Misery, meaning, and the opportunity of incarceration. *The Howard Journal* 59, 1, 44–64.

Wright, K.A., Morse, S.J, and Sutton, M.M. (2021). The limits of recidivism reduction: Advancing a more comprehensive understanding of correctional success. In J. Gould and P. Metzger (Eds.), *Big Ideas in Criminal Justice Reform.* New York University Press.

Yehia, B.R., Schranz, A.J., Umscheid, C.A., and Lo Re III, V. (2014). The treatment cascade for chronic hepatitis C virus infection in the United States: A systematic review and meta-analysis. *PloS one* 9, 7, e101554.

Zgoba, K.M., Haugebrook, S., Jenkins, K. (2008). The influence of GED obtainment on inmate release outcome. *Criminal Justice and Behavior* 35, 3, 375–387. Available: https://doi.org/10.1177/0093854807311853.

5

The Path Forward

This chapter summarizes the evidence from the preceding chapters and presents conclusions and recommendations pertaining to the study committee's two-pronged charge: (1) evaluating existing measures of success for those returning from prison, including but not limited to the cessation of criminal activity, and (2) considering alternative measures of success. As this report suggests, there is great promise for improving our measurement of success among individuals released from prison, and better measurement is a necessary, if not sufficient, condition for improving post-release policy and practice.

In presenting its conclusions and recommendations, the committee recognizes that persons with lived experience of incarceration and practitioners who work with them have unique insights regarding the conceptualization and measurement of post-release success. Formerly incarcerated individuals and reentry practitioners have made valuable contributions to each chapter of this report. The study committee strongly recommends that their experiential knowledge and expertise inform the design and implementation of each of the following recommendations. Ensuring that the perspectives of all key stakeholders are taken into consideration throughout research development is critical to increasing the relevance and effectiveness of any resulting intervention programs and can help to empower populations that have been stigmatized, marginalized, and ignored.

FROM RECIDIVISM TO DESISTANCE

Recidivism refers to a return to criminal activity. However, most recidivism measures are based on administrative records of actions taken by the

193

criminal legal system, including arrest, revocation, conviction, and incarceration. These measures therefore reflect the *interaction* between individuals and the criminal legal system and not necessarily engagement in criminal behavior that may go undetected by criminal legal system actors. Nor do such measures account for the greater likelihood that some individuals may face arrest due to their identity or location and others may be arrested and convicted despite being innocent. In addition, as discussed in Chapter 2, recidivism rates differ depending on whether they are based on the records of those entering or leaving prison. Most persons who have been to prison do not return to prison, while roughly half of those released from prison at a given time, many of whom have been in prison multiple times, are likely to return. Finally, recidivism rates typically include technical violations of the conditions of community supervision that may not constitute criminal behavior for the general population (e.g., missing a parole meeting or failing a drug test). In these ways, current recidivism measures risk being both under- and over-inclusive.

Referring generally to a "recidivism rate" based solely on administrative data sources invites misinterpretation and policy responses that are not appropriately tailored to the actual circumstances of reoffending or to the specific purposes of research and interventions. One common misinterpretation has been mentioned: assuming that persons who have been in prison will probably return. Policy responses may be misinformed by common recidivism measures, which do not record changes in the frequency or seriousness of criminal activity by persons released from prison—the focus of our first recommendation.

A robust body of literature on desistance has demonstrated that the cessation of criminal activity, like other behavioral changes, is incremental and may involve setbacks. Despite this, recidivism is typically measured in a binary manner that distinguishes between people who are and those who are not rearrested, reconvicted, or reincarcerated after release from prison without adequate description of consequential changes in post-release criminal involvement. Measures of desistance offer a more nuanced, complete, and realistic view of the cessation of criminal behavior.

Viewing any return to crime as failure obscures how cessation of criminal behavior actually occurs and fails to recognize positive progress, such as longer time elapsing between crimes or fewer serious crimes committed. For example, using existing measures of recidivism, someone previously convicted of armed robbery who is arrested or convicted on a misdemeanor charge for shoplifting would be labeled a recidivist. An alternative measure from a desistance perspective would acknowledge setbacks in the process of desistance and count less serious criminal activity as a potential indicator of progress. Moreover, focusing only on criminal activity neglects other signifiers of progress, including change in life circumstances, self-view, and feelings of hope that can result in reduced involvement in crime over time, eventually leading to the cessation of criminal behavior.

Conclusion 1: Recidivism rates based on administrative records reflect the interaction between individuals and the criminal legal system. These measures reflect decisions by legal authorities and not necessarily an individual's return to criminal activity.

Conclusion 2: Because cessation or reduction in criminal behavior often occurs as part of a gradual process that may involve setbacks, measures of desistance from crime offer a more realistic account of an individual's reduction in criminal activity.

Recommendation 1: To ensure more precise and accurate use of the construct of recidivism, researchers, policy makers, and practitioners should (a) specify the exact actions taken by legal authorities (arrest, revocation, conviction, incarceration) included in their measures, (b) clarify the limitations of the data used to measure these actions, and (c) supplement binary recidivism measures with measures of desistance from crime, such as the frequency and seriousness of offenses.

MEASURING SUCCESS

As emphasized in our conversations with formerly incarcerated individuals, correctional officials, and service providers for crime victims and survivors, recidivism does not capture important, positive post-release outcomes that facilitate social integration and individual well-being. A more meaningful conception of success views post-release outcomes through the lens of healthy adult development across multiple life domains in addition to criminal involvement: education, employment, housing, family and social support, and mental and physical health. Such a broad conception of success involves a heightened sense of personal well-being, which is not generally captured in administrative records. As such, the measurement of post-release success should include reliance on self-report data and standardized psychological instruments that provide indicators of post-release success not contained in official records. Examples of existing instruments discussed in Chapter 4 include the Cantril Self-Anchoring Striving Scale, 100 Million Healthier Lives, and Well-being in the Nation instruments. Other measures include the National Institutes of Health's PhenX Toolkit.

Conclusion 3: Post-release success involves multiple life domains (e.g., health, employment, housing, civic engagement) and not simply involvement in the criminal legal system. Success entails a heightened sense of personal well-being, which is best measured on the basis of self-report surveys and validated assessment instruments.

Recommendation 2: Researchers should review existing measures and, as needed, develop and validate new measures to evaluate post-release success in multiple domains, including personal well-being, education, employment, housing, family and social supports, health, civic and community engagement, and legal involvement.

Barriers to Success

Success following imprisonment cannot be understood without attention to the social context into which people return. An individual's environment after release can support or undermine their ability to successfully return to society. What resources and supports, if any, are available in an individual's neighborhood to facilitate success? In what ways are the organizations that provide these resources and supports attentive to or dismissive of the needs of returning individuals? How do local or state policies and practices impede progress and eventual desistance from criminal behavior?

Given persistent racial and ethnic inequalities in health, housing, education, and employment—and the disproportionate incarceration of Black, Brown, and Indigenous populations—how is post-release success for historically marginalized groups shaped by structural inequalities within each of these systems and the community at large? Without understanding how community contextual factors and existing policies support or hinder an individual's return from prison, opportunities to identify and potentiate success after incarceration are missed.

Measuring structural barriers and systemic inequalities that impede success can include recording the residential address (or other geographic identifiers) in intervention studies and program evaluations of individuals returning from prison. Linking the geographic data to existing small-area measures, such as the Area Deprivation Index, would enhance understanding of how community socioeconomic conditions affect an individual's potential for success following release from prison. Researchers can also track whether individuals are subject to particular state or local regulations that restrict employment, housing, or public assistance for those with criminal records, local or state variations in what constitutes a technical parole violation, and the level of police surveillance in their community.

Understanding how institutions and organizations hinder success or facilitate it is equally important, especially concerning how systems that provide health care, food, transportation, education, and employment support the needs of individuals released from prison. Linking data from correctional systems to other administrative data from state and local government could increase understanding of how different sectors support the success of individuals following release. For example, some studies have linked data from correctional systems to substance use treatment, opioid overdose, and cancer tumor databases. These studies demonstrate how linkages with health systems that compile data on the social determinants of health can better serve people who are being released from prison.

Moreover, linkages can be made between administrative data from various systems and data from well-being inventories and ongoing longitudinal surveys such as those discussed in Chapter 4. To be sure, such data linkages would need to be carefully designed and monitored, with input from individuals with a history of incarceration, both to protect privacy and to avoid coercive surveillance leading to repeat encounters with the criminal legal system.[1]

> **Conclusion 4:** The existence of community-level and policy facilitators of and barriers to success can be documented in studies that link data on post-release success and local socioeconomic conditions, policies that restrict access to employment, housing, and public benefits, and structural inequalities that disproportionately affect persons of color.

> **Recommendation 3:** Researchers should review and, as needed, develop new measures of facilitators of and structural barriers to post-release success that link data across multiple domains, including personal well-being, education, employment, housing, family and social supports, health, civic and community engagement, and legal involvement. These measures should reflect the particular needs and experiences of historically marginalized groups.

NATIONAL STANDARDS FOR MEASURING POST-RELEASE SUCCESS

Linking data across multiple recordkeeping systems would facilitate the development of national standards to measure success among persons released from prison. By establishing a standardized, minimum set of demographic, social, economic, and legal data to be collected by local, state, and federal agencies, national standards would enhance the comparability of evaluations of post-release outcomes and the quality and utility of administrative data for monitoring success across multiple policy domains.

---

[1]See the two-volume National Academies (2017) report *Federal Statistics, Multiple Data Sources, and Privacy Protection* (https://www.nap.edu/catalog/24893/federal-statistics-multiple-data-sources-and-privacy-protection-next-steps).

These standardized uniform success measures would supplement, not replace, the local measures correctional agencies use to monitor their performance. As noted in Chapter 2, the local measures can yield best practices in the measurement of success to inform the development and refinement of the national standards.

A model for this kind of standardized data repository is the Uniform Crime Reports (recently superseded by National Incident-Based Reporting System), which provides harmonized crime classification and coding procedures for local law enforcement agencies. In addition, national standards for measuring post-release success would benefit from the kind of continuous updating by the World Health Organization of its International Classification of Diseases (ICD) codes used in research, treatment, and disease prevention efforts. The ICD also harmonizes data across different systems and levels of government.

More immediately, the academic community could develop a website of core success measures, instruments, and validation studies from multiple administrative domains that is accessible to researchers, practitioners, and policymakers. The website and accompanying communication among researchers and practitioners would begin to establish norms around common measurement and provide guidance on how to address gaps, errors, and other data issues when measuring success across diverse information sources. Such a toolkit could be developed by a combination of partnerships between private foundations and government agencies.

Conclusion 5: National standards for measuring success among individuals released from prison would augment the comparability of program evaluations and the utility of administrative and other data across multiple policy domains. The development of a website containing core measures and instruments would hasten the eventual development of national measurement standards. These efforts can be supported by federal agencies and private foundations committed to improving success for persons released from prison.

Recommendation 4: The National Institute of Justice, Bureau of Justice Statistics, Bureau of Justice Assistance, National Institutes of Health, and other federal agencies and centers whose missions are central to the success of persons released from prison should (1) convene interdisciplinary research advisory panels to assess data, methods, and recommendations for measuring post-release success; (2) request grant proposals from researchers and practitioners, in collaboration with formerly incarcerated persons, to review existing measures of success and develop and validate new measures as needed; and (3) consider questions relevant to the measurement of post-release success in existing survey protocols such as the American Community Survey and data collection efforts in other domains such as education, labor, and health. In order to carry out such activities, additional funding will be required. Private foundations committed to improving success among persons released from prison should support this evaluation independently or in partnership with federal agencies. Governmental and private support should be directed, at a minimum, to the following issues:

a) The quality of records from legal and other social institutions used to monitor post-release success;

b) The utility and feasibility of linking records across multiple administrative domains;

c) The utility and feasibility of linking existing administrative data with instruments measuring personal well-being;

d) The development of a website containing core measures of success across multiple administrative domains and the role of qualitative as well as quantitative research in the development of these measures; and

e) The eventual development of uniform national standards for measuring post-release success.

CONCLUSION

Five overarching themes emerged from the committee's deliberations on improving the measurement of success among persons released from prison:

1. Current binary measures of recidivism do not adequately reflect the continuation or cessation of criminal behavior and should be augmented by measures of desistance from crime that, at a minimum, account for changes in the frequency and seriousness of criminal activity.

2. Post-release success is multifaceted and cannot be adequately measured by indicators of criminal involvement alone.

3. Persistent group inequalities require that measures of post-release success take into account the needs and experiences of historically marginalized populations.

4. The perspectives of persons with lived experience of incarceration and practitioners need to be part of all efforts to improve and implement new measures of post-release success.

5. Improving measures of post-release success will benefit formerly incarcerated persons, the communities to which they return, and society as a whole by supporting policies to facilitate post-release social integration, enhance personal well-being, and improve public safety.

While the committee was not asked to consider how better measurement would lead to better outcomes for individuals, communities, and public policy, the fundamental objective of upgrading the quality and utility of social measurement, particularly in areas of significant public concern like the criminal legal system, is to enhance individual and social well-being. Faulty measurement serves no good public purpose. Our recommendations for improving the measurement of post-release success, if implemented, can inform the development of effective policies to increase the health, safety, and security of formerly incarcerated persons and their communities.

Appendix

Committee Member Biographies

Richard Rosenfeld is the Curators' distinguished professor emeritus of Criminology and Criminal Justice at the University of Missouri-St. Louis. Rosenfeld has written extensively on crime trends and crime control policy. His current research focuses on changes in crime rates during the U.S. coronavirus pandemic. He is a fellow and former President of the American Society of Criminology. He received his Ph.D. in Sociology from the University of Oregon.

Robert Apel is a professor in the School of Criminal Justice at Rutgers University-Newark. Much of Apel's research is at the intersection of crime, the criminal legal system, and the labor market. This research seeks to better understand the work-crime relationship, the impact of criminal justice involvement on long-term employment, the comparative effects of the labor market and the social safety net on crime, and the efficacy of employment-based reentry programming. He received his Ph.D. in Criminology and Criminal Justice from the University of Maryland.

Elsa Chen is a professor of political science at Santa Clara University. Her work focuses on criminal justice reform, reentry from incarceration, criminal record expungement, the implementation and effects of mandatory minimum sentences, and racial and ethnic disparities in sentencing outcomes. Her current research examines policy reforms associated with the de-escalation of mass incarceration and prisoner reintegration into society. Chen served as Santa Clara's Vice Provost for Academic Affairs from 2016 to 2020. She has served on the Executive Board of the American Society of Criminology (ASC), chaired the ASC's Division on People of Color and Crime, and served on the U.S. Department of Justice, Office of Justice Programs' Science Advisory Board and the ASC Policy Committee. She teaches public policy, criminal justice policy, housing and homeless policy, research methods, and American politics. Chen received the Santa Clara University's College of Arts and Sciences 2015 David E. Logothetti Award for teaching excellence.

Jennifer Cobbina-Dungy is an associate professor in the School of Criminal Justice at Michigan State University. Cobbina's areas of expertise center on police-community relations, youth violence, and concentrated neighborhood disadvantage, with a special focus on the experiences of minority youth and the impact of race, class, and gender on criminal justice practices. Her research also focuses on corrections, prisoner reentry and the understanding of recidivism and desistance from crime. Her mixed-methods qualitative and quantitative research predicts recidivism and desistance outcomes and also explores offenders' perceptions regarding how they manage reentry and integration back into the community. Her scholarship is centered on improving the reentry outcomes of individuals with a felony record and/or has been formerly incarcerated. She received her Ph.D. in criminal justice at the University of Missouri–St. Louis in 2009.

Ronald F. Day is a vice president of Programs at the Fortune Society. Day is passionate about reentry, promoting desistance, dismantling mass incarceration, and addressing the stigma of incarceration. He provides oversight for Fortune's Education and Employment Services, and for Individualized Correction Achievement Network (ICAN), a New York City Department of Correction (NYCDOC) initiative that provides pre and post release services to people incarcerated in NYC jails. He formerly served as the AVP of Fortune's David Rothenberg Center for Public Policy (DRCPP), which advocates to reduce reliance on incarceration, promote model programing for the incarcerated population, change laws and policies that create barriers for successful reintegration, and foster a just and equitable criminal justice system. He is the former host of Fortune's original show Both Sides of the Bars on Manhattan Neighborhood Network. He has a Ph.D. in Criminal Justice from the CUNY Graduate Center/John Jay College of Criminal Justice, and a M.P.A. from Baruch College (CUNY). He was also formerly incarcerated.

DeAnna Hoskins is president of JustLeadershipUSA. Hoskins has been committed to the movement for justice, working alongside people impacted by incarceration for nearly two decades. She was formerly the senior policy advisor over corrections and reentry with the Department of Justice (DOJ). In this capacity, she represented DOJ's strategies and priorities and oversaw the Second Chance Act portfolio of grants, The National Reentry Resource Center, and Residential Substance Abuse Treatment programs. Hoskins was designated as the interim deputy director of the Federal Reentry Interagency Council by Attorney General Loretta Lynch. She has experienced the reentry system from all perspectives as she is herself a previously incarcerated individual who has successfully transitioned back into the community, ultimately receiving a pardon from Governor Ted Strickland. She holds a M.A. in criminal justice from the University of Cincinnati, bachelor's degree in social work, and is a licensed clinical addictions counselor and certified as an Offender Workforce Development Specialist.

Cecelia Klingele is an associate professor at the University of Wisconsin Law School, where she teaches courses in criminal law, Constitutional criminal procedure, policing, and sentencing and corrections. She is also a faculty associate of the Frank J. Remington Center, the La Follette School of Public Affairs, and the Institute for Research on Poverty. Klingele's academic research focuses on criminal justice administration, with an emphasis on community and institutional corrections. She has served as Associate Reporter for the American Law Institute's Model Penal Code: Sentencing revision, External Co-Director of the University of Minnesota Robina Institute's Sentencing Law & Policy Program, and co-chair of the Academic Committee of the American Bar Association's Criminal Justice Section. She received her J.D. from the University of Wisconsin Law School. Klingele then served as a law clerk to Chief Judge Barbara B. Crabb of the United States District Court for the Western District of Wisconsin, Judge Susan H. Black of the United States Court of Appeals for the Eleventh Circuit, and Associate Justice John Paul Stevens of the United States Supreme Court.

William J. Sabol is a professor in the Department Criminal Justice & Criminology at Georgia State University where he teaches and conducts research on corrections, sentencing policy, and crime statistics. During the past 30 years, he has held positions in government, private sector research institutions, and universities, including serving as the director of the Bureau of Justice Statistics. He earned his Ph.D. from the University of Pittsburgh and was a Fulbright Scholar at Cambridge University's Institute of Criminology.

Faye S. Taxman is a professor at the Schar School of Policy and Government at George Mason University. She is a health service criminologist. She is recognized for her work in the development of seamless systems-of-care models that link the criminal justice system with other health care and other service delivery systems and reengineering probation and parole supervision services. She has conducted experiments to examine different processes to improve treatment access and retention, to assess new models of probation supervision consistent with Risk, Need and Responsivity (RNR) frameworks, and to test new interventions. She has active "laboratories" with numerous agencies including Virginia Department of Corrections, Alameda County Probation Department (CA), Hidalgo County Community Corrections Department (TX), North Carolina Department of Corrections, and Delaware Department of Corrections. She developed the translational RNR Simulation Tool (www.gmuace.org/tools) to assist agencies to advance practice. In 2019, she received the lifetime achievement award from the American Society of Criminology's Division of Sentencing and Corrections. She has a Ph.D. from Rutgers University's School of Criminal Justice.

Christopher Uggen is Regents Professor and Distinguished McKnight Professor of sociology and law at the University of Minnesota and a fellow of the American Society of Criminology. He studies crime, law, and justice, firm in the belief that sound research can help build a more just and peaceful world. His writing on felon voting, work and crime, and harassment and discrimination is frequently cited in media. Current projects include a comparative study of reentry from different types of institutions, employment discrimination and criminal records, crime and justice after genocide, and the health effects of incarceration. His outreach and engagement projects include editing *Contexts Magazine* and *TheSocietyPages.Org*. He received his Ph.D. from the University of Wisconsin in 1995.

Christy A. Visher is professor of Sociology and Criminal Justice at the University of Delaware and Director of the Center for Drug and Health Studies. Over the past three decades, her research has focused broadly on crime and justice topics, including prisoner reentry, crime prevention strategies, and substance use disorders. Visher designed and implemented the path-breaking, longitudinal study of men and women released from prison, "Returning Home: Understanding the Challenges of Prisoner Reentry". She was also Co-Principal Investigator for the multi-site Evaluation of the Serious and Violent Offender Reentry Initiative. Her most recent research projects examine the strategies for improving the day-to-day environment for people who live and work in prison, the efficacy of using cognitive behavioral therapy in correctional settings to reduce misconduct and rearrest, and interventions to link probationers to health care providers. She has published extensively on prisoner reentry. Visher has an M.A. and Ph.D. in Sociology from Indiana University, Bloomington.

Emily Wang is an associate professor in the Yale School of Medicine and directs the Health Justice Lab. The Health Justice Lab is a collaborative, innovative, interdisciplinary team focused on improving the health of individuals and communities who have been affected by mass incarceration.

The Lab has studies ranging from the epidemiology of incarceration and cardiovascular health to mitigating the community impact of gun violence using a participatory approach and assets-based framework. Wang has cared for thousands of individuals with a history of incarceration and is co-founder of the Transitions Clinic Network (TCN), a growing consortium of 30 community health centers nationwide dedicated to caring for individuals recently released from correctional facilities by employing individuals with a history of incarceration as community health workers. Wang has an M.D. from Duke University and a M.A.S from the University of California, San Francisco.